In Love with Islam, Believing in Jesus

To my friend Sarlath
& O/ive
May God bless you And
your family.

Rick

STUDIES IN THEOLOGY
SOCIETY AND CULTURE

Series Editors:

Dr Judith Gruber
Dr Norbert Hintersteiner
Dr Declan Marmion
Dr Gesa Thiessen

Volume 17

PETER LANG

Oxford • Bern • Berlin • Bruxelles • New York • Wien

Original French edition
Amoureux de l'Islam, croyant en Jésus
by Paolo Dall'Oglio,
with the collaboration of
Églantine Gabaix-Hialé

Translated by Richard Kimball,
Marie Salaün and
Masha Refka

In Love with Islam, Believing in Jesus

PETER LANG
Oxford • Bern • Berlin • Bruxelles • New York • Wien

Bibliographic information published by Die Deutsche Nationalbibliothek.
Die Deutsche Nationalbibliothek lists this publication in the Deutsche National-
bibliografie; detailed bibliographic data is available on the Internet at
http://dnb.d-nb.de.

A catalogue record for this book is available from the British Library.

A CIP catalog record for this book has been applied for at the Library of Congress.

Original French version: *Amoureux de l'Islam, croyant et Jésus*, Paolo Dall'Oglio,
© Les Éditions Ouvrières/ Éditions de L'Atelier, Paris/ Ivry-sur-Seine, 24.09.2009

Cover image: Carole Lozano.
Cover design by Peter Lang Ltd in collaboration with Marija Kovač.

ISSN 1662-9930
ISBN 978-1-78997-996-1 (print)
ISBN 978-1-78997-997-8 (ePDF)
ISBN 978-1-78997-998-5 (eBook)

© Peter Lang Group AG 2023

Published by Peter Lang Ltd, International Academic Publishers,
Oxford, United Kingdom
oxford@peterlang.com, www.peterlang.com

Richard Kimball, Marie Salaün and Masha Refka have asserted their right under the
Copyright, Designs and Patents Act, 1988, to be identified as Authors of this Work.

This publication has been peer reviewed.

Contents

RICHARD KIMBALL

Introduction to the English Translation

On the day that Fr. Paolo Dall'Oglio disappeared, 29 July 2013, I was studying *Early Christian Arabic* with Sidney H. Griffith at the Catholic University in Washington D.C. This summer module was part of my PhD research concerning the exploration of the use of the Qur'anic appellation and designation *ahl al-kitāb* [the People of the Book] by Arabic-speaking Christians. The *People of the Book* is an appellation that governs relations between Muslims and the followers of other monotheistic faiths whose scripture Islam recognises as being revealed by God.

During the course of the summer Griffith told me about Fr. Paolo and his community, how he first met members of Deir Mar Musa al-Habashi Monastic Community back in the 1990s at a Louis Massignon conference held in Notre Dame University, which he had helped organise, in collaboration with Herbert Mason and David Burrell. Through these contacts Griffith came to know and respect the work of Fr. Paolo. They met face-to-face later at a conference in London and then again at a dinner held in a Jesuit residence in Georgetown with a few others who were also very much involved with Muslim-Christian relations and the life of Louis Massignon. On both occasions the two gentlemen had the opportunity for long talks that Fr. Griffith described as inspirational. I was very impressed with what Fr. Griffith had to say about Fr Paolo, as well as the community of Deir Mar Musa al-Habashi. This was my introduction to Fr. Paolo Dall'Oglio, his life and *Amoureux de l'Islam, croyant en Jésus*.[1]

As soon as I started reading *Amoureux de l'Islam* I knew that I would have to incorporate his ideas into my research as an example of modern contemporary use of *ahl al-kitāb*. Yet, as I scanned the pages for the term, I realised to my surprise that Fr. Paolo used the appellation quite judiciously,

---

1   Henceforth to be referred to as *Amoureux de l'Islam* in the introduction.

perhaps even Jesuitically. Typically Fr. Paolo expressed a deep understanding of the scope and implications of *ahl al-kitāb* when it suited his needs, but would ignore the limitations when it did not. For instance, he accepts that Islam requires Muslims to acknowledge that God established Christianity, and that dialogue and conviviality between Muslims and Christians is the expected and preferred relationship between the two faiths. However, when it comes to the thorny issues of intermarriage and conversion, he opts for the more secular foundation and shifting sands of human rights to progress his arguments, knowing full well that these areas are clearly regulated under "terms and conditions" for *ahl al-kitāb*. For Fr. Paolo it would seem that the logical product of dialogue and the sacrament of daily life necessitates respectfully challenging the existing boundaries. The more I read and heard about Fr. Paolo from friends and acquaintances, the more I was won over by his insatiable passion to bring Christians and Muslims together, kicking and screaming if necessary, away from their respective isolationist comfort zones, and, as Fr. Paolo would say, away from the "dialogue of the deaf".

Amoureux de l'Islam encompasses more than the words and philosophy of Fr. Paolo Dall'Oglio. The book also captures many of the hopes and aspirations of those of the Community of Deir Mar Musa al-Habashi in Syria, the sister monasteries of the al-Khalil Community in Iraq, Syria and Italy, as well as the Christians and Muslims around the world who dare to look beyond the haze of social and theological constructs that divide us.

In order to bring *Amoureux de l'Islam* to the English speaking and reading world, I knew that I would need help. Although growing up in Maine and learning to speak French with les Québécois, seven academic years of French, followed by two years in Tunisia with the U.S. Peace Corps, had enabled me to work through his text for my own purposes, my language skills alone would not be adequate to capture and translate Fr. Paolo's thoughts, aspirations and humour. Fortunately, I was able to draw upon the service of Marie Salaün. Marie was lecturing in Galway and working at the French Institute at the time. She played an instrumental role at the genesis of this project through her correspondence with Églantine Gabaix-Hialé, who collaborated with Fr. Paolo in the writing of *Amoureux de l'Islam*, and the French publishers Les Editions De L'Atelier, from whom permission to translate the text for publication was required. Nevertheless, as we worked our way through the text, we found some of Fr. Paolo's ideas were quite elusive and highly nuanced, especially where he employed expressions and ideas that are in the pioneering stages of interfaith relations. We recognised early on that we needed to enlist the services of someone with closer ties to Fr. Paolo and his community in order to bridge the gap between a translation of mere words and our hope of capturing the spirit of Fr. Paolo's message. At the suggestion of Nayla Tabbara (President of Adyan Foundation) we approached Masha Refka who knew Fr. Paolo and who had often stayed at Mar Musa on retreat, and who also shares sympathies with the al-Khalil Community's approach to Muslim-Christian relations. Thankfully Masha not only accepted but also embraced the challenge. Masha's contribution has been invaluable from the start, not just for her comprehension of Fr. Paolo's ideas but also with her relentless stamina and attention to detail, infused no doubt by her love and respect for Fr. Paolo.

Over the course of this project we enlisted the advice and support of several people. I would like to begin by thanking Sidney H. Griffith for sharing his thoughts and memories of Fr. Paolo and his community. Little did he realise that he was sowing the seeds that would eventually lead to this translation. Nayla Tabbara and Fadi Daou were always there for us offering advice and support. Tabbara reviewed our project proposal, alongside my dear friend Ali Salim. Their recommendations were instrumental to Peter Lang Publishers accepting the project. Martin Whelan (Diocese of Galway) offered advice and clarification on the use of a few theological terms that aided in our translation. Jens Petzold (al-Khalil Monastic Community, Deir Maryam al-Adhra in Sulaymaniyah, Kurdistan, Iraq) and Sr Carol Cook Eid (Deir Mar Musa) likewise helped us understand how Fr. Paolo viewed and incorporated certain philosophical concepts like "*conscience identitaire*" into his ideas. Shaun O'Neil (*A Church of Islam: The Syrian Calling of Father Paolo Dall'Oglio*, 2019) was the first person to proofread a complete draft of the text. His counsel and suggestions are very much appreciated. My friends in the Religious Society of Friends, Rachel Cave and Joe Fenwick, assisted in proofreading our later drafts. Their efforts and advice are also greatly appreciated. Thanks is also due to Greg Sheaf from Trinity College Library for his valuable assistance regarding technical issues with the referencing software. At this stage I would also like to thank Anthony

Mason, Norbert Hintersteiner, Declan Marmion, Gesa Thiessen, Judith Gruber, Shruthi Maniyodath and all concerned at Peter Lang Publishers who patiently waited for us to complete this work.

I would like to gratefully acknowledge financial support for the publication of this book from Fr. Murt Curry and the Galway Jesuit Community, as well as from Bishop Michael Duignan and the Diocese of Galway.

Finally, we have just a few comments to make concerning references. "TN" denotes translators' notes. We strove as far as possible to allow the words of *Amoureux de l'Islam* to speak for themselves; however, on rare occasion we felt it necessary to explain a phrase, a term or to direct the reader to source further information regarding the discussion of a particular subject. Unless otherwise stated all Biblical references are from the Jerusalem Bible, English edition, since Fr. Paolo generally used the French edition. Unless otherwise stated all Qur'anic references are by Abdullah Yusuf Ali. Wherever possible and unless otherwise stated the English translation of Vatican encyclicals and Epistles are taken directly from the official Vatican online archive: <https://www.vatican.va/archive/index.htm>.

تقبل الله منا ومنكم

(May God be pleased with our Deeds and with Yours)

Acknowledgements (French Edition)

Together, Églantine and Paolo, we would like to offer our heartfelt appreciation to Mr Régis Debray who kindly accepted to write the preface for our work. We are also grateful to Kabira Nait Raiss, Raphaël Denamur and Diane de Pas who were very much involved in this reflection. Thanks are also due to Arielle Corbani, who believed in this difficult project from her very first visit to Deir Mar Musa and who actively participated in improving the text of this edition. Lastly, we would like to offer the entire Community of Deir Mar Musa our gratitude for their Islamophilia in practice without which dialogue would be in vain. It is to each one there that we would like to dedicate this work.

Preface

Signed by any other than Father Paolo, a defence statement with such a title would be called out as dandy provocation or as confoundingly naive. The restorer of the Deir Mar Musa monastery and its eleventh-century frescoes has a sense of the Beautiful, but is no aesthete. The monastic Arabist and founder of a mixed community in the middle of the desert, tried and tested in Syrian and Middle-Eastern ruggedness, is no dupe. This heir of Father de Foucauld and Louis Massignon is not out to attract customers through fanciful exaggeration: he speaks of what he lives and knows from within. Islam is not, for this European of Syriac rite, a topic for university studies or a romantic fascination. He tackles head on a difficult, ambitious and shifting religion, by turning his back on the two opposite idealisations that compete for our image of Islam: the Andalusian garden of olden days, a force for the Good, and the cutthroat Afghan of today, a force for Evil. In order to respond to the observations of the Congregation for the Doctrine of the Faith, which verged on admonishment, he so to speak doubled the bet, and not without panache. As if he wanted to bend back the stick of Islamophobia with his Islamophilia, in order to straighten it.

Everybody knows that Islam, the civilisational backdrop for Political Islamism (which has killed a hundred times more Muslims than infidels) has implicitly become, since the Iranian revolution of 1979, then explicitly since 11 September 2001, the public enemy number one of our collective unconscious. This bogeyman culture, which we love to hate, constitutes the precious cement of our Western consensus. Suffice it to look at our magazine covers, the store fronts of our bookshops and the editorials of our favourite newspaper to find an unsurpassable concentration of malevolent "*isms*": fanaticism, terrorism, antisemitism, obscurantism, clericalism, despotism, male chauvinism, let's abbreviate the list. For anyone other than

Father Paolo, myself being neither an Islamophile nor an Islamophobe, but rather an incompetent and distant observer, I never would have considered prefacing a work thus entitled. No matter how much the secular and republican mind kicks up a fuss against the stereotypes of their social milieu, they rather tend to lend an ear to those who would put forward, as side notes or as stigma, the statutory inequality of women, the petrification of time, the tyranny of transcendence and the uncritical idolatry of a text signed by God, the Qur'an.

Paolo Dall'Oglio does not blindly and unilaterally praise Islam. He does not detail, as a historian would, the legacy of Islamic civilisation to universal culture. He does not dwell, as a sociologist would, on the European vision of the Muslim world. As a spiritual man of Catholic allegiance, he seeks to engage in conversation, by asking himself why, in the family of Abraham, only the Christians would have faith, and Muslims only beliefs. This effort towards a dialogue of reciprocity has become rare. Lebanese abbot Youakim Mubarak had started it from the Maronite perspective. He takes over, from the Roman point of view. Instinctive paranoia cannot in fact replace a well-argued reflection. Let us be reminded that during the century-long Wars of Religion between Catholics and Protestants, the warring parties would take the time to engage in debate and polemics, discussing this or that theological point. I am by no means a theologian, but I must take notice that a citizen and *a fortiori* a *politique*, whichever side they are on, to the east as to the west of the Mediterranean, are confronted, whether they like it or not, by each other's biases and theological options. And I am grateful to Father Paolo, this migrant who voluntarily left his native cocoon to have no other homeland than hope, for going beyond the pious rhetoric of the conference and tackling the core, even at the risk of playing the thankless role of go-between, without relinquishing an iota of his own faith. Accusations of relativism and syncretism do not scare him. He holds that a dual belonging such as his own, straddling West and East, could facilitate in the long-term the surpassing of certain dogmatic contradictions between Islam and the Church. In his eyes, the Spirit of God is still at work, and certain fecund provocations susceptible of creating an effervescence of ideas and overturning torpors contribute to this work. The facts did not prove him wrong: the Roman Magisterium listened to him, without constraining him to make honourable amends.

Let us remember that this Jesuit is a missionary who takes on the risks of the mission without batting an eyelid. He is one of the Church's light-horsemen, the traditional pioneers of inculturation. Muhammad is not Master Kong, Allah is not the High Sovereign and Paolo Dall'Oglio is not Matteo Ricci. Rome is no longer appalled, merely circumspect and cautious. The Rules of his new Community have been approved. Be that as it may, it is tempting to draw a parallel with the Chinese Rites Controversy of the seventeenth century. In the Chinese fortress, Matteo learned Chinese, donned the bonze's habit and strove to reduce the incompatibilities between the Christian vision and Buddhist culture, even Confucian culture. The papacy accused him of styling himself son of Heaven, not of Jesus Christ. Nobody would accuse Paolo of styling himself imam. Our adventurer of faith, who made the option for the poor his own, knows how far to take "accommodation": he may be daring, but never irreverent, and always the priest celebrating Mass in Arabic. Let us add that this disciple of Ignatius of Loyola is oblivious to "pious fraud". He does not wish to circumvent this or that decision-maker by deploying astronomical seductions, like Matteo with the Chinese Emperor. He is neither a *politique* nor a man of power. His integrity is that of the prophet, not the schemer, and as we know prophets are more gifted with wounds and hassles than with religious titles and honours.

They sometimes make a mess. They do not possess the authority of a title, or the strength of numbers. Their only strength is their dynamic and their trust in the movement that shakes things up. The game is far from over. European Islam is already not the same as it was yesterday. The Christian world can also change tomorrow, because of and by virtue of an accepted coexistence. Such would be the wager of a possible and mutual symbolic transcendence, between two types of societies both admitting to their own imperfections. That this convergence is historically possible, it is permitted to doubt. That it is the ideal of a man of faith who puts this ideal into practice at the crossroads of two worlds, one can, and one should only rejoice for it.

ÉGLANTINE GABAIX-HIALÉ

Introduction to the French Edition

Some desert crossings will lead to an oasis. On the improbable road
that takes you from Nebek, a Syrian town 80 km north of Damascus, to
the Monastery of Saint Moses, Deir Mar Musa in Arabic, you will see
nothing but scorched land, a few black plastic bags carried by the wind
and herds of goats guided by timeless Bedouins. In the minibus which
rocks and rattles, the driver will ask you where you come from, and will
mutter a few words of welcome in your language. You hesitate for a few
moments, wondering what has brought you to the middle of the desert,
but the motor has stopped. This is it. All you can do is lift your head and
gauge the distance you still need to cover. Endless steps, which delight
in circumnavigating the mountain and embracing its form. The monastery is there, rooted in the mountain like a king's throne, arrogantly
overlooking this nothingness that encircles it. A naked, divested king,
with nothing to offer but what is brought to him. You climb the steps
one by one, because not only are they numerous but they are also large
and high. You hesitate again, but the minibus is gone, and you have
no other choice but to keep climbing, for "the desert has closed in on
[you]".[1] Breathless, undoubtedly sweating, you bend down to cross the
threshold, in a gesture thousands of years old, humble and monastic. In
the house of God, one enters with a bow. Suddenly engulfed in darkness, feeling your way, you follow the light to reach the terrace. "*Ahlan
wa sahlan*" [welcome], will be the words that receive you.

---

1   Exodus 14:3. Biblical quotations in the original French are from *La Bible de
    Jérusalem*, Paris, Le Cerf, 1984. TN. Unless otherwise indicated, the Biblical quota-
    tions in English are from The Jerusalem Bible, 1968 by Darton, Longman & Todd
    Ltd and Doubleday and Co. Inc.

History of Saint Moses and the Monastery

According to later accounts, Moses the Abyssinian was the son of an Ethiopian king. But the only kingdom he wished to win was the kingdom of God. He abandoned crown, honour and marriage and went to the Holy Land via Egypt. He later settled in Qara, around ten kilometres from the monastery, where he became a monk. Then, he became a hermit, and took up residence in one of the caves in the mountains surrounding the monastery, natural grottos, as if nature were by design making hermitages to encourage vocations. Moses was martyred by Byzantine soldiers. It is told that when his family came to claim his body, his right hand miraculously separated from his arm. It was kept as a relic and is today conserved in the Syriac church in Nebek. Moses, Musa in Arabic, became *Mar*, meaning lord, and thus saint. Christian hermits in the region started coming regularly to these grottos to pray and created a small monastery that took the name of the saint: Mar Musa al-Habashi (the Abyssinian or Ethiopian).

According to archaeological investigations, monastic life there dates to the mid-sixth century and followed the Syriac rite of Antioch. The current church in the monastery was built in 450 Hijri (1058 CE) according to the inscription on its wall, which begins with these typically Qur'anic words: "In the Name of God the Merciful, the Compassionate."

The Frescoes

After crossing the threshold to the church, you have the strange impression of being surrounded and spied on from all sides. The walls are populated by figures with vivacious and warm colours. These frescoes are among the best conserved in the Middle East, and date to the eleventh and thirteenth centuries in three successive layers. The most recent restorations allowed the reading of the date of the third layer: "Completed in the year six hundred and four [Hijri, 1208 CE] by the hand of the decorator Sergius son of the priest Ali, son of Barran. May God have mercy on him and all those who come to this blessed oratory and may they be healed. Amen."

The layers are superimposed with astonishing harmony. In the nave to the right, the second layer stages Jesus' presentation in the temple, while above the altar, to the east, the third layer depicts Christ Pantocrator surrounded by the apostles and at the very top, the Annunciation. Among the gaps, one can make out the remains of the first layer, recently identified as representing the Forty Martyrs of Sebaste around the Archangel Michael. Above the four pillars, the Evangelists are enthroned, copying their Syriac texts from a page contemplated in the Heavens. Everywhere, you see prophets, Church Fathers and saintly martyrs on horseback. Women saints are the focus in the intrados of the arches. The most striking image is to the west, that of the Last Judgement. Adam and Eve seem to be watching over their children. The Apostles of the Christ-Judge play the role of viziers on precious cushions around the throne of the Cross, on a royal carpet. The fresco then divides into two parts: to the right, Paradise and the saved; to the left, Hell and the souls of the damned, where one actually notes an overrepresentation of the clergy...

The Monastery: Abandonment and Restoration

In the fifteenth century, the Monastery was partly reconstructed and enlarged. Subsequently, the hermits who would gather there on Sundays must have experienced some difficulty living together, even for a single day, and the monastery was abandoned. In the mid-nineteenth century, once its ownership went to the diocese, or rather the Syriac Catholic Eparchy of Homs, Hama and Nebek, it fell into ruin. The local parish struggled to keep it as best they could, as the inhabitants of Nebek, Christians and Muslims, would often visit with reverence.

In 1984, spurred by a young Italian Jesuit and with the aid of the Syrian government, the local Church and a group of Syrian and European volunteers, the Monastery's restoration began. But by which strange turn of events did this young Jesuit come to lose himself in these desert lands?

A Jesuit Falls under the Charm of a Ruin

Every article on the Monastery of Mar Musa begins as follows: "Once upon a time, there was a young Italian Jesuit." Today, this Jesuit is no longer young, and all he retains from that Italian is this sanguine temper of his. And even this, the gestures, the words, the outbursts, one can no longer be sure if he takes them from his native Rome, or his adoptive Syria. But since this is how legends begin, and since the legends of Paolo Dall'Oglio and Deir Mar Musa are intrinsically linked…

Itinerary of a Committed Jesuit

And so, once upon a time, there was a young Italian Jesuit… In 1977, then a 23-year-old Roman novice, he declares his desire to offer his life for the salvation of Muslims to his Father Superior.[2] His vocation is heard and taken seriously. He is sent to a torn Lebanon to study Arabic. He applies himself to it like a madman; with this passion he still possesses today to get to the bottom of things. He returns to Naples to study Philosophy for two years, and from there he goes to Jerusalem to study Hebrew. Once back, his dream is realised, and he is sent to Damascus. He immerses himself in the Syriac rite, according to him the closest to the rhythm of the prayers of Muslim sheikhs, and decides to be ordained as priest according to this rite. (Since the Chinese rites of Mario Ricci and his companions in the seventeenth century, Jesuits prioritise a profound adaptation to the context of their mission.) Somewhat by chance, in 1982 he discovers this abandoned monastery. It will mark the beginning of a human, spiritual, archaeological and pastoral adventure, which lasts to this day. Guyonne de Montjou has told this story in her admirable book: *Mar Musa, Un monastère, un homme, un désert*.[3] In it she renders Paolo's free discourse,

2   TN. In the Jesuit Order this role is generally carried out by the Master of Novices.
3   Guyonne de Montjou, *Mar Moussa, un monastère, un homme, un désert* (Paris: Albin Michel, 2006).

his commitments, his doubts, his love of Islam and the thousand twists and turns that make Mar Musa's rebirth a miracle.

The Community of al-Khalil Today

Paolo Dall'Oglio has been fighting for twenty-five years. He fights to restore the monastery, the frescoes, to bring in water, electricity and telephone lines. He fights to tackle the desertification of the valley. He also fights for recognition by the Vatican and local Church of the Community he has founded.

Birth of the Community

It is a mixed ecumenical community dedicated to Muslim-Christian dialogue. Jacques the Syrian was the first to join Paolo. He was barely 20 years old. He took a liking to this Italian who was crying out in the desert, and who in fact still is. They have been by each other's side ever since. Jacques is currently a priest in Qaryatayn, a desert town next to Palmyra, and takes care of the Monastery of Mar Elian. From a monastic point of view, he is affiliated to Mar Musa. Then came the others, companions for a few years or, in the case of those who stayed and became monks or nuns, for a lifetime. The Community took on the name al-Khalil, "God's Friend", the Biblical and Qur'anic title for Abraham. After more than fifteen years of procedures, of reticence on the part of the Diocese and the Vatican, of misunderstandings, tenaciousness, sometimes discouragement, the Rule of the Community was approved by the Vatican in 2006. Real joy ensued, and especially, gratitude. Today, ten members make up the Community: Jacques; Houda, a Syrian, and one of the first women to join; Jens, a German Swiss who had stopped at the Monastery on his way to Samarkand, and never left; Boutros, a cheese maker from Hassakeh on the border with Iraq; Dima, the youngest member to have taken religious vows; Jihad, a young Maronite Syrian; and three novices: Youssef and Dany, both Syrian, and Diane, a young French woman. Jens, Jihad (now a priest) and Dima are all studying theology at the Gregorian University in Rome and return to the Monastery for holidays. Houda, who completed her five years of study last year, now lives in the Monastery full-time.

Symbolic Presence, Incarnate Exchange

Every Friday in spring, hundreds of Muslims picnic at the foot of the Monastery, then come up to drink tea with the Community and to admire the church frescoes. Their restoration was completed in 2003 by an Italian-Syrian team. It is always the occasion for a fruitful exchange between the two communities, in the spirit of Abrahamic hospitality. The interreligious seminar in August in a way theorises this daily exchange by bringing together imams, pastors, priests and believers around various themes. Most recently, they gathered to discuss the interpretation of sacred texts. Father Paolo receives invitations to conferences in Syrian Muslim institutions, Sunni as well as Shiite. He is a privileged interlocutor for his knowledge of Arabic and of the Muslim world. The al-Khalil Community believes that building Muslim-Christian harmony is also a means to slow down the emigration of Eastern Christians to the West.

Daily Life

At 7 a.m., the Community gathers on the terrace of the men's monastery to drink *maté* (an infusion mainly consumed in South America and Syria). Between 7:30 and 9:15, they pray in the church, and Paolo conducts a catechism that lasts for as long as its subject requires. At 9:30, it is time for breakfast with visitors, guests for a week, a month, a year, the workers and friends. Breakfast consists of tea, tomatoes, jam and the Monastery's goat cheese. From then until 14:30, everyone goes about their business. Boutros makes the cheese and enjoys teaching the process to those interested. He decides the daily menu and manages the food supply. When no one else is available, he cooks, sometimes with debatable skill… Jens, whose heart belongs to God and computers, fixes the daily computer issues, manages the library files, updates the website… He also enjoys discussing politics and philosophy in different languages. Houda receives the visitors, listens to them and advises them. She is also responsible for managing the accommodation. Jihad, a polyglot, welcomes everyone and sometimes disappears to study or play the flute and the violin. Dima acts as Paolo's secretary, working with him on the Monastery's innumerable projects and the accounting. When she is given the time, she bakes delicious cakes. Youssef and Dany, the novices, are a little bit everywhere: in the goat pen, the cheese room, the kitchen, welcoming guests or learning English with the tourists. Diane, a trained agricultural engineer, gathers rose petals to make jam. More generally, she oversees the plantations, sometimes doing a rain dance. As for Paolo, he is everywhere at once – on the building site of the women's monastery with the workers; with the goats in the pen; in the office seeking funds and writing up projects, letters and reports; in the church to explain to the tourists the story the frescoes are telling; in the garden with the tomatoes growing like olives; or in the new shop. He is often away from the Monastery, with the Jesuits with whom he still belongs, or at a conference in Damascus or Europe.

Lunch is generous and must satiate everyone. Rice, pasta and burghul constitute the main staple, plus cooked vegetables. Fruits are offered for dessert. Once a week, to the cats' great delight, chicken is included. Visitors volunteer to do the dishes. After lunch, everyone is free to do what they wish. In reality, most continue the morning tasks, especially when visitors are numerous. At 19:00 it is time for an hour of meditation. The Monastery plunges into absolute calm. Whatever their faith is, everyone is held to silence, or else, if they have an irrepressible need to speak, they can go to the mountain. At 20:00 there is Mass in Arabic, with translations by Paolo or Jacques, depending on those gathered. The rite, Syriac Catholic, will surprise Latin Catholics. We take off our shoes before entering. Like in a mosque? Yes, but above all, as it has always been the case in the churches of the East, to preserve the carpet. We sit on cushions on the floor. For the Western Christian neophyte, hearing God being called Allah is always disconcerting. Sometimes, towards the end of Mass, around 21:30, the Community begins chanting invocations that borrow from Sufi chants. Dinner is modest, not that the other meals are opulent, but this one is particularly so. On summer nights, when the sun has gone to smart skins elsewhere, visitors, friends, guests and the Community members can stay together a while, talking on the terrace, in a tower of Babylon where people finally understand each other...

Hospitality

The Monastery of Mar Musa acts not only on the local and national levels. Abrahamic hospitality is inscribed in its walls. Visitors, who spend a day or several weeks, belong to all nationalities, cultures and faiths. The West meeting the East also builds harmony. Through its simple and ascetic way of life, the Monastery does not depart from the local lifestyle, and shares it with the visitors who partake, often joyfully, in the work of the Community: cooking, laundry, cleaning and agricultural work. When they extend their stay a little, they take charge of welcoming new arrivals and join in the prayers and Mass with the Community. "Many tried their hand at living at Mar Musa. They can be recognised all over this earth by the citadel they carry in their heart."[4] How can one narrate these intersecting lives? How can one know what brought them here? Old French Catholic families with their children, young travellers who meant to just pass through, who stayed a little longer and "too bad about Palmyra!", pilgrims on their way to Jerusalem on foot or by bicycle, their eyes washed out by the thousands of kilometres already covered, groups on tour parachuted here without really knowing where they landed,

4   Montjou, *Mar Moussa*, 157.

perennial travellers who no longer know how to stop and who sometimes stay for six months, expats or students of Arabic fleeing the hustle and bustle of Damascus or Aleppo for a weekend and life-long friends who return to Mar Musa as if returning home. They are Europeans, Americans, Asians and Australians. Only Africa remains underrepresented. Muslims of course come and visit, Arab or Western; Christians as well, whether Orthodox, Catholics, Protestants, sometimes Evangelicals and Anglicans; not to mention Buddhists, Hindus, Shintoists, atheists, agnostics, seekers of a God who conceals himself. It is a sample of humanity, privileged no doubt, as they are free to travel, but who here meet Syrians with torn lives, as well as Iraqi and Lebanese refugees who travel to escape. There are also prison torture survivors, those bruised by the incomprehension of their families and the seekers of impossible loves. The Monastery of Mar Musa is traversed by all the world's cries; it absorbs them, hears them, listens to them, and, like a mother, takes them on her breast to console them.

The Monastery's Projects

Like its building, Deir Mar Musa cannot be approached directly; you need to go around it to reach it, choose an angle to tell its story, if only because dreams are born there every day. Environmental projects are as important as cheese making, or as the new publishing house. Father Paolo together with Adib, a layman who moved to Nebek with his wife in order to be close to the Community, have already translated and published pages from the works of Father Charles de Foucauld and Louis Massignon, both of whom inspired the Community's charism. There is also the library, the new buildings and, below, the visitors' centre with its meditation space for all, which is soon to rise like the sacred heart of the park; the olive and almond trees; and Abraham's path, from Urfa in Turkey to Hebron in Palestine, the "little" brother of the Camino de Santiago, materialising under the impulse of American Sufis and the support of the Dalaï Lama, Jimmy Carter and others... The pilgrims are already on the march, halting here as they follow in the footsteps of Abraham.

Reward

In November of 2006, the Community received the Euro-Mediterranean Award for Dialogue between Cultures by the Anna Lindh Foundation. Its theme was "Interfaith dialogue and mutual respect among people of different beliefs". Father Paolo went to collect this first award in Finland, from the hands of the Minister for Foreign Affairs. In February of 2009, the Universities of Louvain and Leuwen granted Paolo an Honorary Doctorate for the activity of the Community in favour of Muslim-Christian dialogue.

The Origin of This Book

In 2005, in the heart of winter, it was so cold that year in Syria, Paolo asked if I would help him write his defence, to respond to the questions from the Vatican's Congregation for the Doctrine of the Faith. In fact, when the moment came to ask Rome for the approval of the Constitution and Rule of the new Monastic Community, an official query had been addressed to him about comments and articles deemed somewhat unorthodox.

And so that winter, Paolo and I locked ourselves in the library of the monastery. If I had known what awaited us, I might have declined the offer. In order to put it down into intelligible French, I had to understand everything he dictated to me. The difficulty came not from his French, which he knew better than I, to my often great annoyance. Rather it came from his thought process, at once powerful and complex, sinuous, bewitching too, with its sentences that could cover fifteen lines. Towards the end of each day, oppressed by so many words and by the failing gas heater, I would convince myself: never again. In February of 2006, the good news came: the Rule of the Monastery was approved, and suspicions of heterodoxy were filed away in the archives.

As we went down the steps of the monastery shortly before my departure from Syria in June 2006, Paolo proposed that we make a book out of our exchange. Forgetting a little too quickly to which point writing the previous text had been a struggle, I accepted. One and a half years later, I again climbed up these steps one by one to collect his thoughts and shut myself up in the desert with him.

I had spent two years in the monastery, sent there by the Service de Coopération au Développement, where I was the librarian, Paolo's secretary and responsible for the cat community all at once. I was Catholic through a long-forgotten baptism, an atheist by comfort and conformism, and yet gripped by numerous doubts about my nihilistic certainties. Going to live in this Monastery was an opportunity for me to present God with a challenge. A challenge and a search that I encountered in many of the Monastery's visitors. And so it was not so much as a Catholic that I confronted Paolo's thought, but as the bearer of my contemporaries' commonly shared questions, with a mixture of mistrust, lack of culture, curiosity and attraction to these two religions. And yet, Catholic theology is not completely unknown to me, and if I was sometimes naïve and provocative with my questions, it was to try and clarify all that in me and in others was a barrier to the Christian faith. I also wanted to understand why, in spite of his attraction to Islam, Paolo had remained a Christian.

During one of our interviews, Paolo stopped to ask me whether I believed in his vocation as a desert monk dedicated to Muslim-Christian dialogue. Rather distractedly, I answered "yes". Then I thought about his question again, which deep down was one about faith. How can one encounter a religion other than through those who practise it, doubt it sometimes, live and share it? Is not the witness of faith more convincing than any theology? Yes and no. Let us say that they are complementary, and that a true dialogue cannot be nourished by vague affirmations, sensations and feelings. And so, do I believe in your vocation, Paolo, in your desperate dreams of dialogue? I do not have the precise answer. Like many travellers that I met at the monastery, I have no illusions and carry no utopia within me. We lack the radical hope that in one leap would make us see further. We lack prophets, unless we are failing to see and recognise them. But I believe in this fragile Community that keeps questioning itself, in this prayer that you raise up in the desert, in this hospitality you offer at the risk of bad encounters, at the risk of discovering how alike we all are. I believe that beneath the jumble of this world, a tidal wave carries us towards harmony.

Applied Theology

Paolo's theology is not pure abstraction. It is incarnated here, day by day, in Mar Musa. It feeds on the exchanges, conflicts and sharing that are born here. It acquires its full meaning only at the heart of this monastery, but it tends towards the universal, for here all cultures, religions, belongings and identities intersect without dissolving. Certainly it is easier to live in harmony in the middle of the desert, than at the heart of a city, the place of encounter, where dialogue is still sometimes difficult. All the same, it seems to me that something here plays out that goes beyond the conditions of everyday life, a possibility we can believe in.

If, at the risk of being shocking, Paolo Dall'Oglio says that he feels himself to be Muslim in a certain way, it is out of solidarity, a desire for communion, and ultimately empathy in the face of painful divisions. Solidarity with a Community that suffers and causes suffering; communion, even if the term appears improper, theologically at least, with a religion that has kept on questioning Christianity, provoking it, purifying it as Paolo would say, by curtailing its universalist hopes; finally and above all, empathy, because Paolo lives, works, thinks and debates with and within a Muslim society, his adopted land and family, and because true understanding can only be born from sharing everyday life in the heart of this Middle East torn by its contradictions. The importance and role of monasticism in Islam and the notion of conviviality are part of the basic and essential elements of the dialogue initiated by the Community of Mar Musa. This dual belonging, Muslim-Christian, which Paolo claims for himself and which is a notion that he will clarify in these pages, is the condition for going beyond the dogmatic and theological contradictions between Christianity and Islam, in order to break fixed identities, which are the source of so much rigidness. It is also a going-towards, illustrated by the expression "Church of Islam", incarnated by the experience of good neighbourliness and founded on Abrahamic relations, particularly the relationship between Abraham and God. By analogy, recognising the title of Prophet for Muhammad does not entail Paolo abdicating his Christian faith, nor does it entail, by an easy renunciation, the search for an improbable and superficial harmony. Rather, it entails considering that prophecy begins with Christ much more than it ends with him, and recognising the special relationship that Muhammad experienced with God. And lastly, the study and comparison of Muslim and Christian eschatologies allow for building a common future and politics, founded on a shared hope.

These are some of the questions that will be addressed here; momentary snapshots of Paolo's thought process, which is constantly in motion, questions itself, and which here has taken on the risk of allowing itself to be considered as if fixed. But faced with the rise of exclusivist theologies, it seemed important and necessary for both of us to express and share this thought.

Methodological Remarks

The text that follows is entirely Paolo's, and so the "I" is his. "We" refers to the Community, or the Catholic Church, depending on the context. I tried to transcribe his thoughts as best I could, which he dictated to me or shared with me, without including my questions, even if they can be guessed sometimes. For the sake of clarity, I introduced each chapter. If this book is the result of long discussions, this does not mean that we agree on everything. It is clear that his words are his own, and do not necessarily reflect the ideas of the Community of Mar Musa, the Jesuit Order to which he belongs or the Syriac Catholic Diocese of Homs, Hama and Nebek.

CHAPTER I

The Monastery of Mar Musa, a Work of Dialogue

Syria is a country with a Muslim majority. Approximately 75 per cent of the Syrian people are Sunni Muslims, 10 per cent are Shiite from Alawi or Ismaili and Twelver denominations, not forgetting the Druze. Syria would be nearly 10 per cent Christian. It is a symbolic estimate, since we know that many have already left the country. These Christians, most of them Armenian Orthodox, Byzantine, Syriac and Assyrian, also include Catholics (Melkite, Armenian, Syriac, Maronite, Chaldean and Latin, not forgetting a few Protestant communities). The Monastery of Mar Musa is a part of this complex mosaic. It is a Syriac Catholic rite Community, even if its members also come from other Christian traditions. The Community presented to you in this book is an ecumenical community of men and women devoted to dialogue between Christians and Muslims.

Monasticism, an Ideal Christianity for Muslims

On cultural and religious grounds, the Monastery of Saint Moses intended to rediscover a few essential aspects of the ancient monasticism of our region. This is due to the Community's conviction that this monasticism is the one form nascent Islam was familiar with, has known and protected since the seventh century CE. The Eastern Christian monasteries, especially the ones bordering the big deserts, are aesthetically and spiritually part of the Muslim symbolic world. This is also true, in a broader sense, for the entire Eastern Church within the Muslim political-religious structure; but monasticism benefits from an especially favourable Qur'anic status because it is considered, in a way, as the ideal Christianity.[1] In practice, the rediscovery and the renewal of monastic life in an Eastern Muslim-Christian context, encouraged and guided by the apostolic letter *Orientale Lumen* and the post-synodal Exhortation, also become efficient for dialogical missionary work: Christian service and missionary witness in a Muslim context, supporting its spiritual progress, with the aim of greater harmony between Muslims and Christians in the country and for the service of the Kingdom of God.[2]

1   "… and [We] bestowed on him the Gospel; and We ordained in the hearts of those who followed him Compassion and Mercy. But Monasticism…they invented for themselves…", Qur'an 57:27. "… because amongst these are men devoted to learning and men who have renounced the world, and they are not arrogant.", Qur'an 5:82. The original French edition used Jacque Berque's translation: *Le Coran, Albin Michel, 2000* for Qur'anic citations. Also, as expressed by Massignon: "Because with Islam having come after Moses and Jesus, with the prophet Muhammad, with the negative announcement of the Judgement of death which will befall all of creation… Islam even has a positive mission, by reproaching Israel for believing itself privileged … it also reproaches Christians that not all of them recognise the sign of the Holy Table, and with not yet achieving this Rule of monastic perfection, "*rahbāniyya*", which alone realises in them the second birth of Jesus and anticipates within them through the coming of the Spirit of God, the Resurrection of the dead of which Jesus is the sign. This double claim of Islam towards Jews and Christians who abuse their privileges as if these privileges were theirs alone, this incisive warning like the sword of divine transcendence, the unconditional recognition of which alone can perfect their vocation of sainthood, is an eschatological sign…" Louis Massignon, *Les Trois Prières d'Abraham* ed. Daniel Massignon, Patrimoines Islam, (Paris Le Cerf, 1997), 141–42.

2   *Orientale Lumen*, The Light of the Orient, is an apostolic letter by John Paul II, 1995. This letter was prepared by the Congregation for the Oriental Churches, presided at the time by Cardinal Achille Silvestrini, a man of dialogue who saw in the renewal of monastic life an important means of encounter with the Orthodox Churches and mystical traditions of the other religions. It is not surprising that he supported the Monastery of Mar Musa in its early stages. "Monasteries will be able to become prophetic places where creation becomes praise of God and the commandment of Charity lived concretely becomes an ideal of human coexistence, within which the human being seeks God without barriers or obstacles, and becomes a reference for all, carrying the in his heart and helping them seek God." … Monks will be, as they were before, guides and spiritual teachers, and their monasteries ecumenical and interreligious meeting places." *A New Hope For Lebanon, 57.*

Way of Life

In fact, as we choose to return to the local people's modest way of life (food, clothes, hospitality, managing and organising space), not only do we express our solidarity towards them, keeping with Jesus and the Church's choice to favour the poor, not only do we follow Charles de Foucauld's school of thought and its divine simplicity of life in Nazareth, but we also return to the Eastern way of life that has been shared for centuries by our Christian and Muslim brothers in the region. In this way, we criticise today's Western globalisation that fascinates local Christians more than Muslims in percentage terms, and that concretely widens the cultural gap between the two communities.

Arabic Language, Community Language

Language is a means towards authentic inculturation. In Deir Mar Musa, we speak Arabic. The non-Arabic-speaking members of the Community steadfastly commit to learning Arabic. The liturgy is celebrated in Arabic. We try to broaden our knowledge of the religious language of Islam, and we make the effort to translate and express through it our Christian hope and experience. It also helps the local Christians to rediscover a common language with Muslims, for dialogue, understanding, respect and mutual love. It should be noted that the religious Arabic language was for a long time deeply shared by Christians and Muslims. The Ottoman and most importantly the colonial period separated the religious language into the Muslim Arabic language and Christian Arabic language, since especially for Catholics, it is often translated from Western languages. The abundant Arabic Christian literature, which developed through the centuries alongside Muslim literature, is a true treasure; it knew how to deeply and faithfully express the mysteries of Christian faith through expressions directly borrowed from Muslim religious language. Eastern Christians mainly made that possible by greatly participating in and promoting the translation into Arabic of the Greek and Syriac culture from pre-Muslim civilisation.

Understanding Islam

In preparation for inculturation (Cf. Chapter 5), the community committed to the effort of understanding Islam. Among other things, the monastery's library developed a strong interest in culture and science subjects related to the knowledge of yesterday and today's Islam. Besides, monastic catecheses that, in Arabic, deepen the knowledge of the reservoir of faith, tend to show the possible connections, analogies, differences, possibilities of comprehension and complementary enrichment with the religious culture of Islam. Interreligious seminaries also take place as opportunities for plural engagements. Arab-Muslim Sufi music is also used with discernment during celebrations. With discernment because we must adapt to the religious sensitivities of people present, coming from different backgrounds. The care to value Eastern Christian traditions and to respect local Christians' sensitivity remains a priority. The members of the Monastic Community, depending on their skill and charism, are encouraged to know Muslim texts, not only for their cultural enrichment, but also to develop their ability for Christian spiritual dialogue, in accordance with our own vocation in the service of harmony between Muslims and Christians.

Solidarity towards the Muslim Community

Practising hospitality, day after day, is also a great opportunity to existentially deepen one's relationship with Islam. All of this is called to transform into prayers, intercession. The monks and the nuns of Deir Mar Musa carry the *Ummah*, the Muslim Community, in their heart when they stand before God during meditation, communal prayer and the Eucharist and receive from the Spirit of God insights, advice on how to love more and better, as well as the energy to do so. The effort is to keep making our ecclesial dimension more theological. What I mean by theological is the affiliation to the Church centred on faith in Jesus. This dimension must take precedence over any other ground, be it sociological or cultural. A church consciousness stems from this, which pushes us to become more deeply spiritually united to the destiny of the Muslim world, our chosen homeland, because of the universal love of Christ. This conduct will not be naïve and blind to the contradictions and failings of this context, but they are seen from a logic of solidarity and a desire for constructive reforms. Muslims are our family!

Solidarity towards Eastern Christians

This solidarity towards Muslims does not at all signify a lack of solidarity with the destiny of the local Christian populations. Quite the contrary, a prudent and conscious rapprochement between Christians and Muslims generates good support for Christians too, that they can recover the joy and sense of remaining in their ancestral homeland. Local Christians are at home in Deir Mar Musa and, along with the monastic community, take part in the Muslim practice of hospitality. We are talking about practice because it is a concrete experience that does not pertain to theory, but to a traditional elaboration of neighbourly relations between Christians and Muslims.

Inculturation

The common practice of environmental responsibility (the fight against desertification, sustainable development via responsible and cultural

tourism) and social responsibility (participation in social activities pro-
moted by local non-governmental organisations) constitutes another dimension of dialogue and inculturation in Deir Mar Musa. We are trying
to harmonise our commitments with the prevalent Muslim vision, while
still contributing the ferment of our own vision.

Where exactly do we want to go with the inculturation process and
in the practice of dialogue in the Muslim world as a Catholic Monastic
Community? Would it be acceptable to local Christians with pre-Islamic
roots? Would it be acceptable to the Church? Would it be tolerable for
Muslims themselves? In the East, time is notoriously long... And so is
the time of inculturation. Besides, this Monastic Community must not
lose sight of the fact that it has an internal religious role too, towards local
Christianity with its ecumenical complexity. It is a role of listening, spiritual support, catechesis, consolation and help on different levels. It may
also be a prophetic role... This role requires patience and discernment. The
witness of charity is more important and efficient than demonstrating a
great aptitude for cultural adaptation.

The monastery will stay as it is, a Syriac, Eastern, Christian monastery,
a place of prayer and spiritual welcome with a relationship to Islam in the
form and substance of conviviality, which is a concept that we do not at
all consider opposed to inculturation. The big upcoming historical, social
and cultural changes are going to guide us, as we go along, in the light of
God's Spirit, to modify our current way of life in a way that is faithful to
our charism. The one criterion of cordial openness and sincere obedience
to the shepherds of the Church, local as well as universal, is what will
guarantee over time that we are working for the Kingdom and not for our
own illusions.

Maybe someday, elsewhere in the Muslim world, if God blesses our
Community with a number of holy vocations, with approval and encouragement from the Church, it will be possible, with prudence and courage,
to do more for the inculturation of the faith in the Muslim context and
to lay the foundations of a more consciously Muslim-Christian Church
(Cf. Chapter 3). All the same, we think that, in general, Deir Mar Musa's
method is good and suitable in today's context of minority Churches in
the Muslim world to live the Christian mission there with more hope.

It seems timely to me to underline the theological value of conviviality within the local Arab culture, dialectically shared, in its Muslim-Christian being. Beyond any dogmatic consideration, there is the simple fact of living together. The human dimension, as a value that all take part in recognising and building, remains what is immediately available to everybody's good will. The quality of day-to-day gestures is the basis on which we can build that sense of companionship that comes from "breaking bread" together, of conviviality, supported by the relational rites of neighbourliness.

CHAPTER 2

My Relationship to Islam

As a novice, Paolo Dall'Oglio, decided to dedicate his life to the "salvation of Muslims", and so he developed an intimate knowledge of the religion. It is within this intimacy that his theology blossoms and that the Monastery of Mar Musa develops. As for his relation to Islam, he defines it as a dual sense of belonging. A dual sense of belonging that finds its source in Christ and can only find its way in a Church in motion.

Bosra and the Temptation of Conversion

In 1978, I was a young Jesuit studying in Beirut. The city had remained calm almost all winter and spring. I had a sore throat by dint of pronouncing Arabic gutturals! During that period, the structure of barricaded communities of Lebanese society deeply hurt my desire for inculturation in the Muslim world. As summer came, immediately after my exams, I wanted to go to Egypt, passing through Syria and Jordan and avoiding Sinai, still under Israeli occupation. On my way south of Damascus, I stayed in a hostel in Bosra, an ancient Roman city, then Byzantine and later Arab. In the evening, as I found the mosque, I thought I recognised an ancient church made of black stones. I stepped into the yard, where two young men welcomed me and we started talking about religion. I told them after a few exchanges: "I am dirty after a day's travelling, I would like to pay my respects to the mosque, the house of God, by performing my ablutions." They gave me a jug of water and guided me to the toilets to do a basic clean-up. When I came back, we sat down on the stone benches facing the ablution font and they taught me the words and gestures of the ritual

purification. When the time of the evening prayer came, men and children
filled the mosque and invited me to join the prayer. I felt a very strong attraction to do so, as well as a duty not to deceive my hosts. I thought that
they would not be able to understand my attitude of open-mindedness to
Islam for the sake Christ, but that they would simply have been delighted
with a conversion. How could they conceive of what I already felt as a dual
sense of belonging? Then I asked if I could just stay on my knees behind
the group, which the young imam pleasantly allowed me to do. It was like
a first time… The beauty, the universality, the gentleness, the truth of the
Muslim prayer revealed themselves to me in their might. There I was, with
these country people, and at the same time, I was in every mosque in the
world. Muslims say that praying is like finding yourself between the two
hands of the Merciful, like God in the Bible kneads clay with both hands
to form man. It is simply like this, in that mosque in Bosra, amongst those
believers, that the mystery of the Muslim prayer came into my own life of
prayer. It is in this town, where Muslim tradition reports that the monk
Bahira recognised in a very young Muhammad who was crossing Arabia in
his uncle's caravan, the Prophet ("*salla Allahu 'alayhi wa sallam*", Peace Be
upon Him), that I touched the authenticity of the Muhammadan way. It
is there that I discovered the strength it has, to have passed on from generation to generation through an astonishingly efficient pedagogy of rites of
sure symbolic strength and undeniable purity.

After the prayer, everybody remained seated for a catechetical conference, the topic of which could only be the conversion of a young European
man! For their preoccupation was to open the Islamic path of truth and
happiness for me, through this hyperconsciousness of being on the only
righteous path. The imam asked me what prevented me from becoming
Muslim on the spot. It was obvious from my moist eyes that I had been
within reach of the mystery. I answered that I had been a Muslim from my
childhood, since my dad, on the highest point of the Abruzzo Mountains,
would open his hands and my heart to the amazed recognition of the One
God, the Creator, and would ask the rivers, the valleys and the stars to praise
the Lord with his children. I wasn't among them to change religion, but
to share this praise. And also, that I was a *raheb*, a monk, by vocation and
imitation of Jesus! And there is no monastic life in the Muslim tradition!

I learnt later as I read Louis Massignon that my argument was a bit weak since some Sufi Muslim branches had wanted to create the authentic monasticism as it is praised in the Qur'an.[1]

I never went back to that mosque, nor met those believers again, but that is where my Muslim initiation took place.

A Dual Belonging?

I experience my relation to Islam as a sort of belonging. But let's be clear, my Christian faith doesn't find itself masked, or lessened by this belonging, on the contrary it professes itself to be orthodox, whole and true to its own dynamic. When I say that I belong to Islam, it is because from a cultural, linguistic and symbolic point of view, I feel deeply at home in the Muslim world.

The question is not only folkloric or ritual. It is about participating in the Muslim way to experience the world as actually being willed and created by the One God at this precise existential moment. It is receiving deep down in one's soul the testimony of the Truth, the only Truth. It is a movement of submission, of placing oneself in God's hands, of radical paradoxical trust in Allah who unifies the personal being and the universe, to the point where the theological affirmation that God alone is self-existing and that one's own existence is absolutely contingent, becomes something

---

1   Cf. Louis Massignon, *Essai sur les origines techniques du Lexique de la Mystique musulmane* [Thèse d'Etat complémentaire: Lettres: Paris: 1921–1922/ Paris: Librairie Paul Geuthner, 1914–1922.]. "How, exactly, is *rahbāniyya* defined for writers of Arabic? It is life in a hermitage and a vow to abstain from sexual relations. It may include even abstaining from eating meat, and forty-day retreats, as well as wearing a hair shirt... In reality, the Arab monastic life is based on vows of chastity and seclusion: it is the eremitic life. Islam is so little opposed to it that a temporary vow of chastity is imposed on pilgrims during their stay on sacred ground in Mecca. All the orthodox schools of jurisprudence allow the *i'tikāf*, pious retreat" (English translation from *Essay on the Origins of the Technical Language of Islamic Mysticism*, translated from the French by Benjamin Clark, University of Notre Dame Press, Indiana, 1997).

one is continuously aware of. The absolute as well as the contingent are included in the Mercy of the Unique One who embraces all.

I desire to be part of Islam, to dedicate myself to loving it, and first of all to loving Muhammad, may God's blessing be upon him and his *Ummah*.

This dual belonging to Islam and Christianity is always based and centred on the original relation to Jesus and his Church. My attitude is not different from Saint Paul's "I made myself a Jew to the Jews … To those who have no Law, I was free of the Law myself … I made myself all things to all men (1 Corinthians 9:20–23)". It is in this way that I always spiritually understood this mission towards Islam which I received. If in a certain way I declare myself Muslim by grace and evangelical obedience, it is because the charity of Christ encouraged me to a committed-rootedness, although so incomplete and unsure, still feeling my way, in the cultural world of Islam, therefore in its religious and spiritual world as well. I am Muslim because of Christ's love for Muslims and for Islam. Muslim, in accordance with the Spirit and not in accordance with the letter, "the written letters bring death, but the Spirit gives life" (2 Corinthians 3:6). Jesus and the Apostles in his wake were indeed Jews, but they interpreted their belonging to the people and to the religion of the Bible in the freedom of the Spirit and not in the fundamentalism of the letter. Therefore my relation to Muslim law, to the Qur'an, to the prophecy, is always measured, discerning, judged and guided by the Spirit of Christ. In other words, I experience that Jesus who lives in me is prompted by his charity to meet Islam in all its dimensions.

But what is this need, this desire, the reason to go to Islam in this way? Why not simply make the Christian tradition meet Islam to organise world peace? And "To you be your Way, and to me mine" (Qur'an 109:1-6). Why not accept to simply belong to one religion amongst the others? The answer requires an open attitude, intrinsically linked to the mystery and to the self-consciousness of the Church. What could it be?

Christianity Is a Movement

Jesus did not immediately found a religion. He initiated a community in motion, inside the Jewish religious world. It is this movement that we are interested in, a movement that of course can only exist within a certain religious world. For example, in the Gospels, Jesus' polemical attitude towards the Sabbath is blindingly obvious. The text depicts miracles, as well as other acts clearly against the Law that Jesus explicitly accomplishes on Saturday to irritate his contemporary coreligionists. This does not mean that Jesus doesn't celebrate Sabbath with his disciples, but his attitude is a Jewish reinterpretation of his own Jewish tradition! Likewise, the early Church experienced that this movement, this force of reinterpretation that is the very life of Jesus, the way Jesus transforms the world, could spread to other circles outside Judaism. Gradually, the Christian Community felt pushed by the Spirit of Jesus to take root in religious cultures other than Jewish, such as the Greek, Armenian, Egyptian and Latin cultures, etc.

In this way becoming a Christian is not so much about not belonging to a community that establishes prohibitions (dietary or others), as it is about integrating a community in motion, driven by the charity of Christ to meet everyone. Through the Church, each Christian is led to the priorities of Jesus, his logic and his style in his communion with God the Father in the Spirit. I feel very traditional on this point, "missionary", like Saint Paul who wanted to win everyone for Christ.

But where does this authority of Jesus come from, this freedom that allows him to reinterpret the Law and the Prophets and claim to accomplish them? It lies in his relationship to God the Father in the Spirit. For a disciple of Jesus, it is about delving deep within themselves to where the soul bears the imprint of the sacrament of Baptism. That is where the soul has been united to the self-awareness of Jesus of Nazareth. It has been sealed by his act of consecration to God the Father for our salvation. Through the event of the gift of faith, the disciple is transported to the space and the time of Jesus. The disciple is united to the soul of Christ, they participate in his intention and choice and they actively attend the renewal and the accomplishment of the world he achieves. In the Christian vision, this participation is possible because God joins us in our spiritual inner self, and introduces us through that into the life of Jesus of Nazareth. Jesus is the act of God to meet mankind, and by the Christian initiation, especially through the sacraments, the disciple has access internally to the life of Jesus.

The Church Goes to Islam

A great fear of syncretism troubles today's Church. I will not go to Islam on my own, to make my own alchemy of cultural syncretism. The movement of Jesus invigorates the Church, and it is within this Community that I go to Islam, with curiosity and attention to the work of the Spirit of God in the *Ummah*, the Muslim Community. The Church goes to Islam in anticipation of the coming Kingdom of God. Therefore, it's not that there is the Church and the Christian religion on the one hand, and on the other, the *Ummah* and the Muslim religion standing alongside the other religions in anticipation of a coming Kingdom of God in view of a final harmonisation. No, in the Christian experience, the final Kingdom is already, essentially, united and present in the Church in motion. The final harmony of the Kingdom happens through a pilgrim Church, the leaven and the lever for setting in motion all those religious realities towards the accomplishment of the Kingdom. This Kingdom is not only the glory of the Church, but also and just as much, the glory of the peoples and religions which the Church gathers by the grace she will receive.

I can already hear those who say this is a Church-centred vision of history, preventing the other traditions from developing their own vision of the final harmonisation of human pluralism. I admit this pitfall but, according to my experience, it is not the way things happen, quite the contrary. The Church does not mean to monopolise the future, and Islam has its own vision of the future. The Church can only perceive the completion of its mystery in a respectful and appreciative harmony with the completion and the accomplishment peculiar to the religious traditions in their plurality. It is the reconciliation of the plural visions of the future that creates the harmony of a future in common.

Ummah and Church, Impossible Links?

Islam unequivocally claims to be impervious to the mission of the Church. The shock that Islam represents is crucial in the history of the Church.

The evangelising mission of the Church has been stopped and repulsed by the Muslim wave. Therefore, a dual sense of belonging is always affected by this chronic opposition between *Ummah* and Church. It is unacceptable for either side, because both communities feel a strong need for an exclusive demarcation of the criteria of belonging. If you are a Christian, you cannot be a Muslim, and vice versa. A Muslim cannot be invited to receive Communion during Mass because that would imply accepting assertions about Christ that would separate them from Qur'anic monotheism. Likewise, a Christian could not fully and publicly participate in the Muslim Qur'anic prayer because just by doing this, they would separate themselves once and for all from the visible Church and join the Muslim Community. Since as a matter of fact, the *Shahada* prayer holds the official confession of the Islamic faith that implies obedience to the Muhammadan revelation.

The fact that those principles are often not strictly implemented in the churches and the mosques, for proselytism and irenicism purposes, does not invalidate the reciprocal awareness of dogmatic incompatibility... At least until today. The future belongs to God and to our good intentions.

Islam Perceived as a Rival Community

Islam was born and developed with a strong awareness of being a Community other than the Church. As for the Church, she immediately saw Islam as a rival and polemical Community. There are too many dogmatic and symbolic principles that are at once shared and interpreted differently. This constantly leads to siding entirely with one or the other of the Abrahamic families!

By the way, this is also the case with Judaism. If a Jewish person recognises Jesus as the Messiah, they can still feel Jewish, even very deeply. Since the Second Vatican Council, the Church would not mind it: consider, for instance, Cardinal Lustiger, or Saint Edith Stein. But the Jewish Community does not have the same line of reasoning and will tend to consider a baptised Jew as a soul that only ignorance can excuse. In the same way, the Christian Community will keep asking them to prove that they wholeheartedly accept the evangelical newness and the Church as a community and society.

This also holds true for Islam, since according to Muslims, the newness is the Muhammadan prophecy. They would not want a converted Christian to be ashamed of their Christian roots, quite the contrary. They would consider that by accepting Islam, the Christian has found their fulfilment.

The Dual Sense of Belonging Is No Relativism

I do not hide from my Muslim friends my conviction that my dual sense of belonging is sound, nor do I deny this to Christians. I understand it has to be explained in order to avoid unnecessary scandal. Believing that a dual sense of belonging is possible means and implies, at least in perspective, believing in the possibility of going beyond the theoretical and dogmatic contradictions between Islam and the Church. I feel it is right to place Islam and the Church side by side here because both the Muslim and Christian sense of belonging aspire and strive for a final unity that actually is their starting point. In a sense, it is only an apparent dual sense of belonging, because by traversing this duplicity, I want to belong to the sole Kingdom of God. Maybe I could say it differently: I belong to the Church for I am part of the mystery of Christ-Church; this mystery lives in me, not in solitude of course, but in a communal experience of Church. And I belong to Islam because the Church in me goes to Islam, wants to meet Muslims and wants to acknowledge the work of the Spirit of God in the Muslim religious experience. And still it is possible to respect the will of Islam to be Islam, and to not be absorbed by others at the expense of theological contortions.

Moreover, in some ecclesiastical circles, attitudes can be found where the dual sense of belonging does not result from a missionary apostolic activity of the Church but from the loss, or the fading, of Christian faith. As when it is said, for example, that Jesus Christ is the symbol for Christians of a universal salvation performed by God in various ways in all religions, or that religious traditions are diverse ways to reach God and therefore are more or less equivalent, or finally that the Word of God showed itself in Christianity through Christ but differently in other traditions. And so a person's dual belonging can come from the fact that they found themselves, because of their religious history, for geographical or cultural reasons, at the junction where two religions meet. So they receive spiritual nourishment from both, by picking and mixing what suits them best. It is quite a widespread tendency today within the *New Age* galaxy, for example. What these tendencies have in common is that the unique truth would eventually just be symbolic, not historical, transcending those cultural mediations that are only images of the unique truth. As such, the one initiated into the ultimate truth would lift those mediations like veils, once useful on the way, but eventually neither necessary nor definitive. We can recognise here a new gnosis chapter in the history of the Church. Besides there are Christian theologians who see Islam as merely another avatar of the gnostic danger to the Christian faith. By the way, I will say the time may have come for the Church to consciously open dialogue with gnostic tendencies.

The Dual Sense of Belonging Must Be Rooted in the Mystery of Christ

However, having an authentic aptitude for inculturation can help the disciples of Christ to rediscover, in its fullness, faith in the Redeemer for every person and all human reality. In fact, the opposite, that is to say the idea of remaining barricaded in inherited religious forms considered as impossible to update, unduly fixed or even fossilised, causes the loss of faith in Christ for a lot of people, especially the young, and prevents people from discovering it.

For the disciples of Jesus, the possibility of a dual sense of belonging is always rooted in their union to Christ in the Church, the first and last mystery of their life. It is therefore a belonging by faith, pertaining to the absolute, to the Church, and a derived, subordinate, apostolic belonging, due to the charity of Christ, to those we were sent to. All the same, one can wonder if a dual Muslim-Christian belonging is not somewhat naively understood as dressing the faith of the Church in the garments of Muslim culture.

Faith and Culture, Transcendence and Nature

In a way, every Christian has a dual belonging and bears a dual dynamic. The first dynamic is one of radical personal commitment in the dimension of faith, which represents the perspective of culture's openness to transcendence. The second dynamic wants to give spiritual experience its full expression within history and society, where human nature implies a being-there, engaged in the world. On the one hand, Christians give a cultural body to their faith, they express it in all aspects of their lives, and on the other hand they give a dimension of faith to their culture. Here the term "culture" is on the one hand opposed to nature, and on the other hand opposed as well as dynamically linked to faith, understood as supernatural. That is to say, faith goes beyond nature, in a higher and deeper way than deliberate cultural production. The Christians know that if they distinguish faith from culture, it is because at the height of their cultural world they experience transcendence and faith as an access to the absolute, which fractures the frame of their world. And yet, the transcendence of culture by faith is not an extra-cultural or an extra-natural phenomenon. On the contrary, it is in effect, the cultural awareness of a limit surpassed.

To return to the subject of Islam, the Church in its process of inculturation has the considerable task of learning to express herself through this encounter while at the same time remaining fully conscious of the assistance and consolation of the Holy Spirit; and of doing so while she tries to open herself to her endeavour of evangelical and eschatological preparation for the nation.

I am aware that what I propose is a theological opinion that must be verified within the Church, but I reflect on Islam in its historical and post-Christian being, and in its certitude of constituting the achievement of revelation. I am not deluding myself as to the dogmatic difficulties, apparently unsurmountable, such as the Muslim refusal of the Holy Trinity, the Divine Sonship, the Incarnation and more than anything, the Cross. But the theological virtues of faith, hope and charity encourage us to renew the efforts of interpretation so that the Church can go beyond these difficulties.

The Three Functions of Islam

When Christian theology attempts to state its case about Islam's part and function in the history of salvation, in the path of humanity towards God, it is called upon to distinguish and to recognise the importance Islam could have, either in relation to the Church – conversion, reform, deepening of the conscience of its own mystery – or in relation to the maturation of human spirituality – the cultural and spiritual unity of humankind, aesthetical, economic and social, and political organisation. I present here three non-exhaustive functions.

Islam as Completion of the Revelation

Islam is the last great religion that appeared on Earth, the last great Community of believers. The journey, the human phase of "production" of the Holy Scriptures seems to end by and with the Qur'an. It is like a phase of humanisation was ending to let another one begin. From a phenomenological point of view, we can agree on this, even without being a believer of one or the other religion. Humanity is not expecting another Book, despite the constant production of new holy texts that create new religious groups that look like aftershocks from a big earthquake. After Islam, we are no longer expecting another major revelation to show us the final, common, complementary or dialectical truth that would lead the religious traditions, as converging approaches, to a final harmonisation. Few people nowadays are expecting the advent of another big, structured religion or are hoping for a big, universal prophet. In that sense, Muhammad is the last one. This does not mean that the prophetic dimension of humankind has forever run dry, quite the contrary. It is to be rediscovered like a responsibility shared by each one of us.

Islam as Faith and Natural Revelation

Louis Massignon notes that "if Israel is rooted in hope, and Christianity devoted to charity, Islam is centred on faith".[2] Islam understands its mission as bringing back the community of mankind to recognising the original, natural revelation, the object of natural faith. Muslims consider Adam, and therefore every single man, each person, as the one to whom God is communicating a revelation. In the Qur'an God reveals to Adam the names of the created things, whereas in the Bible God is curious to know how Adam is going to name the creatures.[3] We can bring the two visions into opposition and theorise about the free Biblical man and the Qur'anic man to whom names are dictated. But here exactly is the methodology that outrages me: comparing in order to judge! To me it is magnificent to see that the Qur'anic concept, directly aligned with the Biblical concept, offers a meditation on human rational activity as being, from the beginning, a revealed thought. Man united to God, God thinks in him and human thought becomes revelation. Islam brings the person back to the Creator and a relationship is established. For the Muslim, God is the Other in the fundamental and original relationship. Abraham, the friend of God, remains the Islamic model of the relationship to God, where God takes the initiative and offers His Covenant. Islamically speaking, this Alliance, this Covenant, is pre-eternal.[4] It has been there

2   Massignon, *Les Trois Prières*, 98.
3   Cf. Qur'an 2:29–33 & Genesis 2:19 respectively.
4   "The Qur'an formulates a kind of final closure of the revelation through a pre-Mosaic regression; it is no longer the Christian idea of the Biblical text as "body

since God offered humanity to be His partner. Pre-eternal doesn't mean a state before time, but simply outside time, atemporal and, according to me, the ultimate dimension of every instant. In this way, the Alliance presents itself as the goal of every instant. God is perceived by us as the one who offers this Alliance as the final objective of our existence and invites us to answer responsibly.[5] Islam brings us all back to this original and final dimension...

Islam Perceived as a Challenge

A third dimension of Islam could be defined as difficult, not to say punitive, or more accurately, corrective. Since its beginning, Islam was perceived by Christians as a terrible challenge. By the Jews not so much, for they saw their cousin Ishmael thwarting the Christian Byzantine Empire and reopening the way to Jerusalem for the sons of Isaac and Jacob. But for Christians, it was immediately an unprecedented scandal! On the one hand, the very idea of a Christian empire was doubted because a large number of Christians suddenly had become subjected to Muslim control in the birth places of Christianity to the east of the Mediterranean, then southward all the way to Spain. Islam was perceived as a wall that isolated Christianity in a continental cul-de-sac, cutting it from its African and Asian future prospects. This way, the ambition of Eastern Christians to retain their power by baptising the new Muslim empire was thwarted. We are still here today, despite the fact that Islam as well had to face defeats when falling behind in technology and social institutions, had to

---

of Christ", ...it is not the Jewish idea of the special pact of alliance... No, it is the simple reminder by a warner of the primitive Covenant of humanity and its frightening final Judgement." Massignon, *Les Trois Prières*, 91–92.

5   "When thy Lord drew forth from the Children of Adam, from their loins, their descendants, and made them testify concerning themselves, (saying): "Am I not your Lord (who cherishes and sustains you)?" They said: "Yea! We do testify!" (This), lest ye should say on the Day of Judgement: "Of this we were never mindful", Qur'an 7: 172.

face crises due to Western colonial empires and along with them Western ideologies expanding their grip on a territory they felt was theirs; not forgetting its own internal contradiction concerning globalisation and the foundation of the state of Israel. Today's suicide terrorist attacks are indeed a tragic symptom of discontent and radical unhappiness of the Arabic nation as well as of the entire Muslim Community. It is useless to state that terrorists are not "real" Muslims. It is often said that wanting to combine the exercise of violence with the glory of God would be blasphemy! The horror of sacralised violence does not justify excommunications. Our religious traditions have always justified the use of violence. Each community would better recognise the still existing roots of these violent drifts, these tendencies that reside in them, inside their own traditions. This soul-searching would force us to rediscover the deep roots of our hatreds and therefore to make responsible choices.

The Eschatological Challenge

It is interesting to note that in general, fundamentalists, whether they are Christians, Jews or Muslims, are haunted by a fever for the end of History. According to these fundamentalists, as of now, all the signs of the end of the world are gathered. The Antichrist, or the fake Messiah, is now at work to secretly gather the conditions for the final victory. Secretly, because he would like to have eternal ultimate power. The victory of the Righteous ones, the Muslim Mahdi (the anticipated "rightly-guided one"), the Jewish Messiah ("the anointed one") and the triumphant Christ prevent him from obtaining it. The name of the battle place is known, it is the plain of Armageddon in the Holy Land. Gog and Magog are ready to unleash themselves on this civilisation that thinks it is immortal, to re-impose the original, pre-moral chaos.[6] And all this is the beginning of the end. It is paradoxically in this setting that the radicalisation

6   Ezekiel 38 & 39; Apocalypse 20:8; Qur'an 21:95–96

of the ongoing conflict between civilisations could be explained. The idea of the clash of civilisations immediately refers to Samuel Huntington's theory.[7] I do not believe it is necessary to develop this point here. Let us just not forget that for a huge majority of Muslims, as well as for Jews and Christians, religion is the constitutive element, the centre and source of identity awareness, both personal and communal. It is hard to know which proportion of Muslims are guided, in their ideas, in their political commitment, by an eschatological perspective of a fundamentalist type, but it is also to be linked to the situation of tension and conflict that a local community can experience more or less dramatically. In general, situations of war facilitate eschatological and fundamentalist visions.

Each one believes that they are on God's side and considers that the other is on Satan's side... With some amusing detours sometimes, like this Shiite leader who found that "our enemy" Bush, the demon, had been used by God to eliminate Satan in the person of Saddam Hussein! The other, the enemy, is considered as subhuman and therefore can be eliminated. The definition of a human being is from now on linked to belonging to a religious community that categorises beliefs as either true or false and therefore someone's humanity as true or false. Let us set this idea aside and go back to the fact that there is a shared, although distinct, expectation. This is not the place to write a tract on comparative eschatology, but even so I would like to underline that in the story of the end, in an eschatological point of view, nobody is expecting any other major event than the end itself, launched by a Kingdom of peace and justice, established by this anticipated one, in a different but similar way, by all the children of Abraham. I mean the anticipated Messiah of the Jews, the anticipated Christ of the Christians and the Mahdi expected by the Muslims. Our different eschatologies draw different "political programs" and offer different visions of everybody's future. Many elements remain common to the three religions:

– The advent of the end following a series of catastrophes.
– The patience of the righteous in an increasingly perverse, difficult and cruel world.

7   Samuel Huntington, *Le choc des civilisations [The Clash of Civilizations]*, (Paris: Odile Jacob, 2007).

- The final advent of a superhuman from our own Community who reveals everybody else's fake beliefs.
- The establishment of a penultimate, millenary, just and peaceful kingdom, the Resurrection.
- The Final Judgement and the final realisation of the Kingdom of God.

Within each religious group, there will be literal interpretations predicting dates and so on, and symbolical interpretations that differ slightly less from the sciences. My goal is not to ridicule all this, quite the contrary, I would like to draw from it the symbolic elements that could be subjects of dialogue, the language of a shared hope. A hope held by a mutual political responsibility that I persist in calling Abrahamic.

Islam, a Bulwark against Christian Totalitarianism

To my mind, the immense merit of Islam is to have thwarted the imperial Christian political project. It is the project for a humanity shaped by violence, rallied around a power that justifies itself by "true" dogmas. In such a way, the truth of the dogmatic system is granted by ecclesiastical structures and it falls to them to bless and consecrate a society where privilege, injustice and discrimination often become the norm.[8] From the Period of Enlightenment and secularism, this system entered into crisis and a democratic system was put in place, with all its weaknesses; a system that, to many people's minds, realises some of the important evangelical values, such as equality and solidarity. A system that lost a lot, by the way, of the sacred dimension of family, of social and political life. The Western world finds itself disenchanted and waiting to be re-enchanted. Compared to the modern Western world, Islam is a reminder of this holy dimension.

8   Saint Paul's Epistle to the Galatians 3:27–28: "...and there are no more distinctions between Jew and Greek (no privilege), slave and free (no injustice), male and female (no discrimination), but all of you are one in Christ Jesus."

I am aware of the risk of amalgamation and simplifications that can lead to an ideological drift. I bear, I experience, I endure a scandal and a fever. The scandal is the Church's failure in regards to evangelical poverty, in regards to being a disciple of Jesus of Nazareth, the Son of God, which can only be demonstrated through practising this discipleship. And a fever, an eagerness for the Church, its beauty, its faithfulness... This very fever prompts me towards Islam. I am not converting to Islam because conversion is to God. But the relation to Islam breeds a crisis in me and a challenge that I feel is in the same line as the scandal I feel.

In this way, Islam created a wall against the fundamentalist totalitarianism of Christian Europe, and also represents a criticism of Western lay secularism. By saying this, I would not want to consecrate an idealised vision of Islam because, let us admit it, the history of Islam is made of serious contradictions and suffering. I believe much more in the reciprocal functions of criticism and inspiration of the culturally different religious bodies towards one another. It remains essential to recognise that in the history of Islam, there is a substantial tolerance towards the Jews and the Christians. Since the first Muslim society, "contracts" of tolerance have been agreed with the People of the Book (the Jews and the Christians). Of course, specific taxes were established for them, which were linked to their privilege to not to participate in war. However, to be honest, I still have to admit that I feel Muslims' tolerance is based on the recognition that the Jewish and Christian communities were established by God, the only Master of History and of its conclusion.

There have also been drifts of power in Muslim history and it is very healthy to have Muslim historians listing them and describing their horror. Muslim historians are sometimes accused of being unable to cast a scientific and critical eye on history, even religious history. It is true that when they are critical and differ from partisan chronicles, historical sciences are recognised accomplishments of modernity. But thinking that all Muslim historians today have an attitude of justification and apologetics is a myth among other myths.

The Christian Crisis of Conscience in the Presence of Islam

Christians are stuck between the double scandal of the sincere refusal of Judaism, pre-Christian in its roots, to believe in the Son of God the Saviour, and post-Christian Islam's same refusal. I am speaking as a Christian: the healthiest thing Islam gave to us was to have thwarted us in relation to the sacralisation of power. Islam halts the pretension of Christianity to constitute the perfect, final, eschatological society. First of all, in medieval and Renaissance art, Christ was represented as an emperor. The Antichrist looks very much like him in terms of the signs of power! The mystery of God's humility becomes the icon of Moloch in power.

The contradiction between being a disciple of Jesus of Nazareth and belonging to the Church of power is a drama that led Charles de Foucauld's evangelical soul to purify his Catholic faith, his belonging to Western Civilisation, to his French nationalism and even to his aristocratic origins in the depths of the Muslim desert.[9]

Many people say that Muslims are not any better regarding the sacralisation of power and practice of violence as an act of worship. This is true, even though there is no ordained priesthood in Islam. That said, we cannot confine all the searching and suffering of Muslims to such a description. Indeed, I am struck by how many young Muslim believers possess a great religious eagerness for justice and a true capacity for criticism towards the sacralised powers in their society. The legitimacy of violence, motivated by a religious political programme, is the subject of an open debate within Muslim society. My Muslim friends, whom I met in the East as well as in Europe, tell us that Muslim religious terrorism is a tragedy for Muslim society before being a danger to the West.

It is harder to accept that religious violence is truly part of our common cultural baggage (in Gandhi's India, Hindu violence is raging)! It outrages me to hear Christians say that the violence of the "Crusaders" has nothing to do with "true Christianity". Amin Maalouf shows us to what extent

9   Jean-François Six, *Charles de Foucauld autrement* (Paris: DDB, 2008).

the Crusades are an integral part of our European and Christian historical reality, while the catechesis of the lofty souls tries to demonstrate the
foreignness of both Christians and the Church to violence throughout
Christian history.[10] Violence and sacralised power are part of both of our
histories and I don't want to excommunicate anyone. Thank God, there is
a reciprocal thwarting effect that brings about a crisis of purification for
all of us.

Within its own cultural space, all of Christianity was placed in a deep
crisis by fascist, nationalist tides and by communism, which paved the four
continents with dead bodies. Colonialist movements aligned themselves
with Catholic and Protestant affiliations to serve national and imperialist
interests. And Islam considered itself a victim of the West in all its expressions, including liberalism. Perhaps in an even more universal way, Islam
perceived itself as besieged by the most contemporary of Western expressions of power, that is to say, liberal economic imperialism combined with
the secularised consumerist model; especially considering that oil capit-
alism deeply penetrated the Arab-Muslim world. In the eyes of many pious
Muslims, here lies one of the most serious and dangerous challenges the
Muslim Community has to face. The 2008 global financial crisis that caused
harm to the entire world's resources was interpreted by many Muslims as
the natural consequence of an unfair and amoral system, based on interest
loans and the artificial profits it involves.

I feel it is my duty here to repeat that Islam's history does not escape
total blame regarding the sacralisation of power. This power has also been
linked to the caliph whose role was to govern the Community in the name
of the Prophet. Often, Muslim religious titles were attached to the totali-
tarian power structures of Asian empires. Muslim history, like Christian
history, seems to be experiencing a desire for purification of authority's
eagerness for power, a desire to reclaim justice, a desire for assisting the
most disadvantaged in society in the name of the pure, true religion.

While globalised Western power causes a crisis for the sacralised
Muslim powers, the Muslim world, perceived as a whole, rises up against

---

10   Amin Maalouf, *Les croisades vues par les Arabes* [*The Crusades Through Arab Eyes*]
      (Paris: J'ai Lu, 1999).

the Western Moloch (capitalist system monopoly, single social model, nuclear arms control...). There is reciprocal functionality here as well...

Nowadays, the consumerist wave, the commodification of all things human wash over us just like Gog and Magog, striking all that is spiritual to the point where the spiritual need itself becomes the object of a commercial activity. Indeed, the popular movements in Latin America, the liberation theologies, provoked an internal crisis within the Christianised Moloch, recognised as such by Oscar Romero, bishop and martyr. Still, it is Islam that until now represents the greatest, the most shockingly unassailable rampart against the Western World with its supposed Christian roots.

Islam and Church in Relation to Asian Wisdom

Islam entered South-East Asia mainly though trade starting in the eleventh century. The Islamisation of Indonesia, the country with the largest Muslim population worldwide, did not occur through armed invasions, but instead through the example and penetration of a Sufi-inspired civilisation. On the other hand, in Central Asia, Islam entered by armed force. In both cases, people's hearts were also conquered by Islam's beauty and spirituality as by the coherence of its civilisation. In South-East Asia as well as in Central Asia, the advance of Islam seems to have been stopped by Indian and Chinese cultural hegemony. Even if occasionally Islam deeply pierced the heart of these civilisations, they were not massively Islamicised. In Asia as in Africa for that matter, Muslim penetration was in turn halted by Western colonialisation.

I think statistically the very limited spread of Western Christianity, allied with the colonial powers, in Indian and Chinese Asia is due to these communities' deep resistance to such a form of foreign imperialism. Something similar can probably be stated about the resistance of the same communities to Muslim empires.

Paradoxically, there has been a strange complicity between Islam and Christianity in Asia. Generalising is always bad, and there are books filled with fascinating stories of more or less successful inculturations and osmoses between the Muslim and Christian religions in Asia. On the Christian side, we can recall the names of great Jesuits like Mateo Ricci, Roberto de Nobili, Vincent Lebbe and Henri le Saux. On the Muslim side, it is more of a long-term adaptation phenomenon and widespread folkloric cultural synthesis. The Mughal civilisation is a good example of this. It is notably true that the colonialists demonstrated a large incapacity to recognise the spiritual value of Asian wisdom, just as Muslims demonstrated a real difficulty in recognising the authenticity of Asian religious experience.

Islam thwarted Christianity in its Western fiefdom. The Christian colonialist short-sightedness took care of the rest. Thus, Muslims and Christians were as if allied to spare China from baptism as well as from the *Shahada*! Deep down, it saved the depths of the Asian spiritual experience that is necessary for the metaphysical future of mankind.

Dual Belonging, One Unique Belonging

I state loud and clear my belonging to the Catholic Church, led by the successors of the Apostle Peter. I also claim the necessity for every generation to participate in the fight for the purification of the Church from the control of idolatrous structures. I am tempted to make the same statement for Islam. It is less about breaking with the *Ummah* than taking part in a renewal of Islam that roots itself in the sincerity of the Prophet and his first Companions. The fruits of this renewal are today carried by the desire for authenticity and justice for disadvantaged Muslims, *mustad'afù l'ard* [the oppressed of the earth].[11]

My belonging to Jesus of Nazareth prompts me to belong to Islam. The fight against fundamentalism, against the manipulation of religion by the powers-that-be, must transcend religious affiliations… In other words, it should interest the Christian as well as the Muslim world…and everyone else! It is time to stop attributing all fundamentalism to the Muslim side

---

11   TN. *Mustad 'afù l'ard* (various translations of this term are possible including the poor/vulnerable /oppressed of the earth), translation assisted by Dr. Nayla Tabbara.

in order to justify and promote our own fundamentalist fevers. Just as it is about time Muslims do the same and stop blaming the West for every internal problem within their Community. Quite the contrary, it is in our best interests to join forces in a context of common belonging to a postnational and, at least in a certain way, post-religious humanity.

My dual belonging is the governing principle of my life. The Church, passionate for universality and in love with the spiritual richness of the people, sent me to pour the batter of my Christian identity into the mould of Islam. It implies a necessary effort of communication to explain this evolution of identity to the Church as much as to Islam.

If I try to summarise the meaning of this dual belonging, I could say that it resides in the contextualised and existential dynamic of in-depth study and in the necessity of moving beyond any fixed crystallisation of identity. We are looking at our reflection in flowing water. The reflection of our identity is constantly modified by the water running towards the valley. It is not necessary to arrive at a static definition for a communal self-perception. But it is essential to open up and participate, dialogically, to the advent of the One in the contingent multiplicity of His thousand-faceted glory.

CHAPTER 3

A Church of Islam?

In ecclesiastical contexts, Paolo Dall'Oglio was often criticised for using the expression "Muslim-Christian Church" in articles and conferences. Today, he would rather use the expression "Church of Islam". Beyond the obvious oxymoron of the expression, it signifies a way to go towards the other that would break fixed and reductive identities. A "going towards" that would not be an absorption, nor a simple blend, but a deep inculturation, just as respectful of the identity of the Christian Churches in a Muslim milieu.

A Church for Islam

Even before wondering if the words "Muslim-Christian Church" or "a Church for Islam" could be accepted in the Church and even someday recognised by Muslims, we need to say straightaway that these terms absolutely do not signify some sort of blending and compromise between Christianity and the Muslim religion, produced by some encounter, or a name for a religion formed by cultural and religious blending.

I now tend to distance myself from the expression "Muslim-Christian Church", even if I consider it as correct from a dogmatic point of view, for it can be misunderstood by the Christian side and even more by the Muslim one. The fact remains that it is necessary to find a name for a community that would gather the disciples of Jesus living in a Muslim milieu, born in, sent or pertaining to this context where they choose to put down roots and with which they want to engage, in anticipation of the coming Kingdom of God. Besides, it might be necessary to underline that the expression

"Muslim-Christian Church" is analogous to established expressions such as "Judeo-Christian Church" (Christians with Jewish origins who do not separate themselves from their Jewishness) and "Ethno-Christian Church" (Christians without Jewish origins who acquired a full right to ecclesiastical citizenship without actually embracing Jewishness). In this case, "Church" simply means "assembled community"; otherwise, there would be a repetition, and the expression "Christian Church" would be redundant.

Perhaps it would be more appropriate to say "Church of the Jewish nation", "to the Jewish nation", bearing or assuming Jewish roots. One also speaks of the "Church of the Nations", the same way as one would speak of the "Church of France" or of the Mongolian nation. In this way "Church of Islam", an expression proposed by Melkite Patriarch Laham, would be the most appropriate.[1] Because it does not imply a blending but a reality in which Islam, as well as the Church, remain themselves in the face of the elements shaping their communal self-perception.

In this situation, Muslims certainly struggle with assimilating Islam to one of the nations because they consider themselves as *Ummah* (Community, or "nation") that understands itself as supranational and postnational, in other words a "religion". It truly is here that this question becomes interesting because the Church does not only want to blend with ethno-linguistic national identities or, differently, with local communities sharing the same narrative but also, and just as much, to blend with much deeper and vast religious identities.

It should be pointed out right away that one of the essential elements defining ecclesiastical self-perception is universality, Catholicity, as a participation in a diverse and plural cultural identity that forms a sole and unique ecclesial body.

A specific or a local Church will be catholic, universal, or it will not be ecclesial. The opposition between Church of Islam and Catholic Church would be analogous to an impossible opposition between an Italian or a French Church and the Catholic Church. In a timely manner the Catholic Church revived a Church that professes itself Judeo-Christian in Israel,

---

1   *Oasis* Magazine, March 2006, "The Church of the Arabs: A Special Responsibility", Mgr. Gregorios III Laham, Greek Melkite Patriarch of Antioch, p.104.

with its own bishop who prays in Hebrew and lives at the rhythm of the People of Israel, following the example of the early Church of Jerusalem. This Christian Community in a Jewish milieu is certainly called upon to the communion of charity, justice and sharing with the Arab-Palestinian Church, the direct and uninterrupted heir of Jerusalem's early apostolic Church.

Simultaneously, there are Christians of different origins (different geography, family, religion), who are aware that they want to embody the Church of Christ in a Muslim milieu. Some of them were born in this Muslim milieu, others have ties to it, while others emigrated or were sent there. Their community does not want to be opposed to, nor in competition with this Muslim context: they want to support it. Is this pure fantasy? It is not, it is a theology of the Church, directly built on the advances of the Second Vatican Council.[2] These Christians are conscious of being a Christian Church for Islam, or a Church of Islam.

The Church is always contextual, and its catholicity is a communion of plural contexualities.

Are Muslims shocked by the expressions "Church for Islam" or "Church of Islam"? Will they suspect an attempt to incorporate Islam into the Church? I often heard Middle-Eastern Muslims referring to the Arab Christian minorities as "our Christians", the Christians of our Muslim societies, who form with us a single cultural, but also cultural community, for we love the One God in different ways. The Melkite Patriarch Laham, who resides in Damascus, has been criticised for using the expression "Church of Islam", but I have not heard negative reactions from the Muslim side. Is this about "incorporation"? It is and it is not! It is, because in Christian theological language there is precisely the matter of incorporating the entire universe into the body of Christ, in anticipation of the coming Kingdom of God, or rather it is Christ who incorporates it. And it is not, because the question is not to devour otherness in order to assimilate it, but on the

---

2   Cf. Appendix p. 196–203. "Explanatory Note on the Particular Vocation of the Monastic Community in the Muslim World", where the texts of the Magisterium on these issues, starting with Second Vatican Council, are cited in a coherent manner.

contrary, to fall in love with otherness, in this case Islam, to interact with it
and participate in the joy and glory of its accomplishment and fulfilment.

I want to recall the ecclesiological aim of my words. Is there, or
will there be a Church aware of being fully, sacramentally, doctrinally,
disciplinarily Catholic; and with that, precisely and because it is Catholic,
a Church also capable of being "Muslim-Christian"? The problem is not
with the expression, to which I am not attached, what matters is the mission I am consecrated to.

The Sacrament of Good Neighbourliness

There already exists a local Church deeply inculturated in the Muslim
milieu. It is embodied by the historical Eastern Churches in the Arab,
Turkish and Persian milieus etc. I would like to insist on the theological
value of neighbourly relations: the sacrament of neighbourly relations.
The fourteen centuries of common life shared by Eastern Christians and
Muslims, not forgetting the Jews, immediately occur to me. In day-to-
day life, through and despite the cultural and dietary laws that separate
communities, a true conviviality and commensality takes place. The
theological aspect comes from the fact that it is impossible to live side by
side with people you consider as being under Satan's power! How could
you imagine living together, playing together … and believing that your
playmate is doomed to hell? Furthermore, how could you live in mutual
esteem and also consider the religion and faith of the other to be futile?
Beyond the dogmas of mutual condemnation, neighbourly relations signify a benevolent hope towards one's neighbour and indicate a way for
the future wherever Christians and Muslims share the same space of life
and work. I have often noticed differences in the theological considerations of Eastern Christians towards Muslims, be they bishops or simple
believers. In general, the ones who belong to homogenous and protected
areas (districts, regions, Christian villages) tend more easily towards traditional statements of blind rejection of the Muslim revelation, whereas
the ones who have experience with neighbourly relations from an early

age would rather lean towards a quest for theological justifications of the legitimacy of their neighbour's Muslim belonging, and even of its foundation: the legitimacy of Muhammad.

In the village of Yabroud there lives a Christian family that, from generation to generation, spins goat hair to make tents for Bedouins … There, the neighbourliness falls within a business relationship with nomadic Muslims. The family's old patriarch told me one of his dreams. He was in a *majlis*, a gathering of men under a tent, and the Prophet of Islam was there. The patriarch's child comes in and makes a gesture of contempt towards the Muslims present. The patriarch disciplines his child and brings him by the hand to show consideration and respect to the Prophet, who then blesses them with a kiss. Abou Youssef, the patriarch in question, said that when he recounted his dream to his Muslim friends, they kissed him on the head because the Prophet had visited him in a dream!

The problem is that neighbourly relations are in crisis. Participation in a mutual local culture crumbles before the validation of conflictual cultural models. For example, fifty years ago, Christian and Muslim women from the village of Nebek used to dress the same way, covering their heads but not their faces, rarely wearing black outside periods of mourning. Today, under the influence of their travels, of television, etc., Christian girls westernise to the point of caricature and the Muslims go "Saudi style". The common space narrows and the tradition of sharing is forgotten. Neighbourly relations, which used to be naturally initiated, must now be deliberately made part of a common catechesis, against the flow. A Muslim-Christian theology of this topic must be elaborated, otherwise the drift of separation and opposition will accelerate. We would like to think in this direction.

It is indeed our duty to recall here the objective difficulties endured by non-Muslim minorities in a legal Muslim milieu that implies limits to neighbourly relations. Before anything, it has to be stated that the only communities Islam legally admits in its milieu are Jewish and Christian communities (as well as the Sabaeans, who tend to blend in, and are thus a minor category) and that it excludes all that could be considered as idolatrous paganism, thus Asian and African traditions in general.[3] Islam is

---

3   Qur'an 2:62; 5:69 and 22:17.

moving forward with regard to this topic and I have heard interesting interpretations based on the respect due to all human communities in the name of the legitimacy of these communities because of Adam, the original authentic human. The important international Islamic Ahmad Kuftaro Foundation in Damascus is in contact with Buddhist centres in Japan. From this contact emerges a whole reflection on the religious authenticity of their Zen friends. This goes beyond the philosophical category of an original natural religion, within the reach of every soul regardless of religious affiliation. This practice of meeting on an existential level inspires the recognition of the other's spiritual authenticity.

Neighbourly Relations despite Discrimination

Christians from Arab-Muslim countries suffer from a discrimination that is difficult to conceal and to keep enduring. A Muslim man can marry a Christian woman, but the opposite is forbidden: a Muslim woman can only marry a Muslim man. What is more, the Christian spouse of a Muslim man cannot inherit from him nor has she the same rights as a Muslim woman has with the children. Acceptable solutions for both sides can be found, but they would have to seek them together. Obviously, there is another question, that of conscience discrimination regarding conversion: everybody is free to become a Muslim; no one is free to abandon Islam. Here too, things are in motion. In general, and by very different argumentations, Muslims think that the death sentence for apostates is not legitimate in present circumstances. Others advocate opening ways to the secularisation of the public sphere based on the concept of citizenship. The reflection of European Muslims can bring a lot to this debate. For the sake of a deep social internalisation, I hope that full freedom of conscience can emerge from an Islamic religious reflection, not against or in spite of the religion itself.

In general, Muslims perceive the question of discrimination differently, because they consider a number of laws issued by Western societies as the expression of a Christian vision, and thus imposed on them. The list could be long: dietary laws, calendar, inheritance, monogamy, dress codes, etc. There can be no absolute rule here, "falling from Heaven"! The solution will only come from dialogue led in a democratic and pluralist framework. Societies have to make choices that remain fluid. Good neighbourliness is a spirit, a dynamic and not a series of rules.

The Church of Arab Christians

There are several groups of who we call Arab Christians today:

- The first group consists of the Arabs who became Christian before Islam. It is a wider and more important phenomenon than one would think. They remained Christian even after the arrival of Islam. Since before the Qur'an, Arabic was mostly the language of an oral culture, Arab Christians used to depend especially on the Greek and Syriac languages in their liturgical life.
- The second group consists of the Christians of Syriac, Greek, Coptic or other mother tongues who adopted the Arabic language in a Muslim context and actively participated in creating the Arab civilisation that is at once Muslim, Christian and Jewish. I would say, as an aside, that it is almost the same for the Jews before Islam, because there were Greek or Syriac-speaking Jews who adopted Arabic subsequently, while others were already Arabs before Islam.

Christians from both the first and second groups have for a greater part Arabised their religious culture and their liturgy. This way, the Arabic language became a language of Christian liturgy and often, in its expressions, is very close to the Qur'anic language.

- The third group of Arab Christians is composed of citizens of Arab nations like Syria, who migrated during the twentieth century, who use their non-Arabic mother tongue in their liturgy and among each other. This is the case for Armenians, Chaldeans

and Syriacs, all survivors of the genocide that marked the end of
the Ottoman Empire, in Cilicia and Upper Mesopotamia. They
became members of the Syrian Arab Republic, while keeping their
linguistic and cultural identity.

- The fourth group includes the Christians who choose to become
  Arabs, because the Church has sent them to express the Gospel's
  dynamic of incarnation and inculturation in an Arab milieu.
  They do so by profoundly embracing this context like a new identity, through a psychological and cultural process that is always
  ongoing. This process would in a way consist of divesting from
  one's original cultural identity in order to take on this new identity, for the love of Christ. This is obviously my case. This has something in common with mixed marriages, especially the ones where
  one of the two partners makes the choice to deeply integrate with
  the cultural identity of the other.

- The fifth group is very hard to define, but it does exist. These are
  the Muslims, (Arab here, but who could be from another nation
  or speak a different language), who choose to be Christians, to
  believe in Jesus of Nazareth and through this very fact constitute
  part of the Church, without abandoning or wishing to abandon
  their Muslim religious and cultural belonging.

Christian Muslims?

My statements might seem vague when it comes to defining what constitutes believing in Jesus of Nazareth. Muslims do not concern themselves with Jesus' death and resurrection, while still believing in him as
Messiah. Indeed, the Grand Mufti of Damascus has declared that all
Syrians are Christian! And yet, they are not all Christian in the sense
understood by the Church, since ultimately, "salvation" comes from believing in the death and resurrection of Jesus. If it were otherwise, the idea
of a Christian Muslim would come across as a Trojan Horse introduced
into the Muslim *polis* with the intention of evangelising. In that case, the

belonging to the *Ummah* would be merely folkloric (a language, a culture, certain practices and symbols).

I accept the risk of potential misunderstanding. I deeply believe that there are collective stories linked to sociological identities. And there, one's relation to the death and resurrection of Christ can be more or less conscious and committed. Further, there is the mystery of personal stories and individual consciousness. They can go either way: belonging to the Church and leaving it, coming to Islam and getting away from it…

Let us imagine now the strong and shocking hypothesis for a majority of Muslims that one of their own would want to belong to the Church. The potential belonging of that Muslim first depends on the capacity of the Church to welcome them, that is to say, to have a theology of Islam that would enable this adoption. Secondly, it would depend on the capacity of that person to synthesise this dual belonging through a reinterpretation of Muslim and Christian dogmatic material. The same holds for their possibility to live their belonging to Christianity without unnecessary and unfair personal heartache concerning their identity. Finally, it also depends on the level of religious tolerance, respect and freedom of conscience practised by the Muslim milieu itself, be it familial, social or legal. Depending on different contexts: either a Paris suburb, Istanbul, Cairo, etc., emancipated international familial contexts, or even traditional milieus strongly characterised by religion, it could prompt the birth of a "Church of Islam" that quietly celebrates its faith within a society that remains deeply characterised by its Muslim religion, and at the same time makes a true space for freedom of conscience.

In fact, most "conversions" from Islam to Christianity today happen with a logic of opposition where one would leave a false religion for a true one, in a more or less admitted process of leaving and rejecting Islam. Actually, this is what partly justifies, in some people's eyes, the violent reactions from the Muslim milieu against any proselytism in several parts of the world. In this way, the failure of evangelisation brings the Church back to the Gospel.

It is a context where, in order to protect Islam, freedom of conscience is not allowed to everyone. Until the Muslim Community itself finds a way to express such a pluralism of conscience as something essential to its own wellbeing, it is possible to imagine a humble and discreet network of men and women who are open about their Muslim identity and centre their lives on the mystery of Jesus of Nazareth as he is celebrated by the Church. Most of them will not know about one another, they will not organise a clandestine Church, they will rather express their belonging to a mystical Church, offered as a hostage of love, like yeast in dough.

I am not expecting a mass movement. My prediction is not only sociological. I would say that I do not wish for a mass movement, I would even be opposed to it, because I sincerely recognise the theological status of Muslim belief and practice.

Besides, I fully recognise the right of an originally Christian person to leave the Church and integrate with the Muslim community as it is currently understood. Apart from that, we should consider the possibility of entering Islam without actually abandoning the Church. I think that there is already a spiritual space for the souls of both Christians and Muslims who, as of now, synthesise the harmonies to come.

Risks of Direct Evangelisation

Some Christian communities today, Protestant in particular, make efforts of direct evangelisation in a Muslim milieu. I do not question the sincerity of their efforts at proselytism, but this approach comprises several flaws. This evangelisation, as mentioned earlier, is based on judging the Muslim religion as fundamentally false. It is a point of view that, after Vatican II, the Church no longer shares.[4]

Moreover, and very often, even if in a Muslim milieu these efforts of proselytism are made in the Arabic language, these Protestant communities remain deeply fundamentalist in their interpretation of the Bible, and much linked to the Western, and often American religious way of life. They are therefore incapable of a deep cultural adaptation, and for this

4   The texts are cited in the Appendices, 196 and ss., especially *Nostra Aetate* and *Lumen Gentium*.

very reason they provoke the cultural uprooting of their new followers. Finally, they lack a vision of progressive hope for the Muslim milieu where they operate. The negative response of the milieu is quite understandable. It is neither likely nor advisable for the Church to establish itself there in this way. Thank God, Islam remains impervious enough. As I am saying this, I do not approve in any way of the violent and more or less subtle repression of freedom of conscience that takes place in several Muslim states. Violent acts also take place in the Western world, within families and in neighbourhoods. However, I am taking the risk to state that the paths towards adopting Human Rights in the Muslim milieu, the way they were formulated by the United Nations, must follow an internal process in Muslim communities and cannot not be imposed from outside. It will follow its own pace and have a particular scale of priorities. Human rights proponents will prove convincing through their universal practices and concrete initiatives, rather than through casting moral judgement while at the same time turning a blind eye to their own conduct. The West of Amnesty International is also the world of Guantanamo Bay... One will respond that the West is pluralistic and complex. Well so is Islam.

Besides, I am entirely aware of the historical impossibility, in most cases, to implant the Church in a properly Muslim milieu by direct evangelisation, with the intention to fully incorporate people and populations of Muslim origin into the visible Church. What is more, the traditional Christian communities that remained in *dar al-Islam* [Abode of Islam], as is the case in the Middle East, in Turkey or in Iran, are generally not very significant from a statistical point of view, and retain a strong awareness of their distinct identity and culture. The relationship to the Other is rarely one of functional reciprocity and often is one of a certain rivalry, or at best, of good neighbourliness despite religious difference.

There certainly are cases where a Christian wants to relate to the Muslim milieu, positively perceived this time, as a Christian. It is more the exception than the rule. More often, authentic national solidarity and shared citizenship enter into crisis with the advances of the re-Islamisation of the state and society, coupled with the endemic emigration of Christians to the West.

The Church Facing Syncretism

In an article that I polemically called *Eulogy of Syncretism*, I tried to
deal with this question from another angle, from the process of cultural
and even religious blending.[5] We have already noted this indeed: be it
Christian or Muslim, faith does not exist separated from a cultural context, and even the distinction between faith and culture, though it is a
theological concept, still pertains to the field of culture. In this way, a
Christian is not able to programme in advance the extraction of their faith
from their education and to culturally reincarnate it in another context,
a Muslim one, for example. It will always be a process where, within the
evolution of our own culture, we make the effort to appropriate another
culture. Because there is no extra-cultural conscience of faith, but only
a cultural conscience of the transcendence of faith. There is no bridge
that could put two cultures in contact without itself belonging, in several
ways, to the two cultures it unites. Hermeneutics is part of the history of
the text. It happens naturally through cultural syncretism, and, when the
question is religious, through religious syncretism.

The Church knew, from the first centuries, how to confront the risk
of syncretism and it had to develop a method for that, a method to safeguard what it judged as falling within the essentials of faith, so that these
essentials were not lost when meeting other traditions. It is in this logic
of syncretism that in the Greek context the Church was able to preserve
itself from the gnostic synthesis of the first and second centuries. Faced
with the mystical philosophies of the ancient world, the Christians had to
defend the originality of the Church's faith in a truly dead and resurrected
Christ, truly divine and truly human.

Today, the Church is open to dialogue but distrusts syncretism:

> We, also as Christians are invited, along the roads of the world – without falling into
> a syncretism that confuses and humiliates our own spiritual identity, to enter into
> dialogue with respect towards men and women of the other religions, who faithfully

5   Albert de Pury & Jean-Daniel Macchi, *Juifs, Chrétiens, Musulmans, Que pensent les
     uns des autres?* (Paris: Labor & Fides, 2004), 75–78.

hear and practice the directives of their sacred books, starting with Islam, which welcomes many Biblical figures, symbols and themes in its tradition, and which offers
the witness of sincere faith in the One, compassionate and merciful God, the Creator
of all beings and Judge of humanity. [6]

The Church condemns syncretism to protect its mission. The fear of
syncretism is not only Christian; it corresponds to the instinct of self-
preservation of identity. The condemnation of syncretism by religious
leaders of different communities can perhaps hide, in a logic of power,
the fear to see the group weakening, and their power weakening with it.
They are maybe afraid to lose their flock and even their jobs! It is also
true that cultural globalisation, with its supermarket-style spiritual syncretism, constitutes a true danger for the richness, the originality and the
authenticity of traditional cultural identities. We now feel that cultural
globalisation causes a loss of depth for every tradition.

We know that there is no such thing as a pure, original culture, which
no element would have come to fertilise or pollute. Except for a few rare
populations who remained isolated for a very long time, we can affirm that
the culture of humankind is syncretic by nature. Religiosity, an essential
dimension of cultural life, is radically and clearly syncretic. Comparative
religion studies abundantly demonstrate this. The Roman Empire, for
example, was syncretic from a cultural and symbolic point of view, while
finding mechanisms in the imperial institution and in Roman legislation
for the cultural integration that was necessary to safeguard the system.

Besides, syncretism is not foreign to the Biblical world. For the
Christian part, it took all the work of modern Biblical criticism in order
to let go of the idea of one pure Bible, preserved from any influence and
exterior contamination. This obviously challenges the revelation. If the
Biblical religion is a revelation from God, from Above, then how could
it blend with the surrounding cultures? Especially given the obsession in
the Bible with separating from these surrounding cultures, to the point of
proposing odious practices, clearly genocidal in nature, as coming from
God. This is evidenced by the texts of Exodus, Joshua, the Book of Judges

6   Message to the People of God of the XII Ordinary General Assembly of the Synod
     of Bishops in October 2008, *On the Word of God*, n.14

and others about the wars by which the people of Israel asserted themselves in the Promised Land. The fact is that today the critical historiography of the Biblical narrative demonstrates that it is an idealised and late reinterpretation of that history. This illustrates that the separation between the Holy texts and the surrounding cultures has always been impossible, and that cultural interaction has always been there.

The Biblical desire to separate from others unfolds in a syncretic framework, therefore a framework of cultural contiguity, of relatedness on the symbolic level and of reciprocal influences. Furthermore, this does not prevent the Jewish Community from elaborating their own markers of identity, constituting in this way their Community as autonomous and separate from the others, while being part, with them, of the same milieu.

There is, finally, a syncretism considered by many, myself included, as negative. It is a synonym of fragility, of superficial identity, of cultural subordination, often in bad taste. It is not easy to give examples because anything can be justified, but I do not feel comfortable seeing representations of the Virgin Mary mixed together with voodoo symbols, with vaguely Hindu iconographies and with photos of a 50-euro-per-session local astrologer. This syncretism is omnivorous, kitsch, lacking in roots or fertile perspectives. It is the syncretism of the global culture of television, of the big international hotels. Within these types of syncretism, some elements, fully meaningful when related to the system of big religious traditions, become consumer products in the supermarket of the most superficial New Age religiosity. Some of my friends are part of quite respectable New Age movements and I sometimes allow, with a smile, the practice of New Age Catholicism in Deir Mar Musa! In fact in our space, there is a bit of the charm of spiritual India which we are receptive to, mixed with Muslim mysticism, thickened by the incenses of Eastern Christianity and the *je ne sais quoi* of Jungian head shrinking to top it off! Nevertheless, we distrust the dangerous and ambiguous type of syncretism that paradoxically combines a universalist pretension with a sectarian spirit.

Religions Facing Globalisation

In my opinion, global syncretism, like popular piety or symbolic globalisation, must be rebalanced by the self-knowledge of the great religious traditions rather than condemned. Assisting and understanding them is providing them a critical service. We have often recognised the humility of the Holy Spirit in coming towards people who in our eyes have the most equivocal religious beliefs.

Today I think that the Church should find a different way to deal with the gnostic currents and the different expressions of the New Age. In the past, the traditional and apologetic attitude of the Churches expressed itself with a mentality in which the true kept defining itself against the false. However, even the most "ambiguous" currents are shaped and cut across by demands that are somehow authentic and answer the true spiritual cravings of humanity. It seems to me that the Church's truth is not a definitive, compact package of religious culture. Quite the contrary, following the example of the antagonistic and relational mystery of Biblical revelation, and therefore also following the example of the Incarnation of the Divine Word that expresses itself in our culture, Christian self-consciousness, always relational, should give up this zeal for defining itself through opposition. It should rather develop a non-violent art, even from a psychological and intellectual point of view, in order to retell its own mystery, as it gradually manifests itself through loving dialogue with religious cultures. It is by trusting the Holy Spirit's faithfulness to the divine Mystery, through all cultural mediations, that the most different relational paths can be travelled without fear. This does not mean that one should always be a concordist, harmonising at any price that which cannot be harmonised. The Church will have to know how to say no, but always with the view of enhancing the histories of peoples. If cultural and religious intermingling does happen, even when we do not want it, then it is better to want it.

It can occur in Deir Mar Musa that we host groups, often numerous, guided by New Age gurus. A few days ago, almost a hundred people came along with their spiritual leader, a charismatic labourer. He had gathered around him thousands of people in Italy on the grounds of his spiritual experience, to initiate them to the universal religion based on mystical experience and not on dogmatic definitions. Simple, honest-faced people who performed dances and Hindu or Sufi songs, coupled with Gregorian chants. In answer to my questions, their leader said he did not think that many from his group would separate from the Church, but instead needed to break the mould of an ossified tradition in order to rediscover the Gospel with fresh eyes. He expressed a loving regard for people with no wish to monopolise them. I went down to Damascus the following Friday to show him a big Muslim centre that practises hospitality towards international groups. Before the midday canonical prayer, I was asked to say a few words. So I asked about the identity of these hard to define groups. We admit the righteousness of their spirituality but we can easily see where it reaches its limits, from the point of view of the richness of our traditions. I said that perhaps these groups are like the cartilage of the knee, they form the flex-ible and elastic joints in the interreligious articulation. Most of them will probably not form new long-term cults, but return to the safe shores of large religious communities with another way of belonging. That is why a large number of people today reject the word "interreligious" in favour of "inter-spiritual" after the Anglo-Saxons imposed the word "interfaith" on us.

Religious Syncretism

Let us go back to the inculturation of faith through religious syncretism. The evolution of the reflection of the Church is always related to more or less opposing, more or less welcoming contexts. History gives us an example of this:

– The ancient Mediterranean Church as it went along admitting the pagans into the Christian faith, was busy demolishing their idols and ruining their temples. But at the same time, the Church knew how to convert the great Mediterranean goddess' pilgrimage sites into Marian sites of devotion, and how to reuse mythical elements in the history of the saints, even at the iconographical level. The

"Church of the Pagans" was and still is as much anti-idolatrous as deeply rooted in the religious culture of the ancient and barbarian Mediterranean civilisation.

– We clearly see how fascinated the Renaissance Church has been by pagan culture and how they tried to produce a new synthesis, while it obviously paraded itself as unsullied by such confusions and blending!

What I mean is that Christian thought is always syncretic, even when it takes place in conscious opposition to a pagan world perceived as satanic. Today we know that this world is entirely worked by the Spirit of God, which does not mean however, that it is entirely good! Human-divine desires run through it. To be faithful to our truth, we no longer need to refuse, often via caricature, the truth of others. We can be faithful by simply remaining well-rooted in the vital, living, charismatic and prophetic current of the Church's conscious awareness of its faith, celebrated in community. It is this vital current that needs to be constantly celebrated! So we are not afraid to take on the language, preoccupations, cultural and religious history of the people and communities that we meet on the way of our Christian pilgrimage. I prefer expressing myself in this way from now on: this movement towards the other is more of a pilgrimage, *a hajj*, than a missionary campaign, let alone a crusade.

Dialogical and Non-conflicting Identities

In a speech delivered to the young people of Lebanon about the identity of the Syriac Catholic Church, I tried to draw out their particular identity from the complex mosaic of identities in the Middle East. I was looking for a discourse on identity that could give them a strong self-awareness without provoking a self-referential drift. If we think that our small Syriac Catholic community, the smallest among the Eastern Christian communities, has something to offer, then we have some work to do on our communal self-perception, otherwise, it will inevitably be diluted by other

larger identities. This work involves following the path of identity crystallisation, starting with an impressive series of cross-fertilisations and at
the same time of oppositions. So I suggested to the group of young people
to move from a conflicting identity to a dialogical identity that would be
aware of the structures of reciprocal functionalities.

Let us outline the history of this small Syriac community. These
Christians came to the faith in Antioch as the Church was spreading
throughout the entire territory of Greater Syria. Essentially, their language was Aramaic, but they also spoke Arabic. They began their journey
by remaining as much anchored in Greek culture as rooted in Biblical
Hebrew. This Church was composite from the start, gathering Jews and
Christianised pagans; it distinguished itself culturally, but not dogmatically, from the other "national" Churches, the Copts and the Armenians.
It later thoroughly Arabicised through its contact with Islam, by refining,
together with Arab Muslims and Arab Jews, a common Semitic culture over
the course of fourteen centuries. Considering all the elements of identity
crystallisation, the Syriac Catholic Church could define itself based on a
logic of opposition, but also on a logic of synthesis and dialogue.

Afterwards, from the sixteenth century onwards, the Eastern Orthodox
Churches expressed the desire to escape from this particularity, perceived
by some as excessive, and to recover a communion with the Universal
Church, not just theologically; in this context, a movement of union with
Rome was initiated. It could have been realised either in opposition to the
Syriac Orthodox identity or, on the contrary, in a spirit of complementary
harmony. The cultural history of the young people I was addressing could
be read as a series of "noes". "No" to Orthodox Syriacs, "no" to Muslims,
"no" to Byzantines and "no" to Jews and pagans. But this would constitute
a hollow identity, because each one of the rejected identities dynamically
carries a constitutive element of the Syriac Catholic identity. Our identity
awareness, on the contrary, should be built on a series of "yeses", in and
by which we acknowledge our Jewish and pagan roots, our Semitic roots,
rediscover the fertilisation of the great Hellenistic culture of the Ancient
world, reclaim our national identity and our participation in the Arab-
Muslim civilisation that has been our true milieu for so many centuries.
In this way, we renew this call to universal openness and to modernity that

Western Catholicism offered us without losing all our previous affiliations. We are aware of the ambivalences and contradictions that characterise this evolution in history until today. But a thread of identity characterised by hopefulness is drawn by this series of "yeses" that echo God's big "yes" to mankind through Christ. We are also aware of what characterises the conflicting dimension of our identity and we choose to take responsibility for it. In this way we would like to offer our gift to human history by the practice of reconciliation and harmony based on dynamic and inter-functional complementarity.

Solidarity with the Local Churches

Some Eastern Christians consider the members of the Deir Mar Musa Community as traitors to the specific national Eastern Christian identity, precisely because they believe faithfulness is demonstrated by differentiation and polemical affiliations. We mainly hope to enable this openness in which the gifts of identity flourish. We carry the richness of our personal histories of identity as well as the identity of the Monastery. The Monastic Community takes on a deep commitment of solidarity with the local Catholic Syriac Church and grows at the same time in its consciousness of Catholic universality, and from its own choices and vocation in relation to Islam. We do not hold a conservative view of history. We do not practise monastic archaeology. We are passionate about history's constant capacity for novelty, which is the most constructive way to be conservative.

It is true that identities often define themselves through opposition. The writer Amin Maalouf points out that the part of our identity we tend to highlight is the one we feel to be the most endangered or threatened, to the detriment of all the other parts:

> Where people feel their faith is threatened, it is their religious affiliation that seems
> to reflect their whole identity. But if their mother tongue or their ethnic group is in
> danger, then they fight ferociously against their own co-religionists.[7]

I consider that each group of people need to create for themselves a set
of traditional or doctrinal elements established as a system that ensures
the group's homogeneity, stability and original identity: "We are this way,
and not that way." Today the world seems to be split along two tendencies.
The first one, widespread and apparently victorious, is the progressive formation of a hollow, consumerist syncretism based on the economic and
technological superiority of the West. While this Western world claims
to sanctify the superiority of its Judeo-Christian roots, at the same time
it also drains their authenticity. Deep down these roots become meaningless, barren and betrayed. Not surprisingly, the New Age movement represents an expression of globalisation, as well as a reaction to the Western
monopoly, and is a manifestation of the thirst for spiritual experiences
that are non-ideological.

The second tendency today is a reaction to globalisation, an attempt
to reaffirm identities and cultural singularities. It also hides behind closed,
self-preserving doctrines that are easily fundamentalist, on the defensive
and often aggressive.

Faced with the increased sensitivity concerning identities, I have often
tried to explain to both Christians and Muslims that, for example, there
is no specifically Christian way to fast apart from the universal value of
fasting on the ascetic and spiritual levels; it would be more Christian to
fast "like the others". That is to say: in a Jewish context, like Jews with the
Jews, and in a Muslim context, like Muslims with the Muslims, etc. As a
matter of fact, historically during the evolution of the Church, it did not
happen this way. We tend to codify and freeze religious forms, and to
forget their syncretic roots in order to make them the historical form of a
so-called absolute Christian way. "We, Christians, fast this way…" Here
is, among others, the challenge of ecumenism among Christians: there will

7   Amin Maalouf, *Les Identités meurtrières [In the name of Identity]*, Livre de Poche
     (Paris: Grasset & Fasquelle, 1998), 19–21. TN. English translation by Barbara Bray
     (Penguin edition, 2003), 13.

be a tendency to put in opposition the forms of worship and expression that they believe to be incompatible and radically different; whereas the interreligious and ecumenical movement can grow in a dynamic of recognition and harmonisation while remaining aware of particularities.

Inculturation Takes on Cultural Complexity

During the past twenty-five years, as we met with Islam, the monastery experienced resistance from the local Church who challenged the legitimacy of an inculturation of the Christian faith in an Arab-Muslim milieu. It seemed like our approach would endanger local Christianity, be it Coptic, Syriac, Byzantine or Armenian. Obviously there are methodological, dogmatic and social difficulties with a radical inculturation of the Christian faith.

Our inculturation would like to go beyond folkloric clothing, carpets spread on the floor, bare feet inside the Church and the common use of Arabic which is also recognised as the Muslim liturgical language. What we should be is the scattered seed that enables the entire dough to rise and be the food of many. What we should do is bear witness to the mystery of Jesus of Nazareth for Muslims, in this dramatic, painful and contradictory period of time for the world of Islam. Eschatologically, that is to say in light of the achievement of the meaning of human history, the mystery of the Church can only be at one with the mystery of Islam. All the harmony of God's work within the different traditions will come to the light of day on that Last Day. It is not hard to imagine a Muslim resistance to this Christian dynamic of inculturation because its method, its dynamic of progress goes against a certain conservative tendency within Islam based on a reified understanding of the revelation's structure. But this is not as accurate as we would think because there is a structure of movement too in the Qur'anic Muslim Community, which renews its dynamic at all times.

The Hermeneutical Principle of Love

Christian love has its reasons, of which human reason knows nothing, and it heralds changes which historians and exegetes cannot foresee. The great mystery of Islam that scandalised the Church for fourteen centuries and that dramatically questions contemporary consciences, cannot be interpreted according to the principle of non-contradiction. It has to be interpreted according to the logic of the hermeneutical principle of love. Since the 11 September 2001, it is no longer permitted for anyone to remain the same, neither in the Muslim world nor in the "Christian world": a brave and eschatological interpretation of the sacred texts is essential. Let us quote Amin Maalouf one more time:

> There will always be different and even contradictory interpretations, however much people study the scriptures, consult the commentators, or set out the various arguments. The same authorities may be cited to tolerate or to condemn slavery, to venerate icons or burn them, to ban wine or allow it, to advocate either democracy or theocracy. Over the centuries, all human societies have managed to find religious quotations that seem to justify their current practices. It took two or three thousand years for the Christian and Jewish societies, which both claim the authority of the Bible, to start seeing that the precept "Thou shalt not kill" might apply to capital punishment; but a hundred years hence we'll be told it was self-evident. The text doesn't change; what changes is the way we look at it. But the text affects reality only through the medium of our view of it, and in every era the eye dwells on certain phrases and skims over others without taking them in.[8]

Eschatological Interpretation

What I mean by "eschatological interpretation" is a reading of the foundational texts, a reading anticipating the future from a moral standpoint that corresponds to our responsibility as believers today. We need to draw

8   Maalouf, *Les identités* 59.

out meaning from the present time towards an ultimate end through our freedom of interpretation and especially of action. There are pages and pages about God's genocidal command to his people as they prepared to enter the Promised Land: what will we do with that? Our ability to perform a paradoxical reading, our open refusal, occasionally, to interpret, our symbolical extrapolation, and our political and moral stand will enable us to take on a true hermeneutical responsibility to build hope in the dialogue in Palestine-Israel. I say "in the dialogue" because our reading of the Bible and the Qur'an is not the only one dealing with the Holy Land. The Muslim readings of the Qur'an are also at stake, as well as the Muslim readings of other scriptural traditions, Jewish and Christian. Exactly like there are Jewish readings of the Bible and other Scriptures, Muslim and Christian... And finally, there is also the secularised reading of history, which makes history as well. This is why we need a new prophetism, a prophetism in dialogue, interreligious, in an always new experience of the action of the Spirit of God, in the sacred space where we meet, the space of our reciprocal hospitality.

As we already said, Islam wants to be true to itself, to not let itself be absorbed by others at the cost of clever contortions of identity. There is an analogy between Judaism's refusal to accept Jesus as their Messiah, a refusal which Saint Paul recognises as playing a part in the mysterious plan of Providence, and Islam's refusal of Christianity.[9] This irreducible wall between Islam and Christianity protects the Muslim community from a premature assimilation that would extinguish its charism, and protects the Church from imperialist temptations. As a result, separation staves off for both of them the temptation to possess the world and imposes a humble dialogue between them. I have no desire for mimetism, nor do I wish to create a fifth column, a secret undercover Christianity. I see that Muslims can accept me as a monk, a disciple of Jesus in love with Islam, not because it is easy for them, but because they glimpse in this what could

---

9   "There is a hidden reason for all this, brothers, of which I do not want you to be ignorant, in case you think you know more than you do. One section of Israel has become blind, but this will last only until the whole pagan world has entered, and then after this the rest of Israel will be saved as well. As scripture says..." Romans 11:25–26.

be the announcement of a final harmony, in God. Some Muslims tend to either withdraw into a rigid hereditary identity or to throw themselves outside, into the big melting-pot. Meanwhile, many Eastern Christians fail to move beyond the logic of defensive identity. This is what leads them to emigration or to isolation today. To me, these attempts at self-protection are doomed because they negate Islam's original input into a mutual social project: they leave no space to recognise the theological status of otherness, which would imply that the "other" means nothing in the history of salvation, that they have nothing original to contribute. To our Christian eyes, Eastern and Western, Muslims would represent nothing more than a historical cul-de-sac. According to this conception, we simply need to backtrack towards the source of fundamental truths that pre-existed the deviation represented by the Muhammadan prophecy, clearly held as false, judged as ill-intentioned or at best, naïve and illusory, which basically means: poor Muhammad got it all wrong.

On the contrary, with the hermeneutical principle of love, on the way to a future depending on mutual spiritual responsibility, the current of hope goes back up through history and announces good news to our ancestors in faith. They shall be consoled of their distress because their children are no longer tearing each other apart. We are not going towards reciprocal assimilations or ambiguous mixing, but towards a shared horizon where a synthesis capable of pluralism in communion is envisioned.

CHAPTER 4

Abrahamic Relationships

In today's ecclesial context, we witness a dual and contradictory movement. On the one hand, the generous work of dialogue goes on with a mutual understanding and the development of authentic neighbourly relations as well as a prospect of harmony. On the other hand, we have to notice the development of a tendency that prevails in traditionalist conservative Catholic environments. It is characterised by pessimism and alarmism towards the evolution of Muslim communities in Europe and by an attitude of exclusion of Islam from the future of "Christian civilisation".

It is necessary to come back to what makes up the foundation of the three monotheist religions. The purpose is not to reduce these religions to what unites them, but really to understand what the place of Abraham, the Friend of God, is in Islam, and to what extent this "soul to soul" relationship between God and the Patriarch can be a doorway towards understanding what the mystery of Islam represents for Christians.

An Abrahamic Community

A rather important consciously anti-Muslim and even sometimes Islamophobic current is developing amongst our Christian brothers. It is germane to this tendency to compare religions to show the superiority and transcendence of the Catholic religion at the expense of others. For instance, they will compare the Biblical Abraham to the Qur'anic one to show how different they are, and how incomplete and distorted the Qur'anic Abraham is. They will do the same with Adam, Moses or Jesus.

Our method is different. We believe in the original participation of Islam in the hermeneutical maturation of semantic fields. Abraham is today enriched with all this complexity of meaning embodied by the Biblical root, Christian mediation, Muslim remodelling and contemporary synthesis.

To what extent can we recognise an Abrahamic ascendancy in Islam? And how does it, or how does it not create an Abrahamic Judeo-Christian-Muslim Community?

It might be important to note that the Judeo-Christian Abraham is different from the Muslim one. Islam is not to be straight off reabsorbed into the Bible. Our Abrahamic histories are rooted together as well as separated through history, often parallel, but also crossing paths and growing apart. We are not looking for a blending of both hermeneutical and symbolic traditions... This blending is often there in historical facts and remains quite inevitable. When it comes to interpreting a Qur'anic text, we must interpret the prophetic vocation of Muhammad with all the specificity and the originality of its relation with the more or less explicit Biblical elements of the revealed text. It really is the case with Abraham, as well as with the Covenant, and the story of Salvation. Muhammad has come into contact with these Biblical elements at some point in time and space.

It precisely is a cultural and spiritual discernment, which will help us trace back the reality of the Prophet of Islam. We will do so based on the Qur'anic text, on the plural and complex hermeneutical Muslim tradition, and on the experience of God conveyed and induced by the text. Our effort of Christian interpretation meets the complexity of the Qur'anic tradition. Our encounter is one moment of the history of the text and its effects. All of this is meaningful because through dialogue, the encounter actually tends to a manifestation-experience of ultimate truth. The awareness of this process is what the German philosopher Hans-Georg Gadamer calls "historically-effected consciousness". That is to say, the interpretative attitude needed so that elements such as tradition, ideology, expectations and so on, which at first glance seem like obstacles to mutual understanding because they generate prejudices, can enter into the dialogical hermeneutic game with its tension between the familiarity and extraneity of the text, the familiarity and extraneity of the other, where human understanding occurs.[1]

A Common Experience of Mercy

We should not search for the religious authenticity of Islam in an impossible concordance with Christianity in terms of dogmas and symbols, even though a large number of analogies can in fact be opportunely found. The Second Vatican Council underlines such common elements: it recalls the Muslim faith in Abraham, our shared monotheism, the shared experience of divine mercy and a common eschatological anticipation.[2] The religious authenticity of Islam is rather to be grasped in the Muslim perception of the sincerity of Muhammad's prophetic vocation. The point is not to find Biblical concepts intact in the Qur'an, but to let the sincerity of Muslims touch us. From my point of view, it is meaningless to try to know if the Muslim idea of Covenant is similar to the Biblical one, even if, from a literary perspective and historically speaking, it obviously depends on the Biblical idea of Covenant.

The Abrahamic Covenant

I am curious to discover the Abrahamic Covenant as it is in the Qur'an and in Muslim tradition.[3] From there, I am interested in facilitating the

1   Paolo Dall'Oglio, *Speranza nell'Islām: interpretazione della prospettiva escatologica di Corano XVIII* (Genoa: Marietti, 1991), 10–13.
2   *Lumen Gentium 16.*
3   A reference to the Covenant is found in Qur'an 2:24 among others; but the Abrahamic prayers that follow are those that define the spiritual tone of this wholly Islamic covenant between God and the Patriarch: "And remember Abraham said: 'My Lord, make this a City of Peace, and feed its people with fruits, such of them as believe in God and the Last Day.' "…"Our Lord! make of us Muslims,

dialogue between these concepts in preparation for the final, yet nevertheless present accomplishment of every Covenant with the One God. The ideas of pact and covenant are very present in the Qur'an, with their Biblical dependency and Islamic originality. The Muslim theology of Covenant has its starting point in the Qur'an with the primordial pact, the Adamic pact. I do not believe I am mistaken to think that still, in the point of view of the Muslim existential experience, what comes first is actually the re-actualisation of both the Abrahamic and the Mosaic Covenants in the Muhammadan prophetic event.

In the Qur'anic text, I do not look for the same theology of Covenant that can be expressed by the Fathers of the Church or by modern theologians based on Biblical texts. I simply find that a good number of Qur'anic verses establish an efficient perspective of Covenant between God and man. This Covenant offered to Adam is successively renewed with Abraham, Ishmael, Moses, the Prophets, Jesus and lastly Muhammad: "And remember We took from the prophets their Covenant: As (We did) from thee: from Noah, Abraham, Moses, and Jesus the son of Mary: We took from them a solemn Covenant…"[4]

Obviously, what is absent, at least superficially, is the Messianic promise as it is formulated in the Bible, because the centre of the Qur'anic experience is Muhammad's prophetic event. Louis Massignon and some of his disciples were considered concordists for seeking impossible harmonies between the Qur'an and the Church's catechism. From one perspective, we can recognise that the method of historical textual criticism is entitled to read the Qur'an in connection with its context without bowing to the dogmatic hermeneutical authority of the Muslim tradition. From another angle, we cannot prevent Christians from re-reading the Qur'an while referring to their own faith-based perspective. Still, I consider it wrong to impose

---

bowing to Thy (will), and of our progeny a people Muslim, bowing to Thy (will); and show us our place for the celebration of (due) rites; and turn unto us (in Mercy); for Thou art the Oft Returning, Most Merciful. Our Lord! send amongst them an Apostle of their own, who shall rehearse Thy Signs to them and instruct them in scripture and wisdom and sanctify them: For Thou art the Exalted in Might, the Wise." Qur'an 2:126, 128–29.

4   Qur'an 33:7.

allegedly "true" readings of the Qur'an that are in opposition to traditional Muslim readings. Reading the works of Massignon is no easy task, but one cannot reproach him for a lack of contextualisation. He contextualises the Qur'an and Muhammadan prophecy within the entire history of the text's effects, from the beginning of the event of the Revelation until Islam's complex present, taking into account the most geographically remote Muslim communities.[5] Along with him and with others, Christians and Muslims in the course of our histories, I recognise a Christological marker in the Qur'an constituted by Issa, son of Mary, that draws history to holiness.

The theme of the Covenant in Islam underlines the idea of God's faithfulness to Himself. In the Qur'an, it manifests in the lineage of the Prophets of Israel as much as in the archaic lineage of Arab extra-Biblical prophetism. It is confirmed as universal in Muhammad, whose prophecy is already close to the Day of Judgement and overlooks it.

It is clear that Islamic salvation history and Biblical salvation history are not identical. However, there is a concept of salvation through faith in the One, Merciful God, starting with Adam, and throughout prophetical history until the Last Day (preceded by the return of Jesus and by the coming of the Muhammadan *Mahdi*, "the rightly-guided one", as well as by the defeat of the Antichrist). This tension of faith constitutes the trajectory of history. It is true that Islam does not develop a concept of original sin comparable to the Christian one. Everything happens through Adam, fall and Salvation. And this divine judgement and pardon are announced by all the Prophets. God saves mankind by renewing the gift of faith that enables mankind to obey God.

5   TN. For clarity the preceding two sentences have been translated in consultation with the Arabic edition, Paolo Dall'Oglio, عاشق الإسلام مؤمن بعيسى, (Dar al-Farabi, Beirut 2013).

Abraham, Model of Faith

The figure of Abraham in Islam is above all that of a great model of faith. He is also the Patriarch of the Arabs, and hence of Muhammad via Ishmael, as well as of the people of Israel via Isaac. Let us remind ourselves here that the Quranic semantic field of the Covenant and of salvation history is clearly different from the Bible's. In my opinion, here lies its charm and its role. This difference constitutes its contribution towards the deepening and broadening of the theological significance of history and existence. From the Christian point of view, this expansion of the work of the Holy Spirit into the history of Islam adds nothing to the essential part of divine salvific work, wholly and definitively accomplished in Christ and the Church as it is taught in the inspired Bible. If this Catholic concept is poorly understood, it would entail that the spiritual development of thousands or millions of future human years will be blocked and held captive by the claim of the Catholic Church, since the Church bases its irreformable nature on the definitive [saving reality] represented by the person of Jesus Christ. But Jesus Christ, thank God, is not the end point of history, but rather a springboard. He is definitive in his act of opening up to every human group and to the universal human community infinite perspectives of free and genial participation in God's work, at every time and in every place.

Ishmael, Son of Abraham

In the Magisterium of Pope John Paul II, we find frequent references to Abraham, and Islam's relation with the Father of believers is implicit in the expression "the three Abrahamic religions".[6] Through their faith in

6   The expression was used by Pope John Paul II in his homily on the 35th World Day
     for Peace, and is cited in the document "Dialogue and Proclamation of the Pontifical
     Council for Non-Christians" (renamed the Pontifical Council for Interreligious
     Dialogue) in 1991. During the public audience on 5 June 1985, John Paul II said: "Among

the prophecy of Muhammad the Arab, Muslims consider themselves the descendants of Ishmael and heirs to the blessings bestowed on him through the intercession of the Holy Patriarch Abraham.

Before Islam, Theodoret of Cyrrhus already refers to the Arabs as Ishmaelites and also as Saracens.[7] Saint John of Damascus speaks of the Hagarenes and the Ishmaelites when speaking of Arab Muslims: "They are also called Saracens, which means divested by Sara. Hagar answered the angel: 'Sara has sent me away divested.' "[8] We are here in the context of the rejection of a new doctrine considered as heretical. For the sake of our argument, we should note that for the Ancients, the identification of the Arabs with Ishmael's offspring was an acquired tradition.

On this traditional basis, but in a context that is free from any heresiological polemic, the great Biblical scholar Cardinal Carlo Maria Martini notes:

> The account we heard is taken from the oldest book of Scripture, the book of Genesis (Ch.21). It tells us of a son of Abraham who was not the ancestor of the Hebrew people as Isaac will be, but upon whom God's blessings were also bestowed. "But the slave-girl's son I will also make into a nation, for he is your child too" (Genesis 21: 13). and at the end of the story, it is said: "God was with the boy" (Genesis 21: 20). The real vicissitudes of Ishmael and his offspring remain obscure in the history of the second and first millennium B.C.E., but it is clear that the Biblical reference concerns a few Bedouin tribes that were settled around the Arabian Peninsula. From such tribes, after many centuries, Muhammad, the Prophet of Islam, would be born. Today, at a time when the Arab world has assumed extraordinary importance on the international scene, and partly in our country also, we cannot forget this ancient blessing that shows God's fatherly Providence towards all His children.[9]

---

non-Christian religions, that of the 'disciples of Muhammad', for its monotheistic character and its connection to the faith of Abraham, whom Saint Paul defined as the Father of our [Christian] faith (Romans 4:16), deserves particular attention…" Jean-Marie Ploux, *John-Paul II, Textes Essentiels* (Paris: Éditions de l'Atelier, 2005), 224.

7   Théodoret de Cyr, *Histoire de Moines en Syrie (History of the Syrian Monks)*, vol. 257, Sources Chrétiennes, (Paris: Le Cerf, 1979), 183, 91, 95, 203.

8   Jean Damascène, *Écrits sur l'Islam (Sources chrétiennes)*, vol. 383 (Paris: Editions du Cerf, 1992), 211.

9   Cardinal Carlo Maria Martini, *Noi e l'Islam* (Milan: Centro Ambrosiano, 1990), 11–12.

In the same perspective of reconciliation, cardinal Kasper recalls that "Moreover, neither Hagar nor Ishmael were ever repudiated by God, who made him a great nation" (Gen 21: 13).[10] In 1076, Pope Gregory VII wrote to the Sultan al-Nasir: "We pray with our heart and with words that after a long life here below, the same God will guide you in gladness into the bosom of the holy Patriarch Abraham."[11]

The self-awareness of Muslims of their Abrahamic origin via Hagar and Ishmael, an origin that is both ethnic and symbolic, is acquired through tradition, is universal and has immense religious significance. Historically, it is an assertion that has been predominantly accepted both in Jewish and Christian milieux, in the East as in the West.

As for the question of Ishmael's part in the promises made to Abraham and in salvation history, I think it good to mention as an example a brief contemporary Jewish text quoted by Father Francesco Rossi de Gasperis S. J.:

> In his book *Yom Kippur, War and Prayer*, (Jerusalem 1975), rabbi and Israeli military chaplain A. Hazàn addresses a lament to Abraham: "Why, oh why did you not wait in faith for Isaac to be born from Sarah, and before him you let Ishmael be born of Hagar? Now Ishmael has too been circumcised, so he too, in a way, is a partner in the Covenant." Is there here another way to ask ourselves where to situate Islam in God's plan? For there is no doubt that there exists a "mystery of Islam", one that Paul could not take into consideration.[12]

These quotes are brought together to defend the legitimacy and significance of the Ishmaelite and hence Abrahamic lineage of the faith of Muhammad, and accordingly of the faith of Muslims. The fact that the vast majority of Muslims have neither Ishmaelite nor even Arab ethnic ancestry changes nothing to the religious significance of the concept.

10   "Réflexions du Cardinal Walter Kasper," *Service d'information, Conseil pontif-ical pour la promotion de l'Unité des Chrétiens [Pontifical Council for Promoting Christian Unity]* II-III (2003): 87.

11   "Reconnaître les liens spirituels qui nous unissent, 16 ans de dialogue islamo-chrétien [Recognize the Spiritual Bonds that Unite Us, 16 Years of Christian-Muslim Dialogue]," *Conseil pontifical pour le dialogue interreligieux* [The Pontifical Council for Interreligious Dialogue] (1994): 4.

12   Francesco Rossi de Gasperis S. J., *Mondo e Missione [World and Mission]*, (Milan, March, 2002).

Eminent professors have found it necessary to demonstrate that Islam's Ishmaelite ancestry only corresponds to the acceptance by a few Arab tribes of the projection onto them of this Biblical concept. Meaning that the Arabs did not look to Ishmael at all, and only started to do so when the Christians and the Jews recounted this Biblical story to them. What is more, others contend that the tribes of Israel invented the Patriarchs as a means to found their unity…

I take up the arguments of my spiritual teacher Louis Massignon, who in the introductory note to his fundamental text *The Three prayers of Abraham* (while recognising the merits of the historical-critical method), asserts the legitimacy of a reading that:[13]

– Internalises the history by which the souls of the Friends of God form connections that lead history to its ultimate goal.
– Knows to find, behind the names and the fragile stories of our symbolic ancestors, the authentic narratives of these figures.
– Considers that Abraham, Isaac, Hagar and Ishmael cannot be known by the chronologies of court historians. They can only be encountered, and oh so effectively, by the humble and trusting human souls who wish to know nothing beyond what God reveals to them.

The Intimate Knowledge of the Patriarch

Massignon's argumentation changes nothing about the dearth of historical evidence. But it is the argumentation of a sociologist of religion who takes into serious consideration a remarkable sociological religious fact: that a given religious group enjoys a devotional knowledge of the intimate soul of its founder, or of one of its most eminent members.

The relationship with the Patriarch and the knowledge of his truth happen in the sharing of an intense soul-to-soul experience, in the

13   Massignon, *Les Trois Prières*, 24–29.

communion of saints, in the adventure of human relationships, in the divine and human poverty of our being here. This relationship is based on trust. The other exists because we have granted and given them this trust. The Abraham-God relationship inspires our own relationship to God, because Abraham's testimony remains effective and alive in the spiritual experience of the community of believers before God. There is a unity between two witnesses, the human and the divine. This unity happens through an alternation of witness for the other, in the other, which brings about the mystical union in the gift of oneself, where God speaks of Himself in me by confessing: "I am the Truth [*ana al-Haqq*]."

In Conclusion: The Path of Abraham

An international, interreligious group of friends are working towards "recognising" and promoting a path of Abraham in the Near East.[14] We would like to propose to the young, as much to those who belong to a religious tradition, as to those who profess themselves post-religious or seeking a post-agnostic spiritual path, to follow the trail of the Patriarch, first in his native Mesopotamia, then in Haran, the site of his calling, now in south-east Turkey.[15] The journey would then continue through Syria and Jordan, and into Palestine-Israel in Jerusalem and Hebron-al-Khalil, the site of the tomb of the Patriarch. They would experience the hospitality of the children of Abraham and would share the testimony of their own spiritual dynamic. We want to found a path of initiation to spiritual harmony, which can nourish the hopes of future generations and assist the young in their choices, those related to an awareness of their identity in a perspective of fraternity, not of competition, opposition and conflict.

14   Cf. www.abrahampath.org
15   Genesis 11:31; 12:5

CHAPTER 5

The Conditions of Inculturation[1]

Inculturation is perhaps the concept that is most manifestly experienced in Mar Musa. And yet, tirelessly, it raises questions. How does
one retain one's identity as a Syriac Catholic monk, without it being
diluted in all the otherness that is encountered? How to commune with
Islam without falling into naïve syncretism? How to be a desert monk
with these incessant and increasing comings and goings of visitors?
How do you manage them? How long will this small Community be
able to carry all this on its shoulders? How do you keep at your project in a country with a future that is always uncertain, on the edge?
The Community does not evade these questions. It carries them in its
prayers, continuously. Sometimes, in the face of all the contradictions,
discouragement seeps in, weariness sets in. What differentiates Deir
Mar Musa from a very hospitable historic building open to the four
winds is the power of this prayer; it is this *rendez-vous* given to God,
each morning and each night, with a rare fidelity. It is the dream of men
and women who do not resign themselves to a clash of civilisations that
would obliterate any possibility of mutual understanding.

Is this evangelism? Yes, but in the strict sense of a life that draws the
necessary love and strength from the source, the Gospels. Deir Mar Musa's

1   I wish to express the immense debt I owe Father Ary A. Rœst Crollius S. J. I owe
him my initiation to the concept of inculturation that he himself developed for the
32nd General Congregation of the Society of Jesus in 1974 that issued a specific
document on the issue. The concept became gradually mainstream in the Church.
Father Ary was a master of going in depth in this dimension of the mystery of the
Church anchored in Jerusalem, and which develops in all places in an original way.
After retiring from teaching at the Gregorian University, he left to offer his heart
and intelligence in West Africa, demonstrating the sincerity of his philosophy.

existence and its longevity cannot be explained otherwise. Inculturation has no other source.

A Missionary Approach

Some have compared our choice in Deir Mar Musa to create a monastic community dedicated to Jesus' love for Islam to Matteo Ricci's missionary stance, which is considered the model of deep cultural adaptation of the missionary project. Matteo Ricci's perspective on missionary work is very appreciated by the Church today, but in other periods was censured and repressed. He symbolises a way for the Church to go towards the other, in their culture and their religious experience, armed with enormous curiosity and the desire to validate it. His name is also linked to the "Chinese Rites Controversy", which the Church resolved in his favour, and hence in the favour of the Jesuit stance. Allow me to quote a few passages from Father Giovanni Marchesi S.J.'s chronicle *La Civiltà Cattolica* on Matteo Ricci's arrival in Peking in 1601. This text shows that the problem of inculturation is truly an essential component of Christian self-understanding. Since opening up to the pagans, which the Acts of the Apostles bear witness to, the Church has been deepening her knowledge of her mystery in the most distant lands, and not without conflict. The Chinese example can be helpful, for John Paul II reformulated the conflict in hope of a reconciliation with Chinese society and the state.

> In the message [that follows], the Pope expresses with much humility, "deep regret", and asks for forgiveness in the name of the Catholic Church for the errors of Christians towards China... John-Paul II said: "...his [Father Ricci] merit lay above all in the realm of inculturation. Father Ricci forged a Chinese terminology for Catholic theology and liturgy, and thus created the conditions for making Christ known and for incarnating the Gospel message and the Church within Chinese culture. Father Matteo Ricci made himself so 'Chinese with the Chinese' that he became an expert Sinologist, in the deepest cultural and spiritual sense of the term, for he achieved in himself an extraordinary inner harmony between priest and scholar, between Catholic and orientalist, between Italian and Chinese...the deep empathy which

he cultivated from the first towards the whole history, culture and tradition of the Chinese people… These sentiments and attitudes of the highest respect sprang from the esteem in which he held the culture of China, to the point of leading him to study, interpret and explain the ancient Confucian tradition and thus offer a re-evaluation of the Chinese classics…first, Chinese neophytes, in embracing Christianity, did not in any way have to renounce loyalty to their country; second, the Christian revelation of the mystery of God in no way destroyed but in fact enriched and complemented everything beautiful and good, just and holy, in what had been produced and handed down by the ancient Chinese tradition. And just as the Fathers of the Church had done centuries before in the encounter between the Gospel of Jesus Christ and Greco-Roman culture, Father Ricci made this insight the basis of his patient and far-sighted work of inculturation of the faith in China, in the constant search for a common ground of understanding with the intellectuals of that great land…the work of members of the Church in China was not always without error, the bitter fruit of their personal limitations and of the limits of their action…For all of this I ask the forgiveness and understanding of those who may have felt hurt in some way by such actions on the part of Christians."[2]

I find it interesting to add that the Chinese Jesuits also characterised themselves by "their refusal to say that Confucius was in hell".[3]

It is important to underline this refusal to "place" Confucius in hell. The traditional, anti-Muslim apologetic stance in the Church has been constant in its rejection of Muhammad's prophecy, which has been often declared satanic and infernal. My impression is that however, there exist diverse attitudes. In the exclusivist and theologically fundamentalist West, it is normal to send all the founders of non-Biblical religions to hell… But in the Christian East, where whether we like it or not we live side by side with Muslims, the sacrament of good neighbourliness leads to a substantial suspension of judgement. Only God will judge! We will be judged according to His unfathomable knowledge of our hearts. We are not authorised to condemn. The "Chinese" Jesuits practise this suspension of judgement

---

2   *Père Giovanni Marchesi S. J., La Civiltà Cattolica 3636 (15 December 2001): 589–89.* For the English text of Pope John Paul II's message: Cf. Message of His Holiness Pope John Paul II for the Fourth Centenary of the arrival in Beijing of the great missionary and scientist Matteo Ricci, S. J. (24 October 2001).

3   Giuseppe Pittau, "Culture in dialogo, L'attualità di Matteo Ricci," *in Vita e Pensiero*, no. Gennaio/Febbraio (2000): 50.

because they discern the Spirit of God in the traditional devotion of the Chinese. Here too, the principle is valid: the bad tree will not bear good fruits, and vice versa.

A More Personal Example

During the late 80s, I spent a few months in the Philippines. It was an opportunity for me to experiment with the Jesuit ideas on inculturation outside a Muslim context. I was lucky enough to be invited by some friends to come into contact with a nomadic mountain population: the Dumagats, *Negritos Remontados de la Sierra Madre*. It was a very touching adventure. The population suffered from cultural and social marginalisation and were being progressively invaded by the majority population that belonged to another Christianised ethnicity. Their language had been studied by Protestant groups, and a New Testament was available. However, most of them could not read. In the region, all sorts of evangelist missionaries in black vests and ties went around, as well as armed members of a clandestine communist organisation. The culture of these forest people was disintegrating. Each year, at the grand dam on the regional river, the Lion's club, an association of elites of American origin organised Mass for the natives and distributed food. I was asked to celebrate Mass for them. I spent all night chatting with the elders under makeshift roofs made of tree branches. During our conversation, I avoided any term specific to Western culture because my translator was having difficulties translating. For example, when I would say *God* in English, he would translate it as *Dios* because the natives knew the god of the colonisers. So, I shifted to the phrase "He who made the sky and the earth", and I started to ask them questions. When I asked them what their story of the moon was, an old man answered me: "Our ancestors certainly knew it, but we are poor and we forgot it. If you know it, remind us of it." I knew from the books I had found at university that they practised the ritual ablution of their children; so I asked them if they baptised their children and they all said yes. Then I tried to find out what they say during the baptism.

Those who were closest to the majority community repeated the magic formula: "In the name of the Father, the Son and the Holy Spirit." Others who lived further inland answered that they were baptised in the name of dad and mom, and those who lived furthest away said that they did not say anything at all! That's when I realised that I was in the presence of a population that was superficially, if at all, Christianised, and that the Mass I was asked to celebrate was an act by the dominant population to solve, as if with a magic wand, a secular failure of intercultural relations. They were all being assimilated through the Mass... With help from a few of them, we built a small cabin, a small altar of interwoven branches on the side of the lake. I had observed that they drank in cut canes and ate in palm leaves. So I asked someone to cut a cane stem for me to make a chalice, and I chose the most beautiful palm leaf for the paten. As the Church does not permit the use of rice and the local drink for the Eucharist, I used the western bread and wine that I had brought with me along with the religion with Mediterranean roots. A hearty traditional meal followed Mass, and the symbolic relationship still took place (note that in the Gospel of Saint John, Jesus multiplies wheat bread once and another time barley bread, and that during the Last Supper, instead of bread, Jesus washes feet... But Saint John is always too complicated!) I read the Gospel texts where Jesus teaches and heals, multiplies bread and fish. All this took place at the side of the lake, and He had appeased the tempest on the lake. I was reading the Gospel in their own language, which I did not understand, as it was transcribed in Latin characters, while they let out magnificent cries of astonishment. To my soul, this was the little Pentecost of the Dumagat people. People of the river, they were already wet. Invoking the name of the Father, the Son and the Holy Spirit was enough to make them part of the Church... We became good friends, and one day one of their chiefs asked me: "How can one become Christian without losing one's ancestral identity?" I answered: "If you and yours are interested in Jesus of Nazareth and his message, you have the right to be Christians while retaining your particularity. You have the duty to guard your ancestral richness so you may share it in the Church. The forest as a hiding place no longer works, you can really feel it (radios were everywhere, televisions were starting to come in). The point is to highlight your knowledge of your environment so it may be protected and saved for the good of everyone. You have all the wisdom required for this mission." In other times, the Church would have been intensely preoccupied with acculturating the new Christians into the Western, consecrated form of Catholicism. They would radically separate them from their ancestral religious culture, deemed demonic by default. God be praised, there have been honourable exceptions in Christian missions with a few good models: Matteo Ricci, Roberto de Nobili, the Reductions missionaries of Paraguay and closer to us, Charles de Foucauld, Vincent Lebbe, Jules Monchanin, Henri Le Saux and Madeleine Delbrêl.

We understand clearly here what a more or less successful inculturation of the Christian faith is. If in 20 years the Dumagats have forgotten their language and are speaking to God with Spanish words, then inculturation would have failed and the worst acculturation would have been enacted by consecrating their inferiority...even within the Church! But if they are proud of their roots, conscious of their particularity, if they have recalled their tales and put forward their wisdom, and if from time to time Jesus would come walking on water and into their canoes, then it's a different matter... Inculturation is never a complete success and always needs reworking, but there is a difference between seeking harmony and pursuing assimilation.

When it comes to Islam, matters are more complex anyway, since Islamic founding texts are consciously post-Christian. All the same, the Church believes in continuing to look for ways to offer witness to Christ in all contexts, including among Muslims; and this in the best possible way for them, looking out for their good, for the valorisation of their experience, and for the greater glory of God throughout their history, all the while engaging in fraternal cultural empathy.

In a Muslim Context

I think we should all be like Matteo Ricci or other Chinese Jesuits in our attitude towards cultures and their spiritual dimension in particular. In our case, it is Islam we are concerned with. Perhaps the difference between Ricci and ourselves is that he hoped to make China a Christian empire. This did not happen for China, and we do not see something similar happening with Islam. While we are guided by Ricci's approach in Mar Musa, we are more directly inspired by the approaches of Charles de Foucauld and Louis Massignon. They were radical in posing the question of the meaning of the Islamic event, of the post-Christian permanence of Islam and its value in the framework of salvation history centred in Jesus Christ.

For Charles de Foucauld, the enigma of Muslim resistance to evangelisation is what pushes the Church towards a more radical imitation of Jesus' humility, of his spirit of hospitality and service... It is a manner that is the opposite of colonial-style missionary militancy. With Louis Massignon, the strictly theological question of the value and function of Islam in salvation history is now clearly posed.

Another story comes to mind about inculturation in a Muslim environment. In 1990 I visited the Carmelite Sisters in Marawi on lake Lanao, in the middle of Mindanao, a large island in southern Philippines, the classic site of Islamic separatist resistance. I spent the night in the room of Bishop Tudtud. He had studied Islam and the Arabic language with the White Fathers in Rome, and had been appointed chief of a new bishopric in an area where Christians were a small minority. In the directory of bishoprics of the Philippines, under the heading reserved for the name of the diocesan head of interreligious dialogue, it was marked, "the entire staff of the diocese". The bishop had just died in a plane crash. I looked at his books, there was Charles de Foucauld, Louis Massignon, Gandhi, Saint Thérèse de Lisieux, Thomas Merton... Al Ghazali, the Qur'an... I felt at home, the man's presence was strong and encouraging, his room radiated hopefulness and one felt a vibrant Church tradition there. He was the one who had asked the Carmelite Sisters to establish a small monastery on a holy hill that overlooked the town, as the contemplative heart of the diocese. There, these women dedicated themselves to praying for Muslim-Christian dialogue, and welcomed people for retreats. The convent, very poor, had refused to close down. I mean they refused external closure, not the closure of the soul, that of radical dedication to divine love. Over the classic Carmelite habit, they wore with a lot of elegance the traditional coloured clothes of the Muslim women in that area. Keeping in mind the somewhat "Spanish" love the Christians of the Philippines have for pious images, we were a little disconcerted to see that in the sisters' little chapel, with its floor covered in mats where they sat in the manner of the people of the country, there were no images, only God's name in Arabic, *Allah*, and the Holy Sacrament placed inside a reproduction of a small local straw house. They explained to me that by renouncing images in the chapel, they were making a gesture of welcome to their Muslim friends, so they may pray together there. The sisters had been kidnapped twice by a group of Muslim resistance fighters involved in the independence struggle in that region. Each time, they were treated with religious respect because of their dedication to God. A few years later, perhaps as a result of the radicalisation of interfaith tension, the monastery had to close down and the nuns had to leave.

How many times must we start over, until a common language takes root and we are able to live together? How many times must the women and men of dialogue, Muslim and Christian, find themselves sidelined by their communities, persecuted, maybe killed, until we exclude violence from our relationships and for the Kingdom of God to come?

Conversion

I do not like the term "conversion" and seldom use it, since our conversion is from sinfulness to God. I prefer the term "adherence": adherence to a tradition, to a teacher, to a community.[4] And it does not imply the rejection of what I used to be, and what I very much continue to be.

I have been asked if I would accept to baptise a Muslim who came to me asking to be baptised. Muslims have asked me to baptise them for different reasons. One gentleman thought that baptism would make it easier for him

---

4   TN. "Adherence" in the sense of taking part in a tradition in conjunction with one's own original affiliation.

to get a visa to a Western country. Others had projected on the Church an intense idealisation that came from a series of disillusionments they suffered in the context of their Muslim family and society. For others still, becoming a Christian meant belonging to the world of Western freedoms.

However, I have also known some people who have encountered, to varying degrees, the truth and efficacy of the Christ-Church mystery. This discovery, rather than turn them against Islam, in fact led them to a stronger understanding of the mystery of Christ in relation to their origins, and with a view towards greater mercy and solidarity.

So, a small community of Muslims around the world, who driven by the Spirit have encountered Jesus of Nazareth, rediscovered God's work within the Muslim tradition. Among them, some prefer not to be baptised and remain on the threshold of the Church, which is what Jewish philosopher and resistance fighter Simone Weil claimed for herself until her dying day.

It is worthwhile to repeat here that I do not feel in me the desire to convert Muslims, even though I have an immense desire to convert myself to God's work within every soul and to serve Him. Some people become Muslim, others become Christian. This is a manifestation of the freedom of God in the face of cultural and theological determinism. The individual's "transversal" spiritual adventure is a measure of the fruitfulness of the openness of the cultural-religious contexts being traversed. On both sides, conversions remain statistically rare.

Offering Communion to Muslims?

At Deir Mar Musa, we painstakingly explain every evening that the Eucharist is reserved for the baptised who believe in the Communion of the body and blood of Christ, Son of God, who died and was resurrected for the salvation of the world. The moment is arduous because mostly the young who are coming from Syria and a thousand other places, recognise the beauty of the sacrifice during Mass, and wish, sometimes pretend to fully participate in the meal of fraternity being offered.

There are Muslims who gladly participate in the celebration of the Eucharist and who have the desire to take Communion. Sometimes they are driven by curiosity or the desire to express friendship and solidarity. It could also be a sign of a transgression that would express a sense of emancipation and freedom from their own affiliation. We should not forget that in churches, it is not generally the custom to ask for a baptismal certificate from strangers at the moment of Communion, and it is rare that the audience is reminded of the conditions of participating in the Eucharist. Some priests do not believe it is their duty to raise a more radical awareness of the meaning of participating in the Eucharist, and tend to simply accept the motivations of Muslim guests. At Deir Mar Musa, we make an effort to explore this delicate question.

We patiently repeat our most courteous explanation of this interdiction, which indicates both our respect for the path of others, and the limit of our own. Yes, in a certain way, the Eucharist is already universal, but the Church can neither delude herself nor deceive her guests.

A long road of conversion to God in dialogue and sharing lies before us. We will skip none of its stages. Once, a Bedouin woman came to us. She had fallen in love with Jesus. In a duly Qur'anic language, she confessed what is essential to the faith of the Church. And yet, baptising her was out of the question… it would have caused a tragedy. One evening, she came to the church for Mass. When the moment came for Communion, she whispered: "Can I…?" I lifted my gaze to her. The black and red embroidered front of her traditional tribal dress was wet with tears. How could I refuse her Communion, baptised in her desire as she was?

How to Preserve Freedom of Conscience?

I have met many people who had been baptised a little too easily by Protestant groups, or by Catholic priests in a hurry to quell their angst before Islam. We found ourselves being subsequently compelled to help these people who were rejected by their socio-familial context and who at the same time were not exactly welcomed into the Christian social setting. This puts these individuals psychologically at risk, and provokes unresolvable human situations.

I do not deny that the Holy Spirit can be behind a Muslim's adherence to the Church. It is legitimate to think critically about the more or less valid motivations for these "conversions", and also about the more or less deep and spiritual knowledge of the religious heritage being left behind. That said, we cannot judge these individuals' conscience or the legitimacy of their actions.

I have the same respect and much consideration for those who "convert" to Islam. We are attentive to go beyond and to subdue the spontaneous feelings of failure and resentment generated by the conversion of Christians to Islam, and against the Muslims who guided and welcomed them. The particular story of each soul demands that we pause before the mystery of its path with God. This affirmation does not prevent us from realistically taking into consideration the less convincing aspects of these personal itineraries, as well as the attitudes of the original context or the new welcoming context.

A few years ago I wrote a long letter to an Apostolic Nuncio to ask that the Holy See promote initiatives for assisting and protecting victims of social and familial persecutions that result from what they choose to believe. If I ask for these initiatives to aim for discreet effectiveness rather than media hype, it is not so much for the sake of sparing Muslim public opinion, as it is to avoid turning the issue of freedom of conscience into a Trojan horse poised to take over the Muslim polis. Apostates have been persecuted throughout the Church's history. If the secular State "imposed" freedom of conscience on Christian societies up until the Second Vatican Council, this is no reason to criminalise Muslim society. It is from within, by endogenous revolution, in an original manner and also by seeking harmony with other important values that freedom of conscience will be discovered in the Muslim world. This will be made easier if the attitude of the Church is not one of conceptual aggression and superficial judgement coupled with a strategic alliance with the geopolitical and cultural enemies of Islam.

A Church of Yeast and Leaven in Gentleness and Transparency

I could baptise a Muslim who, for the love of Christ, wishes to remain Muslim. How I would love to join him in pilgrimage to Mecca! My faith-based choice to be in solidarity with the visible Church prevents me, forbids me until this day from obtaining this grace.

Other believers in Jesus have been able to participate in different capacities in the Muslim pilgrimage, as a prophecy of a final harmony before the Master of Judgement. I was told the story of a Muslim woman who was baptised discreetly, and who had undertaken with her friends the pilgrimage to Mecca, mystically taking Mary of Nazareth as her companion, and saying the rosary while circling the Ka'bah. When Muhammad conquered Mecca, he entered the Ka'bah and asked that all the idols be destroyed, but he saved the image of the Virgin and Child by covering them with his own hands so they would not be effaced. Certain current interpretations have deduced that the Ka'bah was a Christian church. More probably, it was a syncretic temple, since the Meccan merchants wanted to be on good terms with everybody, a kind of small pantheon to house all the gods of their clients.

To resume our discussion concerning these instances of adherence to the Church, I am thinking about the situation of these few Muslims who have discovered Jesus Christ. When it comes to it, these *nasāra*, Nazareans, can very well decide to baptise each other.[5] This would be perfectly valid in terms of Christian canon law. The Muslim ban on switching to another religion prevents priests in Muslim lands from baptising Muslims; the

---

5   *Nasāra* is the Arabic Qur'anic term for Christians. In the past it was co-opted even by Arab Christians. But for a certain while, it has been considered problematic by some among them, who do not want to be assimilated to the Judeo-Christian heretics that the first Muslims would have encountered. Louis Massignon, *Opera Minora: Nazareth et nous, Nazaréens, Nasara [Nazareth and Us, Nazareans, Nasara]* ed. Youakim Moubarac, vol. III, Collection Recherches et Documents, (Beirut: Dar al Maaref, 1963), 490–3. I have learnt to love this Arabic term, *nasāra*, Nazareans, the disciples of Jesus of Nazareth.

ban also extends to religious public practice by any non-Muslim who is not Christian or Jewish by birth. As has always been the case, believers in Jesus can baptise one another. They can retain their sincere adherence to the Muslim religion. Charity compels them to be discreet, and they will not constitute a threat of *fitna* [subversion], against the peace and security of the Muslim Community. In order that this mystical presence of the Church is not perceived by Islam as a fifth column, a cancer, an adapted and specific catechism must be developed. Lastly, it is urgent that the Church explain further her missionary preoccupation and discuss it with her contemporaries. This catechism should help the Christians who come from Islam to root themselves in presence to and in loving solidarity towards the Muslim *Ummah* in the name of Jesus of Nazareth; a radical engagement as evangelical yeast, in anticipation of Issa's return to re-establish justice and peace in the world, as every good Muslim believes.

Muslims sometimes simply respond by asking why must they be baptised to discover Jesus, when they have always known and loved him and his mother Mary according to the teachings of the Qur'an?[6] The easy answer, which is not mine, is to indicate that the Jesus of the Qur'an and that of the Bible have nothing in common besides the mother's name. For even Jesus' Qur'anic name, Issa, comes from Esau the reject rather than from Joshua the saviour. There are entire works on the subject to explain to Muslims and Christians that the Jesus of the Qur'an is not the Church's Jesus, and that when a Muslim discovers the Jesus of the Church, they will abandon the Issa of Islam…

This is not my position, and neither is it the position of a large part of the Christian men and women who encounter Islam. It is true that the Muslim who believes in the Christ of the Church, but wants to remain Muslim, has to ask for the grace to be able to reinterpret Qur'anic material in a way that can be harmonised, even if audaciously, with the Christian

---

6   The list of Qur'anic texts on Jesus and Mary is long, and the bibliography on this subject is rich. Here I quote an already polemical Qur'anic passage, which expresses the state of mind of many of our Muslim neighbours: "O Jesus the son of Mary! Didst thou say unto men, worship me and my mother as gods in derogation of Allah?" He will say: "Glory to Thee! never could I say what I had no right (to say)." Qur'an 5:116.

teachings so that true concord may prevail in their heart. It is a dream of
mine to be able to give an account of this loving reading of the Qur'an,
possible for the disciples of Jesus who would want to attempt it. It will
come, *inshallah* [God willing].

We are not there yet and this is why the priests of Eastern Churches
generally avoid baptising Muslims. The Christian community, recognised
as legal and respected within Muslim society, must be transparent and
sincere while trying to discretely reconcile between the right to individual
conscience and respect for collective Muslim convictions.

The Interreligious Prayer

Saint John's Apocalypse ends with the invocation: "Amen; Come Lord
Jesus."[7] Church time is indeed the time for prayer, for intercession, for
waiting in oration… The Muslim Community is above all an assembly
of oration, summoned to celebrate and give praise in continuous remembrance of divine favours, of His Glory and Infinite Mercy. Is it therefore possible to pray together? Can we together invoke the name of
God, Allah?

One of the questions often raised in interreligious dialogue is deter-
mining whether it is licit for Christians and Muslims to pray together,
without falling into a questionable conflation. This question has been the
subject of extensive discussions in the Church, with the aim of avoiding
murky syncretism. Personally, and alongside the Community of Deir Mar
Musa, we are aware of the complexity of this subject. I want to point out
here that we do not commonly use the term "common prayer" because
that would cause confusion, especially in Arabic.[8] We must distinguish
different categories of common worship.

7   Revelation 22:20.
8   TN. Here Fr. Paolo is referring to *salāt al-jamāʿa*, where jamāʿa refers to the Muslim
     Community in prayer

The first category is that of joint intercession and *dhikr* (remembrance of God), typical of, but not exclusive to Sufism. It is a vast celebratory context which is not, strictly speaking, liturgical, and in which we spontaneously address our invocations and praises to God. This celebration can happen before or after a communal meal. It can take place during a conference, or constitute the conclusion of a meeting. The location and the occasions vary. If we are gathered in a church, then it could take place there. But care is taken not to shock the more sensitive among us, those who are unable to distinguish between the different categories and who get the impression that we have made the two religions into one, and that through this practice, faith gets lost.

The second category of common worship is that of the reciprocal public presence to Christian or Muslim liturgical prayer. Let us repeat that in Deir Mar Musa we explicitly indicate to our Muslim guests that it is not appropriate for them to partake in Communion of the Eucharistic Species (the Body and the Blood of Christ) even as they attend Mass as welcome guests. We underline the fact that partaking in the Communion of the Body and Blood of Christ means and expresses full faith in His divinity, Incarnation, death on the Cross and Resurrection and that in so doing, they would be considered apostates in Islam.

In the same way, we Christians sometimes attend, with pious respect and true intimate participation, the Muslim Qur'anic prayer, *salāt*, without joining the ranks of the Muslims in prayer since this can be easily misunderstood as a renunciation of our Christian faith to embrace Islam.

The third category is operated by the Holy Spirit, when on occasions that are impossible to predict or plan, He makes Himself present in His Grace in the interreligious, interpersonal encounter, by compelling hearts and lips towards shared praise and invocation [*du'ā'*], announcing a future harmony. For, as John Paul II said: "Every authentic prayer is prompted by the Holy Spirit, who is mysteriously present in every human heart."[9]

In his work *Chrétiens et Musulmans: Frères devant Dieu?* [*Christians and Muslims, Brothers before God?*], my teacher, role model and fellow

---

9   *Redemptoris Missio 29, Discours aux Cardinaux et à la Curie romaine* (Address to the Cardinals and Roman Curia), 22 December 1986, n. 11.

Jesuit Christian van Nispen proposes we meet in our faith in God through prayer because "it is God Himself who brings us together and makes us meet one another".[10]

A Harvest of Heads

Once, in Rome, I was in a big church with a Muslim friend by my side, a Sufi master. Summer was ending, it was still hot, and around us the necks of the assembled boys and girls were like a palm grove. Seeing their beauty and dignity, he said to me: "Let us come to a common word, why do you want Christ to be crucified and to suffer, he is God's beloved, God's protégé, God's saint…" I said to him: "Sheikh, I saw you beholding the beauty of these necks and I see that you are preoccupied with our eternal salvation, because you consider that these are pious people, dignified youths, and it would be unfortunate that they go to hell! Well I have to tell you something: you see this harvest? All these youths are ready to have their heads cut off for the sake of the truth of the crucifixion of Jesus of Nazareth." He looked again at all these beautiful young people and said to me: "This is a serious matter, one should reflect on it again, maybe another reading is possible." Obviously, he was thinking about the necessity to reinterpret the Qur'anic negation of Christ's Cross in a way that would make it possible to "pardon" all these beautiful youths.

On another occasion, the same Sufi friend and I were watching the sunset. I had spoken to him about a Muslim boy who had suffered a lot, who came to the Monastery and wanted to become Christian. I wished to be frank with my Muslim friend. I asked him what I should do with this boy. He said to me: "The Lord sent him to you, you must guide him with sincerity of heart." He was crossing a line there, he was going beyond the letter of the Law. He said to me: "I am going to pray", for the sun had set. He went to the bathroom to perform his ablutions while I sat outside.

10   Christian Van Nispen tot Sevenaer, *Chrétiens et Musulmans: Frères devant Dieu?* (Paris: Éditions de l'Atelier, 2009), 138.

I told myself that I should look for water so I too can make my ablutions. I closed my eyes, went to Golgotha, and washed myself with the water that came out from the Lord's side which had been struck by the spear.[11] He came out after his ablutions and found me in tears. He asked me: "Do you want to perform your ablutions?" I answered: "It is done." And we prayed for a long time, intensely. We sat down and he asked me where I had gone for my ablutions. I answered: "To Jerusalem, at the foot of the Cross." He concluded: "I understand. Your prayer is lawful."

Clarification

It is probable that our assertions could provoke some astonishment among Christians and Muslims alike. Some Christians might think that we are afraid to proclaim a more explicit, more courageous evangelical witness, that we are adding water to our wine and giving up on the radical novelty of Christ. Others on the contrary will find that we are inventing another way to evangelise… perhaps not straight-out proselytising but still oriented towards Christianising Muslims. For their part, Muslims will have a lot of trouble to think it licit to attempt a reinterpretation of the Qur'an in order to harmonise it with the Gospel… They will probably think that it makes more sense to reinterpret the Bible in light of the Qur'an!

I want to say and repeat that according to our vision, Islam has a function that is its own. I recognise that it has a role in the spiritual history of humanity. Hence there is no necessity and no urgency to baptise Muslims. This in no way detracts from the Church's mission to love all mankind. This mission remains necessary and always urgent. Still, I believe that in different ways and by different paths, some Muslims can be driven by the Spirit to be disciples of Jesus, as humble and gentle yeast or as delicious spice, by being at one, loyally and in transparent solidarity with the Islamic *Ummah*.

---

11 Cf. John 19:31–37.

CHAPTER 6

The Prophecy of Muhammad

We reach the key question of this book: can Christians consider Muhammad a prophet? It is a sensitive question, one that is ceaselessly put forth by Muslims to Christians, since what is at stake is the recognition of the sincerity of the entire Community and of every soul in it. Muslims ask to be recognised, starting with the first among them, Muhammad. Some non-Muslims would have no problem recognising the prophetic quality of the Qur'anic revelation. Still, this difficulty does exist in the Church, it is traditional and of a dogmatic nature.

A few years ago, Nigerian Cardinal Francis Arinze who was then president of the Pontifical Council for Interreligious Dialogue, came to Damascus. I had the honour of accompanying him on his visit to the Grand Mufti of the Republic, whom I had known since my encounter with Islam in the 1980s. The atmosphere was immediately warm between the Grand Mufti, who had known John Paul II in Rome, and the Cardinal. The Cardinal asked him about the number of Christians living in Syria. The Mufti answered that in Syria, everyone was Christian; it is difficult to believe in Muhammad without believing in Jesus. Then he added: "The Pope has made quite a nice number of new saints. Is it not time to canonise Muhammad, our Prophet?" The Cardinal took a deep breath before answering: "The sainthood of men is the work of God. God recognises and manifests it. The Church has jurisdiction over the baptised only. She cannot officially recognise saints outside of them. This in no way prevents the Prophet's people from recognising him as a saint." I admired the Cardinal's wise response. But here, our reflection must go further.

The Definition of Prophecy

What do we understand by the term "prophet" today? A man who speaks in God's name, who communicates divine decrees and who expresses divine will, even through his actions. In the Bible as in the Qur'an, the authentic prophet is opposed to false prophets who pretend to speak in God's name, or he opposes magicians, seers and poets with inspired mannerisms, but which are false and artificial.

In the Biblical sense of the term, prophecy stops with the conclusion of Biblical scripture. It follows that the Biblical prophets are the ones present in the Bible! In a Christian sense, since Jesus came to accomplish the Law and the Prophets, we no longer expect prophets after him who according to the Gospel is a prophet and more. In the Christian perspective, the entire Biblical prophecy announces Christ, the Son of God, and in this sense stops with him. But the gift of prophecy is one of the gifts of the Holy Spirit to the Church, which instead of stopping with Christ, develops from him. In this way the Church participates in Christ's prophetic charism.[1]

Extra-Biblical Prophecy

Can we speak of extra-Biblical prophecy? We can of course! For even in the Bible it is clearly expressed that prophecy is not only exercised in the lineage of the People of the Covenant. Noah is a universal prophet, and the Jews speak of a law given to Noah for all peoples, which is therefore a universal covenant between God and mankind saved from the Flood. The prophet Balaam is not Jewish, and neither is Job. At the end of the great King Solomon's Book of Proverbs, the Bible retains a small collection of

---

[1]   TN. Fr. Paolo's use of the word 'charism' here is slightly problematic with Catholic theology since the term generally refers to a gift from the Holy Spirit to humanity and is not something that Jesus in his divinity would not receive. ref Fr. Martin Whelan.

proverbs attributed to Lemuel, an ancient Arab king. In many Biblical passages, Cyrus the great King of Persia is described as the envoy, a messiah from God sent to liberate the Chosen People from exile. In the New Testament, there are also non-Jewish, not yet Christian persons to whom God's Spirit manifests Itself.

In the Qur'anic sense, which I do not find opposed to the Biblical sense, Adam is the first great prophet. A great number of prophets were sent to all peoples. And for that matter, individual faith is a divine gift offered to each person so they may believe in the revelation of the Prophets and in the revelation represented by Creation.[2] God's witness to Himself, heard in the innermost self of mankind, pertains to prophecy.

Moreover, in the Biblical vision, there seems to be the desire that the prophetic spirit be shared among all human beings so they may know God, and "so that God may be all in all".[3]

Muhammad, a Great Prophet

That Muhammad was a great leader, a founder, in the history of religions, about this there is no doubt! That Muhammad had an experience

---

2   Psalm 19: "The heavens declare the glory of God, the vault of heaven proclaims his handiwork; day discourses of it to day, night to night hands on the knowledge. No utterance at all, no speech, no sound that anyone can hear; yet their voice goes out through all the earth, and their message to the ends of the world." Qur'an 2:164 "Behold! in the creation of the heavens and the earth; in the alternation of the night and the day; in the sailing of the ships through the ocean for the profit of mankind; in the rain which God Sends down from the skies, and the life which He gives therewith to an earth that is dead; in the beasts of all kinds that He scatters through the earth; in the change of the winds, and the clouds which they Trail like their slaves between the sky and the earth; (Here) indeed are Signs for a people that are wise."

3   Book of Joel 2:28 "After this I will pour out my spirit on all mankind. Your sons and daughters shall prophesy, your old men shall dream dreams, and your young men see visions." 1 Corinthians 15:28.

of communication where he perceived himself as a passive receptacle for
the Divine Word, few also doubt, even if there are many different ex-
planations of this psychological and theological phenomenon, including
within Islam.[4]

For the Church, all that is necessary for the knowledge of God and
mankind's salvation was said, carried out and accomplished through Jesus
Christ. But not with a view to sterilise humanity's charismatic life, on the
contrary! For the Church, the multiform, varied and omnipresent activity
of the Spirit of God in the religious history of peoples is so to say rooted,
measured, mediated and has its final goal in the mystery of Christ, divine
and human.

From the Christian point of view, any prophetic activity by the Spirit,
in any time and any place, builds the Church and belongs to it as seed,
announcement and sacrament of the Kingdom that is to come. So, everything just, sincere and authentic in Muhammad's prophecy belongs to the
Church and is not foreign to her.

Perhaps one day a deeper discernment by the Church of the phenomenological complexity of the Muhammadan reality could lead her to
recognise the sincerity and role of Muhammad. The Church could then
initiate the hermeneutical interpretation of the Qur'anic text and of Islamic
prophecy, which would allow her to dynamically harmonise Biblical revelation with Islam's religious reality.

In the Second Vatican Council, the Church initiated this process of
discernment because she accepted to name some truths shared by Christians
and Muslims, truths that pertain to an authentic knowledge of God.[5]

To what extent are the aspects of Qur'anic revelation, which can be
recognised as true by the Church, mere repetitions of what the Christian
tradition calls natural knowledge? This is a very important question that
remains to be addressed. One should at least recognise that these natural

4   Salman Rushdie, who comes from a Muslim milieu, posed In *Satanic Verses*, in a
     way deemed blasphemous to Muslim conscience, the question of the origin of the
     prophetic phenomenon, and provoked a strong reaction and a critical probing by
     the entire Muslim ecumene.
5   Cf. Note on the Particular Vocation of the Monastic Community in the Muslim
     World found at the end of this book. p. 196.

truths about God, Creation and mankind are the same ones that the Bible presents as knowledge coming from God. The fact that the light of human intellect is able to assert a few fundamental truths does not mean that there is no assistance from the divine Spirit, who is the presence of God's Grace at work, in the Qur'anic reminder of these same truths. Moreover in the Muslim view, one's natural knowledge of God and one's exercise of faith as a gift of divine Grace are inseparable, united in the same act. It is a human act that corresponds to a gift from God.

Does This Mean That a Christian Can Recognise Muhammad as a Prophet?

Christians can grasp the sincerity of Muhammad's prophecy by witnessing how the most sincere and humble Muslims commune with and have intimate knowledge of the Prophet. This is the basis on which a Christian can recognise Muslim prophecy.

Neither historical criticism nor archaeology can give us the answer. Even the dogmatic positions of the Christians who came into contact with the first Muslims are not a definitive judgement on this. It is necessary to take into consideration the Theodoret of Cyrrhus impressive series of sustained scathing theological discussions around Christology, and the general framework of the struggle against heresies, which characterise the history of the Church, particularly in the Near East during the centuries immediately preceding the coming of Islam. It is therefore quite normal that nascent Islam was interpreted in the framework of heresiology, and that Muhammad and his Companions were judged to be the founders of a sect. Saint John of Damascus' position on the subject in the early eighth century CE is well known and has left its impact on the Eastern Churches.

The question of the historical Muhammad must certainly be explored by all possible scientific and academic means. But the question of the Muhammad of the Muslim faith finds its answer within the religious and spiritual Muslim experience, within Muslim devotion and the intimate, mystical relationship between every Muslim and the Prophet.

Matters of faith are treated within the hermeneutical circle of faith. But it is precisely because faith is a dynamic dimension that surpasses the religious structure, that one can, through spiritual empathy and on the basis of one's own experience of faith, in this case with the Christian mystery, attune to the Muslim mystery through the dynamic of Islamic faith.

It cannot be simply a matter of individual process or personal judgement. It can only be an in-depth meeting between two communities of faith, the Church and the *Ummah*. However this remains impossible without pioneers and bridge builders.

The Meeting Space

Do we then simply find our own experience in the other? Yes and no. Yes in the sense that it is through our own faith dimension that the faith dimension of the other can be recognised and understood. No, because the event of my own faith happens within a Christian symbolic, linguistic and liturgical complex, while the other experiences their faith in their religious context. But precisely there is the space of encounter, of discovery, of communication and interaction. It is there that the space of existential dialogue becomes a space of revelation, a prophetic space of genial and gracious production of meaning. After this meeting, when we return "home", we are no longer the same. This opens the door to an increasingly universal spiritual communion.

In his book *Dieu des chrétiens, Dieu des musulmans* [God of the Christians, God of the Muslims] François Jourdan produces a remarkable synthesis of different Christian theological positions regarding the status of Islam's prophecy. He comes to the assertion that "Muhammad is not a prophet for the Christians".[6] I believe that such an assertion only means that

6   François Jourdan, *Dieu des Chrétiens, Dieu des Musulmans* (Paris: Éditions de l'Œuvre, 2007), 54.

the Church will not be imposing the belief in the Muhammadan prophecy on Christians anytime soon! But nothing prevents the possibility that one day the Church could develop discernment around the religious persona of Muhammad, and that the conclusions, which I hope will be positive, of such a discernment may become part of the universal catechism of the Church, for it is universally that Christians meet Muslims. For that matter, the essential part of the positive teaching on Islam in the texts of the Second Vatican Council is already part of the Catechism of the Catholic Church.[7]

Now, if we are to think that the role of prophecy is blocked and sealed in a time defined and closed by the event of the historical Christ, this is the same as saying that Christ's life in Palestine in his day, rather than being a catalyst for events that continuously reopens History, becomes the cut-off point of History.

It seems to me possible for a Christian to first of all recognise that the use of the title of prophet by Muslims is legitimate according to the internal logic of their religious worldview. I generally think that it is not favourable to linguistically monopolise the title of prophet as a technical term exclusive to Christian theology. In my opinion, we can use it respectfully in the context of Muslim-Christian dialogue to begin with, at least as a title pertinent to Muhammad's own historical function within Islam. This does not indicate on our part an out of hand unconditional dogmatic adherence to his religion. Just as it is not necessary to believe in the mystery of Jesus according to Church dogma in order to call him Christ and Messiah, for these appellations can be understood as titles that are part of his name and function in his community. Muslims call Jesus the Messiah, the Christ, and they understand by it something other than what

---

7   The Catechism of the Catholic Church (n. 819–821) quotes the Second Vatican Council, *Lumen Gentium* 16 and *Nostra Aetate* 3 & 4: "Salvation's Design also includes those who recognize the Creator, first and foremost the Muslims who profess the faith of Abraham." Again, it is noteworthy that this is a novelty in the catechetical teaching of the Church. It is possible that one day there will be a more advanced evolution in the consideration of Islam's prophecy. The evolution is not slow, considering that between 1992 and 1995, the Vatican's position regarding the death penalty has been reversed from approval to disavowal (n. 2266).

the Church understands. But not something completely different either. This falls within their rights… The same goes for the title of prophet for Muhammad.

I am not alone in feeling the desire to follow Muhammad's name with the traditional eulogy "*salla Allahu 'alayhi wa sallam*", "Prayer and Peace Be Upon Him". I do not do this only as an act of kindness towards my friends' act of devotion, which would not be so bad, since asking for blessings upon people is always a good thing. It is also an act of devotion on my part before their outpouring towards the person of the Prophet; a devotion that through the ages rises from their heart towards the tomb in Medina, for the confirmation of God's blessing upon him, and for the edification and spiritual reform of his entire Community at all times. And this on the basis of the mystery of the relationship of sincere submission and abundant mercy between the Prophet and his God.

Moses and Muhammad

Muhammad is never named in the texts of the Second Vatican Council. This renders it an open question, whereas for centuries, Muhammad's condemnation to eternal fire was a conviction shared almost unanimously.

The maturation of a missionary theology of the Church as envoy to Islam, through the intercession of the martyrs of the Christian East, Charles de Foucauld, Christian de Chergé and his companions and so many other men and women, allows and will continue to allow the advancement of discernment concerning the Muslim religious reality founded on the Muhammadan experience. Let us also ask for the intercession of the anonymous crowd (and it would be apt to draw up its martyrology) of Muslims who paid with their lives for their religious principle of unconditional hospitality, and who were the victims of the abuse of power always skilfully perpetrated under religious and ideological guises.

Some in the Church believe that we do not have the right to compare Moses' prophecy to Muhammad's. This is true in the sense that Moses is a prophet according to the specific Biblical acceptation, while Muhammad is obviously not. All the same, theology and human thought in general devise useful and legitimate paragons for believers. Had we not the right to seek more or less direct analogies between the facts of world history and those of Biblical history, or between mystical, spiritual and religious experiences of different traditions and similar experiences described in the Bible, then it would be easy to see how the Biblical account would become barren. Unable to be reflected in other traditions, it would be locked up in incommunicability. Even the most dogged opponents of cultural relativism cannot espouse that level of fundamentalism.

Impact of the Muhammadan Prophecy

Muhammad's experience is that of a believer in the One God who, at least from a phenomenological perspective, has exercised a prophetic function. He founded an innumerable Community of believers who received access to the faith in the One, Merciful God through the fire of the Prophet's soul, through his vocation, his existential journey that can never be separated from the Qur'anic account.

The most literalist Muslim currents tend to diminish the importance of the Prophet when it comes to Muslim piety in favour of the idea of Qur'anic revelation as pure and direct divine communication. These currents cannot however separate the revelation from the history of the Prophet, of his first companions and his entire cultural and linguistic entourage without risking rendering the text incomprehensible. The Qur'an and its Prophet form a kind of unity in a way. This is why the *sunnah*, the imitation of the Prophet, is the second source from which flows revealed Muslim Law.

Beyond a psycho-religious interpretation of the Qur'anic phenomenon, it is not difficult for me, a Christian, to admit that Muhammad lived an original and authentic relationship with God. From a certain perspective, this adventure represents every man and woman's truth. In fact, Muhammad compares himself to Adam, and here as well, in this radical response to the intimate call to faith that comes from the Creator, there is no real or crucial difference between a believer and a prophet.[8] This is why he understands himself as someone who is reminding us of an original truth that is essential to every individual in every time and place.

At the same time, the inordinate impact that Muhammad's experience of faith has had on History, his experience of human-divine partnership and human-divine relationship outline his prophetic function. It rests on Muslims and on us with them, it rests on our choice of conscience, our hermeneutical choice (meaning the interpretation of this prophecy), our moral and political choices, to give the Muhammadan prophecy a happy future, a future desired by us and God. Devotion turns the tide of History, and from this movement springs commitment. All the same, I do not claim that everyone can become a prophet and thus risk emptying the concept of its content… Still, it is within the hermeneutical circle of prophecy that sincere souls recognise the sincerity of prophets: the role of prophets before God is to be recognised rather than constructed.

Creative Hermeneutics?

One might think that there is something equivocal about claiming to subscribe to a prophetic tradition while imagining that its truth would depend on one's interpretation. I admit it might appear equivocal to those who need a hermeneutical objectivism detached from their own participation in the advancement of the course of spiritual life and inter-preted tradition.

Let us take the example of Christianity: in what way does it present itself as a truth in itself, and in what way can it be detached from my exist-ential participation? It is true that for Christians, God has laid his funda-mental and final act for us in his Christ, Jesus son of Mary. It is also true however that my access to, my interest in and simply my understanding of this act can never do without my participatory process. Not only as a disciple engaged in the imitation of Jesus, but even more radically in the

8   Qur'an 2:37–39.

cognitive act of faith, of confessing him "my Saviour". The cognitive event is brought about by my act of faith, within my environment, with astonishing productivity and novelty. It grows, so to speak, through my participation. The Kingdom of God comes with my participation.

In a similar way, we can understand how the imitation of the Prophet (*sunnah*) on the part of Muslims is not only the recognition, through engaged participation, of the pertinence of his example in the life of the Muslim believer. More radically, this imitation consists in the act of reproducing in their soul, in a new way, the Prophet's act of faith, the prototype of their own faith. Now there is the added fact that the believer is henceforth engaged in this repetition and re-edition.

Christian or Muslim, I bear the entire responsibility of updating, in the relativity of my time, the message, the example and the flow of grace that reaches me from the cultural environment specific to the historical context, but also symbolic context of the Gospel or the Qur'an. This takes place within the progression of the tradition to which I belong; a history of light, but also an uninterrupted chain of shadows. It is the history of the Church as well as that of the *Ummah*, a history of sainthood and sin, of miracles and debacles.

From my point of view as a believer, the only place from where it makes sense to speak of authenticity and of the experience of truth, the measure of truth of the source to which I am bound, depends on the act of faith. Through this act I project myself into a perspective of hopefulness that makes me the co-agent of my future. An "objective" judgement of Muhammad's prophetic adventure is simply impossible. The only objectivity is that of the magnificent consensus of the Muslim *Ummah*, who offers him a dazzling witness.

What about Historical Objectivity?

Does this mean that one does not have the right to judge the Muhammadan event objectively, historically, psycho-sociologically? On the contrary, in a way there is a right and a duty to do so, because these analytical tools are useful for understanding the context of the foundational religious event. But the soul of the Prophet in its particular time and place is known to God and to different degrees to his friends, his family, his Companions… Believers today have access to a spiritual knowledge of this prophetic soul through the practice of the Muhammadan religion, by obedience, by Muslim worship, the prayer and devotion that make Muhammad alive within his Community. Only his Community knows and recognises him in every era, and only it is authorised to faithfully reinterpret him.

The same devotional structure is found in the Jewish relationship to Moses. Reading André Chouraqui's book *Moïse* [Moses] convinced me that we should adopt the same hermeneutical position when we approach the relation between Jewishness and Biblical prophecy…[9] The Moses of the Jews is accessible to us only via Jewish devotion… It is obviously very important to undertake critical, archaeological, exegetical, structuralist and any kind of study you like! At the risk of seeing the Biblical Moses disappear in a cloud of interrogation points. It is also true that in this way, we will irremediably find three Moses: the Jew, the Christian and the Muslim. But I am fiercely attached to the mystical knowledge of the soul of Moses, that of the persecuted faithfulness of Jewish souls throughout history.

Bewildering Facts

To resume our subject, I would like to give an example here: in Muhammad's life there have been some events that are bewildering to contemporary Christian sensibility, and I underline contemporary. They may also be so for other sensibilities, including Muslim ones. The most cited acts are the bloody slaughter of the men of a Jewish clan in Medina, the Banu Quraydha, carried out with his full approval; the exception made to the law of four wives in order for him to marry a greater number of women by virtue of his prophetic authority; his marriage to a girl who was still a child; his marriage to his adopted son's divorced wife (an issue

9   André Chouraqui, *Moïse* (Paris: Éditions du Rocher, 1995, Flammarion, 1997).

related to Muslim Law's prohibition of adoption); the cruel penalties for certain crimes; and most of all, the combining of these bewildering behaviours with the divine revelation that would come to justify them.[10]

A small comparison of these events with Biblical events would not cause the Prophet of Islam to blush. I apologise in advance for the tone of my remarks. Abraham's behaviour towards his wife Sarah, handed over as a concubine here and there with an *hors-d'œuvre* of lies is not particularly edifying. Neither is his behaviour towards his servant, mother of his firstborn. The genocidal teachings in the Bible are very baffling. It is hard to remember the number of legitimate wives of David and Solomon, not to mention their concubines. This list is not exhaustive... The ethno-religious exclusivism of many Biblical passages requires hermeneutical acrobatics in order to be swallowed... I must confess here that I have real difficulty accepting the widespread position in Muslim apologetics that would see in the weaknesses and limits of God's Biblical men a patent demonstration of the corruption and intentional falsification of the text by Jews and Christians.

Is it true that the New Testament marks a radical moral leap? Asserting this unreservedly in the context of the new Judeo-Christian friendship would be imprudent, clumsy and perhaps even incorrect. Contemporary moral consciousness, while recognising Evangelical novelty, can reproach Jesus of Nazareth with not having freed the slaves, with not having achieved the emancipation of women, not to mention homosexuals! His political programme was somewhat weak in relation to the persecutions of the Roman Empire. He also speaks of Paradise and Hell with astonishingly naive realism. Also, his Hell is so terrifying that one can question his positions regarding human rights! Democracy is not on his horizon. As for the Apostles' attitude, it is not better...

What I simply want to say is that an anachronistic and de-contextualised judgement of the behaviour of our ancestors, while not completely useless, is often unacceptable and even ridiculous. The same stones we throw at Islam can be thrown back at us.

Christians ought to be reminded that Muhammad is to be understood, but not exclusively, in the framework of the model of the political prophet.

---

10   Mahmoud Hussein, *Al-Sîra*, vol. II (Paris: Grasset, 2007), 354–61.

His "cross" is to realistically bear the weight of his duties to organise the civil domain, whereas Jesus corresponds to the model of the prophet who is master of a spiritual school, who does not bear immediate responsibility for the political domain. Let us not compare different phenomena with naive oppositions, let us avoid caricatures.

Thinking that at the time of the Prophet, Christianity had already risen to affirm more advanced moral concepts, and that hence Islam was going backwards, is no argument…The specific environment where the Prophet was born and raised is not an ideal civilised context, but rather a Bedouin, primitive, idolatrous context that Christianity had only penetrated in a very limited and sectarian way. It is an environment on the margins of the great civilisations of the time, uncultured and cruel. It is very different from the monasteries of saint Benedict or saint Basil. And beware, the self-idealising psychological attitude of Western history is still at work in us unconsciously, and the same is true for Muslims. The issue here is to interpret the different stages of the understanding of the Gospel in the context of the different conditions of cultural awareness, without illusions of objectivity… We are all part of the game! It is the spectacular originality of Muhammad's soul in relation to his context that is striking.

For the Jews, the soul and role of Moses are understood well beyond the conditions of his environment as described in the Bible. This prolongation, this expansion of the symbolic complex called "Moses" takes place in Judaism through the concept of oral Law. It broadly corresponds to Tradition in the Church, and in Islam to the Prophet's *sunnah* in conjunction with the agreement of the scholars. Furthermore, faced with the accusation that Christians level against Islam, that of going backwards in relation to Christian renewal by in a sense re-establishing the Law of Moses, the Muslim conscience sees the *Ummah* as the Community of the Middle Way, correcting Jewish legalism without falling into the naive and unrealistic idealism of Christianity. No one is forced to share the vision of others. Still, each Community has the right to position itself relatively to the others, to propose its own vision… But our attitude of comparing in order to demonstrate our superiorities does not interest me. Seeking God's work in the muddy tracks on the paths of human history, this is my passion.

Initiation to the Christian and Muslim Faiths

Let us return to the analogy between Christology and the mystery of the Muslim faith. Christology is not an objective, empirical science. It is subjective in the strongest sense of the word, because it concerns the Christ of faith, experienced charismatically, within an eminently personal relationship, heart to heart, through Grace, by the individuals who form the Church. Through the Church, through the celebration of the sacraments and mysteries of the Divine Presence, we have access to the subject-to-subject relationship with the Christ Son of God, and through Him, with the Father. Here is the initiation to the mystery of divine communion with the One and Trinitarian God. Besides its conceptual dimension, this initiation bears existential, liturgical and practical dimensions. It is not only a matter of entering the cloud of unknowable divinity experimentally, it is also a matter of opening up to the Word, to communication, to explicit relationship.

I feel the urgency here to add how important it is, in the framework of an ascending Christology, to underline the immense significance of Jesus of Nazareth's human, free and voluntary act of self-giving: "This is my body, this is my blood." This stand taken by Jesus' human will, this vow is not only united to the will of the eternal Word. More radically, the human act is also instantaneously the divine act (personal, hypostatic union).

By taking Mary as a model, the Christian believer consciously decides to welcome and to participate in this human-divine act of self-giving that is Christ. He is, for me, the condition of possibility, the cause, the content and goal of self-giving. This is why we say that faith is a grace, it is God's work in me, in the act of my response to Him. The fact that this mystery is the most intimate, the most regal and final mystery of every human soul confirms for Christians the scope of Christ's mystery; but in History, this is not imposed through logic, rhetoric or arms... It is the subject of witness where the works of faith precede and accompany words; witness confirmed by the miracles of the Spirit in hearts and bodies. It is necessary to not grow tired of asking God to be freed from this passionate desire, from this obsession, this psychological thirst to conquer souls, to convince others. The "I am thirsty" can only be legitimately expressed by Jesus from the height of His Cross.

Christian initiation gives us access to the life of Christ, and to the knowledge of the divine act for our sake: his human-divine essence. It is no scandal to understand, through an analogy that is both licit and daring, that recognising Muhammad's prophetic role happens within a similar structure. It seems to me that the experience a Buddhist has of Siddharta Gautama's enlightenment, and hence the enlightenment of every disciple, does not present a radically different structure. These spiritual phenomena are comparable.

In Church history, one notes that the birth of religious groups or orders reproduces this same structure. Even when their founder is well known via vast historical documentation, they can be truly perceived in their charismatic experience only through committed spiritual participation and a journey of novitiate and initiation. This intimate participation in the founding charism creates a group of people joined in solidarity and consciously engaged in the mission of a given church. To give another example, the Sheikh of a Sufi *tariqa* and founder of a mystical brotherhood can be encountered, even if deceased, through a mystical initiation that happens within the circle of the group's religious experience.

Initiation to the Perception of Prophetic Sincerity

One might wonder: where can the space for dialogue be found if only the Christians can speak of Christ and only the Muslims of Muhammad? I would answer that there is an initiatory knowledge that comes from a communal, celebratory journey that introduces the individual to an intimate knowledge of the person of Christ or Muhammad.

Throughout the years and after Massignon, I have sought to learn how to discover the divine flame of Muhammad's prophetic soul by practising the recognition of Muslim sincerity. This happens through the initiatory perception of the divine touch specific to the Muslim piety of my friends and the entire *Ummah,* gathered together by the call to prayer under the dome of the sky in endless ranks.

To be honest, I feel that it is the charity of Christ, to which I was initiated during my First Communion as a child, that drives me to commune with the Muslim *Ummah.* Moreover, Christ's charity is the spiritual instrument by which I am able to penetrate the mystery of the *Ummah…*

In a nutshell, only initiates can understand initiates. If someone were to tell me that this might discourage agnostics, I would answer that it is more important to be helped to enter the sphere of human religious experience through a pathway or a small door, than to try to understand it, *a priori*, from outside. This does not mean that one should stop thinking, on the contrary! The religious sphere requires a different use of the intellect, but not its negation.

Here's another example for more clarity: I was won over by the contemplative attitude of the stone mason of "Gandhara", an Indo-Hellenistic Buddhist monastery in Taxila, not far from Islamabad in Pakistan. I entered a very small cell and there, I was surprised to find a huge statue of the Buddha, which occupied three quarters of the space. The mere fact of being in this still spare corner of the cell threw me into ecstasy. The cell is the soul of the disciple. The Buddha is already there. If his enlightenment had not happened, the world would have sunk into darkness. Now, it was my turn. Buddhahood, the essence of Buddha's enlightenment, filled the soul's cell, and light burst forth! (I ask the forgiveness of my Buddhist friends for this example…I am trying to exit the logic of Muslim-Christian opposition through a third way!)

Islam Faced with the Christian Absolute

Christians are often perplexed by the fact that I invoke "Peace upon the Prophet" with my lips and my heart. We have alluded to this earlier. Father Yves Moubarak, Maronite Father and a dedicated disciple of Massignon, explains somewhere why he himself uses this eulogy and why in his opinion it is licit for a Christian to repeat it.

In fact, asking for "Peace and Mercy upon the Prophet and his Community" corresponds to our being there for them, with them, with a view to the accomplishment of a common destiny. We feel at ease with this vocation and this might be why Muslims feel equally at ease in Deir Mar Musa.

What would be the significance in this case of the evangelical Christian mission and in turn, of the Muslim call or *da'wa*? The mission is not a matter of theoretical information. It is always tied to a witness of life and creates a space of initiation, which allows a person to be gradually introduced into the mystery, aided by divine Grace. All this has to do with the awakening of the person's own, completely unique relationship with the One God.

For the Christian, the salvific divine act is Jesus of Nazareth himself, Son of God, Son of Man. God the Father begets his Only Son by pronouncing the pre-eternal Word of His Mercy. In his humanity, Jesus is the act of the Father and the Son for our salvation. The unique human-divine person of Jesus realises this accomplishment of History by giving life to the Church. This life is the Spirit of the Father and the Son, given to humanity with a view to its participation in the Trinitarian communion. It is this divinisation of humanity that the Church announces and preaches, and it is through this that Christian monotheism is realised.

Universal and Eternal Scope of the Jesus-Christ Event for the Salvation of All

My obedience to God, my conversion to God in faith, is in my case the application, the presence, the effectiveness and the intimate knowledge of the divine act of my salvation, operated now and which is always Jesus of Nazareth. It pertains to the Christian faith to believe and experience that the sincere encounter with God, even the most anonymous one, as it is expressed in any religious tradition, is founded, justified and actualised for each person by the salvific mystery of Jesus of Nazareth, son of Mary. In my catechism, I explain this by pointing out that a Buddhist mother somewhere in Asia two hundred years before Christ, who smiles with pure love and happiness at her child with a religious awareness of participating in the Buddha's enlightenment, smiles only by the power and grace of the act for her sake that is Jesus of Nazareth.

I admit that this example is difficult to understand. One reason for this difficulty could be that many among us are attached to a vision whereby on the one hand, God exists outside History; and on the other hand, He is mechanically subject to the law of historical progression to the point where what precedes Jesus Christ anticipates Him, and what comes after Him is caused by Him, but what is external to Him remains outside salvation and outside the ultimate meaning of the world. Christian experience is more radical than this. The pre-eternal birth of the Word cannot be separated for an instant from the birth of the son of Mary in time, and from the grace of my "yes" to him in the present moment. The humility of Jesus at the moment of his baptism in the River Jordan pleases God the Father who recognises Himself in His child because of his perfect obedience, by which everything was created and tends towards its fulfilment. The crucified and risen Christ is not different, other or elsewhere than the One God who seeks out his children at the furthest point of their ruin, in the hollow of the tomb, in a separation of God Himself from Himself provoked by the madness of His love. There is no God before and God after the Cross. He is since the beginning, always and forever, in Himself and towards us, the One who gives Himself thus. Being a disciple means deciding to mobilise, to engage oneself in the path opened by this definitive event, which is perpetually happening.

For Christian initiates, the previous could serve as a reminder. For Muslim initiates, it could echo some things they know differently. I even advise non-believers not to tense up as if we were speaking of Father Christmas. I would propose to them to perceive how spiritual members of different traditions find ways to express something of the profound structure of the world. If we can liberate ourselves from materialist prejudices we could, at least on a psychological level and by way of projection, see outlined in the visions of the religions a design for world harmony, or for restoring world harmony. Here there is a marvellous unity, which is not impossible to perceive.

The Meaning of the World

I was going down the stairs of the monastery with a young European, and he asked me: "Sir, could you tell me something about the meaning of the world before the end of the stairs?" Very few steps remained when I was able to answer him: "The world is an offering, but because of sin, it became a sacrifice." I tried with these few words to open a tiny window to the mystery for my young interlocutor… I was actually responding to the hopeful expectation I had guessed in his eyes. It is a paradoxical sentence, in the style of the ancient Desert Fathers, to break the cynical structure of materialist education. A shock summary of the Church's doctrine of faith, centred on the thirst for giving that agitates all hearts, and in response to the disarray that the refusal of the gift provokes in all hearts.

Muhammad the Perfect Man

The structure of Islam is not the same, without being completely different from that of the Christian mystery. The perfect act of faithful monotheistic worship by the individual human soul is illustrated, shown and perfected in the Prophet Muhammad, the perfect man. He has been chosen since always for this role and this perfection. The pre-eternal Qur'an, Word of God in God, does not only descend on the Prophet in stages, but read from a certain perspective, it narrates the growth of the faith and obedience to God of the Prophet and of his early Companions, who constitute the first nucleus of the *Ummah*.

In Islam, the central idea is that every created human individual receives by virtue of being human, the possibility to adhere through faith to the divine absolute, perhaps not yet consciously named. This is true since the beginning of civilisation, and is the case for people educated in non-monotheist cultures, or atheists. On the other hand, Muslims express this by saying that God creates every person in the Muslim "state", and that it is their parents who make them otherwise. Muslims believe that every human being in every time and place is created with a real possibility of adhering, through the act of faith, to the Lordship and the Truth of the One and All-Powerful God, Provident and Merciful.

The first model is Adam, which means that deep down, each one of us, every man and every woman, is called to faith. The story of Adam in the Qur'an does retain a definite Biblical echo, but it is not so much related to an original sin that would require a Redeemer. Rather, it is the story of human forgetfulness that entails the need for a lineage of prophets sent to all peoples to remind them of the original, Adamic monotheism. It remains that the call to faith in every human creature, in every time and place, makes us all Muslims in Adam.

The second model is Abraham, because it is he who turns to God by liberating himself from the illusion of idols. He is the herald of faith against disbelief, of authenticity's struggle against deceitfulness, of gratuitousness against self-interest, of intercession in solidarity against self-referentiality, of hospitality against extraneousness. We could say that the entire Muslim religion has an Abrahamic inspiration.

All of the prophets have but reminded all peoples of the divine truth. There has not been a people who have not received a prophet sent to them by God to remind them of their faith, they are innumerable. The Envoys or Apostles like Moses, Jesus and Muhammad, with Abraham as their common Father, are those to whom the act of divine revelation has been entrusted with an explicit and complete reservoir, a large and articulated celestial communication that conforms, is perfectly adapted, connatural and one can say consubstantial with the expectations, weaknesses, capacities and thirst of the human soul of the believer.

Revealed Religion

Revelation pours into the soul of the believer as if in a mould; and the believer pours themself into the mould of religion to take their truest form. In this sense, sending Moses, Jesus and Muhammad is an act of divine Mercy for the world and everybody in it. Revelation is really the gracious divine act of offering a form, a social and individual framework for the relationship of individuals with God, organised into a community of believers. In the Bible, Moses is the prototype of the founding prophet. He projects the anticipation of the perfect model and the perfect type of an awaited successor who will or would be like him. Moses is initial, Muhammad is final.

Jesus has a particular role in Islam. Based on the Qur'an, on the earliest Muslim literature and on successive mystical developments, he is the embodiment of the model of *walāya*, sainthood and closeness to God. Through him and with divine permission, merciful acts and a great number of miracles are performed; his authentic disciples are merciful and humble. But the common element to the three Envoys, Moses, Jesus and Muhammad, is that of the reminder. They represent a divine reminder of the original vocation of human beings and in this sense they are the condition for the event of this return to faith for everyone. They constitute an instrument of initiation, of formation, of organisation and celebration of the practice of faith. By renewing the human being, they renew human society and community, making it the sacred space of obedience to God.

"If Israel is rooted in hope, and Christianity dedicated to charity, Islam is centred on faith."[11] Christianity is centred on charity as ongoing sainthood, and the Qur'anic Jesus is called the Word and Spirit of God. He is all prophecy. In a sense, the quality of prophethood should rather be attributed to his mother, Mary, who "pronounces" him through his miraculous birth. She received this Word through the Annunciation of the Angel, the Spirit was breathed into her and she now offers this "sign of mercy" to the world.[12]

Muhammad therefore represents the final and hence definitive reminder; he resumes and proposes anew the fundamental attitude of a person before God, which is one of faith. All of Islam is based on this concept. The relationship of the Muslim to God can be recognised by Christians as characterised by a sincere consecration of oneself to God in unconditional trust, provoked by an eternal divine calling and a gracious authentic

11   Massignon, *Les Trois Prières*, 98.
12   Qur'an 4:171; 19:21; 66:12.

communication. So it is not a case of "natural" philosophical belief, but of a supernatural, celestial faith. The *fitra,* or natural faith, is not a condition of belief that is independent of divine Grace, but rather the exercise of the primordial faith set by God in the heart of every human being.

Sharâbu l-Fitra, The Drink of Natural Faith

A few years ago, Mgr. Michael Fitzgerald, who was then Secretary of the Pontifical Council for Interreligious Dialogue visited Syria and paid us the honour of coming to the monastery. I took this opportunity to organise with Sheikh Yasser al-Hafez, the Mufti of our region, a meeting with the local Muslim community and representatives of the parish of Nebek. We were all hosted in the home of my good friend the Mufti, shoeless in his living room as if in a place of prayer, Muslims and Christians gathered together. The bishop was warmly embraced, and moments later the Mufti's children distributed glasses of immaculately white curdled milk. The Mufti said: "This is God's hospitality, the drink of natural faith, *al-fitra*, which we receive from our mothers at our birth. Our reunion and our welcome of such a dear guest is happening in the dimension of the gift of faith, which we received immaculate from God, and which the reminder of the prophets helps us renew and purify."

Resumption of the Question of the Mission

There is the impression here of having strayed far away from the evangelical Christian mission and from the Muslim *da'wa*. It is not my intention to muddy the waters. Both communities believe they have received a universal mandate to which they are loyal. In different ways, they consider that every person, from the beginning and forever, is intimately tied through faith to the mystery announced and preached throughout history.

In a sense, both communities hope that by preaching the truth to people, they give them the possibility to fully manifest the fruit of the seed of the Spirit, buried in their hearts from the beginning. Marked by a strong historical and even eschatological dimension, they believe that they inaugurate the End Time where the collective and political dimensions of the mystery of faith will reach their realisation and perfection.

A person's intimate faith would not have a prospective goal without this collective and definitive event. This outlines the obvious fact that these two communities are competitors. But they are also associates by preaching to people all they share in common. It is very probable that the harmonisation of Christian and Muslim hopes is a condition for all mankind to be able to look upon the future with hopefulness.

Aggressive proselytising is considered unworthy of humanity by the majority of Muslims and Christians. Muslims believe that it is illogical, according to the logic of the faith, for a Muslim to become Christian. They consider that the reasons for apostatising could only be malevolent, have a malevolent purpose and be tied to a perverse plan carried out by a visible or invisible enemy. Apostasy therefore causes anarchy or social corruption, and it is hence forbidden. Christians believe that they have the duty to show Christ's entire mystery to Muslims. The contradiction is obvious. We are many who hope that each Community can choose to respect the journey of individual religious conscience.

I believe that the Christian mission is not separate from the exercise of the hermeneutics of charity, that is of understanding the other, while discerning a perspective where the love of Christ, a love that understands, justifies and valorises, could bring that other, as an individual and a community, into the joy of the Kingdom of God. It is also important that the Church be able to see how the Muslim desire to unify the human race in the worship of God rejoins and participates, potentially, to the universality of the Church in its catholicity. It is also always good to emphasise the Abrahamic dimension, Abraham being the common Father to Jews, Christians and Muslims.

Recognising the Prophet

In his preface to François Jourdan's book, Rémi Brague explains that "if a Christian recognises Muhammad's prophethood, one of two things is possible: either they give the term a meaning that no Muslim would be content with, or they are using it in the strong sense of 'envoy'. In the latter case, the Muslim will have the right and even the duty to ask them why, if they admit the truth of Muhammad's mission, do they not submit to the Law he brought and instead remain attached to Jesus' Law, which God abrogated and replaced by Muhammad's definitive one... In both cases, the Muslim will get the impression of being mocked with words."[13]

The interpretations of the Muhammadan prophecy are plural, even within Islam. There are plural interpretive currents with different hermeneutical tools regarding Muslim Law as well. That being said, a Christian can receive the grace of sensing that the Muslim religion is grounded in God, and that therefore so is Muhammadan prophethood. At the same time, this same Christian remains entirely convinced that Christ is their salvation and the salvation of Muslims themselves. Clearly there's a scandal, a difficulty: the Qur'anic negation of the fundamental dogma concerning the Church's Christ, namely the negation of the Trinity, the Incarnation, and the Cross.

The scandal is reciprocal. More sensitive Muslims feel challenged by this Christianity that has not massively aligned itself with the new and definitive Muhammadan prophecy. The majority of Muslims that I meet recognise that there is a divine plan behind this persistence of the Christian faith. They know that the two religions share much in common, and they wish that Christians would recognise the divine foundation of the Muslim religion because of the authenticity and sincerity of the Prophet. In general, they do not contend that a Christian should become Muslim, although they do wish it. It is not a condition for coexisting in peace, friendship and harmony with them. There is the hope that God will eventually gather us together in joy and eternal life. The Muslim is concerned for me because

13   Jourdan, *Dieu*, 19.

if I am not authentically monotheistic, I will not be admitted to Paradise to contemplate the Countenance of God. However, they do pray that God would guide me, and often wish that God would recognise my faith as authentically monotheistic, beyond Christian dogmatic corruptions, in a way in spite of me. Moreover, this same Muslim thinks that in order to be a real Muslim, they themself need to be a good Jew and a good Christian.

If we are used to seeing things as black or white, there is no way out. The most beautiful moments of the day are precisely dawn and dusk, the hour of nuances.

Qur'anic Christology: Is There a Way to Reconcile the Christ of the Church with the Issa of Islam?

The question of the difference between the Qur'anic approach to the mystery of Christ and the dogma of the Catholic Church can be addressed through several interpretive paths. I wish to participate in a process of discernment by the Church that would perhaps gradually be able to reach a reading of this issue framed in a positive vision of Islam, with a future perspective of dynamic harmony, tending towards and drawn by the final manifestation of God, namely the Parousia. In Christian discourse, the Parousia is the final manifestation of Christ, the end of History and the definitive inauguration of the Kingdom.

I believe that I can glimpse a sort of dogmatic rampart in the letter of the Qur'an which separates Islam from the Church in History, to protect its own function. On the one hand, Islam's function is complementary to that of the Church as a reminder of the primary mystery of the One, absolutely Transcendent God. It is not only an issue of celestial mathematics, of God as One or Three. For Muslims, it is about projecting monotheistic faith and celebrating it in the lives of individuals and families in the world. It is clearly a sacred political project. On the other hand, Islam has a function of polemic needling of the Church, who is accused of infidelity, of textual corruption, of associating God with other things. The mere existence of the Muslim Community forces the Church to review, reinterpret and rediscover her own mystery as infinity more inclusive and humble, in the strong and evangelical sense of these terms, and to be more open to the value of other religious communities that resist the universalist absolutism of the Christian pretension.

A Muslim who discovers the mystery of Christ in the plenitude of the faith of the Church is gifted by the Spirit with an interpretation of the Qur'an which is apt to harmonise Catholic theology with Muslim dogma. This is not the domain of naive concordism, and the person in question knows how to carry the cross of contradiction with courage and hopefulness. For example, the Qur'an states that Jesus was not crucified or killed, that it was an illusion. Muslim interpretations of these texts are not unanimous. The Muslim who believes in the mystery of Jesus tells himself: "Faith is not a prerequisite to believe that Jesus was tortured and died." For the most rigorous historians the crucifixion is perhaps the only historically accurate element of the Gospels. However, and this does belong to the domain of faith, we believe that the tortured one, the one who was subjected to the shame of the Cross is a glorious King who draws every human being from the height of the throne of his love, as Saint John says.[14] So it would require faith to believe that his Cross was an illusion, as the letter of the Qur'an says! Only faith sees in the death of Jesus a source of life, and that he who descended to the tomb went there to fight and kill death. It belongs to the domain of illusion to think that the end of his life on Earth is a death and a failure of his mission.

This same person knows very well that such an interpretation is not admissible to the majority of his Muslim coreligionists. This is also true for the Christian interpretation of the Bible. Interpreting the Prophets as fulfilled in Jesus Christ is inadmissible and even scandalous for Judaism. The question is not one of interpretative acrobatics aimed at Judaism or Islam. First and foremost, the Church should once and for all stop considering the other as someone who should be absorbed or conquered. She ought to interpret the religious needs of people and examine the scriptures of religions with the same compassionate attitude, and try to be the disciple of

14 John 12:32.

the one who said: "…learn from me; for I am gentle and humble in heart, and you will find rest for your souls."[15]

On the other hand, I do not wish for Muslims to be locked in a polemical position, and most importantly I do not wish for them to be tempted by polemical violence. I wish for them and for us Christians to be open to the action of the Spirit that can instruct and re-instruct us on how to read all the Scriptures, as well as our history in all its complexity, in order to open us up to the benevolent designs of divine Mercy.

Islam and the Church Faced with the End of the World

A few years ago I was in Qaryatayn, an oasis located on the road to Palmyra, where a residual community of pre-Islamic Arab Christians of Syriac rite has been dying out little by little for fourteen centuries in the face of the rise of Islam. The ancient Mar Elian Monastery was behind me. Before Islam, this monastery had been an important station for the evangelisation of nomads. The monks had come from the north, and had rooted the Gospel in the culture of this Bedouin milieu. Then Islam came. Part of the population became Muslim. Locally, it is told that an accord of mutual protection was signed. The Muslims would protect the Christians, and the Christians would protect the Muslims should the Byzantines return in force. This remains true to this day… As I walked towards this now Muslim town, I kept thinking about the fact that the Church Fathers had developed the concept of "evangelical preparation" to indicate the properly seminal work of the Holy Spirit, not only in the Biblical context but also in the cultures and religions of the nations. I have often heard theologians try to apply this concept of evangelical preparation to Islam. It would prepare masses of men and women through the ways of monotheism, of a particular moral education and written civilisation, to receive the gift of the Church in a mature way… I looked at the tall palm trees along the road. And suddenly, as I looked higher

15   Matthew 11:28–29

and further, a concept crystallised, quite vivid and dynamic in my intellect: "eschatological preparation."

I maintain that it is not sufficient to recognise Islam's goodness and Islam's truth as evangelical preparation, merely a path towards Christ and the Church. By accepting that the Muslim Community sees itself as post-Christian, at least on the historical level, I prefer to speak of an eschatological preparation rather than an evangelical one. The Church is thereby constantly surpassed by the fecundity of its own mystery and forever drawn towards a coming perfection, the source of which is the Christ of yesterday, today and the End of Days.

In the Times, Beyond Time

Consequently, post-Christianities participate in this continuous reinterpretation of the Church in view of the eschaton, the final accomplishment, where "final" is a category of metahistory. By metahistory I mean the breaking up of the chronological succession of time to reveal a deeper, or so to say a more final dimension of our spiritual reality. It is not only Islam that declares itself post-Christian. Judaism is post-Christian, because it continues beyond the time of the Church through its rejection of the Church's claim of constituting the new Israel. Buddhism has a post-Christian consciousness because it refused to be assimilated through Christian proselytism, and so does Hinduism, which flourishes in spite of evangelising campaigns. Secularised and agnostic European culture is also explicitly post-Christian.

The Church should not reject all these different realities out of hand. On the contrary, they push the Church to invoke continuously larger and deeper "pentecosts", manifestations of the Spirit. The aim is to rise together towards horizons of interpretation, of re-reading what we are, which are broader, sublime, and which synthesise our current communal historic consciousness, with a view to an empathic progression that reveals to us hitherto inconceivable harmonies and which, simply, we can only see coming, glimpse and hope for, and which we must commit to building.

Every person carries the gift of faithfulness to the buried treasure of their tradition; but this faithfulness needs the treasure of the other for it to be fully explored.

And so Islam, through its rejection of the Trinity, drives us towards a more dramatic understanding of the dynamism of the One God. It prevents us from settling for a merely philosophical assertion of divine Unity, it forces us to get back on the path of monotheistic contemplation in order to achieve, in worship, the union of all the dimensions of our life with God. It drives us to realise, perhaps in different ways, a recentring of human life in the One God. It equally invites us to build a political monotheism through the re-enchantment of the world, centred in the mystery of divine Omnipresence. We will lose nothing of the mystery of the very Holy Trinity, but maybe we will learn to explain it to ourselves better and differently, with the goal of advancing Islamic-Christian harmony to higher degrees.

The same goes for the Incarnation, because confessing Jesus of Nazareth as the Son of God is not a matter of words. Christians must in the present incarnate, their life must demonstrate the perfect spirituality of divine filiation that takes nothing away from divine Unity and Oneness but rather consecrates its mystery. The Church is capable of expressing the Word in an always new, passionate and loving incarnation within human plurality, which will convince Muslims.

Even more radical is the discourse on the mystery of the Cross, because Christians who are not prepared to die for the other are not convincing when they speak of the crucified Christ.

The three Muslim negations constitute the strongest appeal for evangelic radicality; one that is always new and renewed by the action of the Spirit. To the point where one can, so to speak, unveil the truth of the anti-Christian Muslim assertion as one is progressively driven towards the realisation of the Christian mystery. This is so that our generation may take in its stride this Qur'anic criticism and transcend it.

Other Difficulties

I am aware of the sometimes grave contradictions that can be easily reiterated. Namely it is shocking for Christians to hear the Muslim assertion that Islam is the true Christianity, and that in Islam, everything particular to Christianity has been protected, purified and clarified.

Herein lies a way to go beyond the letter and towards the Spirit, which never dispenses with the letter itself. On the contrary, our position is to seek access, even by way of contradiction and paradox, to a spiritual experience that cannot exist without this letter we are meant to surpass.

Also, there will always be in the East as in the West, Christians who will say that based on the different texts of the New Testament, only false prophets will come after Jesus. I seem to hear the voice of Jesus of Nazareth warning us that we would be mistaken if we were to take even his own words and those of his Apostles literally, even though he knows that we have no other words to help us unveil the face of the Father.

There's an entire theology of false prophecy in the New Testament. It is not surprising that this was applied to the Muhammadan prophecy, which denies the central truths of the Christian faith and has founded a Community that rivalled the Church very effectively… We could stop at this obstruction, but in my opinion that would risk sterilising the prophecy of the Church. We feel driven by the Spirit of prophecy to return to the work of discernment on the prophecy of Islam. Within us, the awareness is strong that only the entire Christian Community in its universality, led by Peter, can rule on this matter with authority. This is the perspective of this entire book.

"Re-figuration"

Christians must purify their spiritual intention before starting prayer, like Muslims performing their ablutions; otherwise their prayer will not be received and will not be a prayer to God. Muslims do this purification through a ritual. Whenever I see a Muslim performing ritual ablution or I take part in it, I remember the water of my baptism. As a foreshadowing, all the sacrifices of the ancient Temple of Jerusalem participate in the unique and ultimate Lamb, the crucified Jesus. Similarly, all these Muslim ablutions, I will not say that they prefigure, but that they "refigure", to my eyes as a Christian, the mystery of the unique and definitive purification obtained for every human being by the humiliation, *kenosis*, of Jesus of Nazareth during the Jordan baptism, the anticipatory expression of the act fulfilled on the Cross.

Why this fixation on humiliation? The Lord Jesus, by asking for baptism, counted himself among the sinners in need of purification. He, the Son of the Holy One, puts himself in a condition of penance, in unconditional solidarity with sinners and receives baptism at the hands of the son of Zachary, John the Baptist, who was precisely of sacerdotal descent, who came from a family of priests and thus had the authority to sanctify and purify.

Muslims have a real difficulty accepting this humiliation of Jesus, God's Envoy. To die a martyr is a glory. But this torture on the Cross is shameful.

Humiliation

In 1997 I was in Assisi, in the magnificent basilica dedicated to Saint Francis, which would later be almost destroyed by an earthquake. My friend, a Sudanese Sufi sheikh, had taken off his shoes at the door and sat at the centre of the nave in his white turban… A university professor had told us the story of Saint Francis along the road. He was now explaining to us the frescoes representing the throne of Lucifer. He showed us the scene featuring the throne of Satan, the Angel of Light, now empty in the heavens, destined to receive the Saint of perfect humility, Francis. The sheikh then cried: "This is of whom our Teacher spoke! In the small *madrasa* of our childhood, a *murid* [seeker] asked him: 'who will come to occupy the place of glory left empty in heaven by Satan, Iblis?' And he answered: 'the humblest among the children of Adam.'"

Humility and humiliation, the question remains open in our religious histories, Christian and Muslim. It is in fact an urgent topic for universal spirituality.

I allow myself to contemplate the inflexible orthodox Sunni Muslim position regarding the rejection of the humiliation of prophets, the well-beloved of God. "A saint of God must not suffer ignominiously, a Judge must not be condemned, a prophet can neither be a penitent nor defeated, for it would mean the defeat of God."[16] And yet I remember that when I was a student at the Faculty of Damascus, the great professor Ramadan al-Buti was giving a commentary on the *sīra*, the life story of the Prophet. He reached the part about the attacks, the insults, the tortures that the Prophet's Community and his first Companions had to endure in Mecca at the hands of their fellow citizens. While he spoke of the humiliations that the Prophet had to suffer to remain loyal to his mission, he was shaken and had to stop, wiping his tears in silence.

Now, my life is teaching me that the only true humility is the one that is given to us through the grace of humiliation.

Biblical Jesus, Qur'anic Jesus

During these last, post-Council years, some Catholic authors have striven to show that the Qur'anic Jesus is not the Christ of the Gospels, and that the same goes for Moses, Abraham, Adam, Mary and the others. Louis Massignon had a completely opposite point of view, and taught that the Qur'an carries something of the holiness of Biblical revelation through the mere fact of repeating these names, the names of these human persons marked by the fire of divine experience.[17] The mere mention of these

16   Massignon, *Les Trois Prières*, 96.

17   François Jourdan, in *Dieu des Chrétiens, Dieu des Musulmans* (Paris: Éditions de l'Œuvre, 2007), 47, also addresses this question by discussing the idea, certainly of Massignonian inspiration, of "a common core shared by the three great monotheistic religions. This seems obvious since all three mention, as we saw, twenty or so names of figures who seem common to them: Adam, Noah, Abraham…Mary and Jesus" 47. "But Louis Massignon posed a vague connection between Abraham and Ishmael and wrote about the Qur'an: 'this Arab edition of the Bible reserved to the physical descendants of Abraham by Ishmael!'" (*La passion de Hallaj* [*The Passion of Hallaj*], Paris, Gallimard, 1975, volume III, 10, fn. 2). "Another disciple, Roger Arnaldez, denies that L. Massignon recognised Muhammad as prophet, contrary to what some would have the master say: his vibrant formulas were often ambiguous"

names who experienced God's eruption in history, in their souls and their lives, would confer legitimacy to the Qur'anic text. I find that this argument is both strong and insufficient. Massignon would probably agree with me that there is another source for discerning Qur'anic authenticity: the discernment of the Prophet's sincerity in his experience of God.[18]

And so it is not surprising to discover that the Qur'an's Biblical figures are in a sense Muhammadan; in fact, this is how Muslims see them, because each of them represents a facet of the unique prophecy, which is so to say resumed and concluded in Muhammad.

The Relationship between Christian Revelation and Muslim Authenticity

Last night, after writing these considerations, I took refuge in the church for meditation and Mass.[19] At the same moment, two million Muslim pilgrims were gathered at Mount Arafat in Makka (Mecca: the name of the city is linked with Bakka, the place where Hagar shed tears for Ishmael) to ask forgiveness for themselves and for their dear ones, at the final station of Abraham and Ishmael's pilgrimage. I felt a deep consolation, because I could see more clearly the ways in which the Sacrament of the

---

50. This entire discussion is resumed by François Jourdan in Annex 1 where he criticises the expressions "Religions of the Book", "common core" and "Islam as a revealed religion". He has the amiability of quoting me: "In the Church, I do not have the right today to say that Muhammad is a prophet... I would like to say to the Church that considering Muhammad a prophet does not affect Christ, in whom I believe" (in Guyonne de Montjou, *Mar Musa*, 211). In this regard it is also necessary to refer directly to Louis Massignon, *Les trois prières d'Abraham*, 89–92.

18   Louis Massignon, *Les trois prières d'Abraham*, 89. "The Qur'an, this silent witness... of Muhammad's sincerity."

19   I'm keeping this temporal indication referring to the month of January 2005, as I was working on writing my response to the observations of the Congregation for the Doctrine of Faith. It was a time of prayer and discernment, where the dimension of the event of a punctual theological "illumination" finds its personal and ecclesial significance.

Eucharist embodies a complete union between Christ's faith in Allah, the Father and Lord, and his work, his act of love for God and for his neighbours, that is all of us![20] The act of worship (I am thinking of its symbolic scope in both Judaism and Islam), the work of the Eucharist (but this applies to all sacraments and to the only sacrament of "salvation", namely the Church) is the efficient divine action that is perfectly suited to the sacrificial salvific intent (death and Resurrection of the Son of God). Through it, from the beginning and for always, the works of faith that express the love of God and others become efficient in regards to salvation, inside and outside the visible Church.

I therefore saw more clearly that the Eucharistic sacrifice offered by the assembly of Jesus' disciples for our pilgrim friends in Mecca is effective in giving the actual act of Muslim pilgrimage its salvific significance, with the plea for the forgiveness of sins associated with the sacrifice of Abraham (he who was justified for his faith) at the forefront. And so, while according to the truth of the Christian perspective, this faith is only possible through God's "Yes" to humanity in His Christ, inseparable from the Church, the Muslims who adhere to the grace of faith in the form of Muslim religion obtain mercy and forgiveness through (and not in spite of) the sacrifice at Mecca. This sacrifice not only re-figures the Eucharistic sacrifice (evangelical preparation) but also expresses a universal and final expectation of reconciliation in divine justice (eschatological preparation). The Muslim faith receives its efficiency from being an act of love for God and for one's neighbour, possible only because of the divine sacrificial Eucharistic act offered to the Father for our sake by the Incarnate Word.[21]

I remember this old lady who brought back a gift for me from her Hagarene pilgrimage: a jar of water from the well of Zamzam, tears of this

---

20   I understand this question of the faith of Christ the same way Hans Urs Von Balthasar understood it (in *La Foi du Christ* [*The Faith of the Christ*], Paris, Le Cerf, 1994). In the history of theology, the question arises: Did Jesus have faith, or does his beatific vision as Son of God render faith impossible, even for his humanity? It is evident that the meditation on Jesus' faith is essential in Muslim-Christian dialogue. While fully human, his faith is entirely united and perfectly corresponds to the cognitive and historical act of divine self-realisation.

21   Acts 10:4, The prayers and alms of Cornelius ascend to God.

mother of intercession and compassion that was Hagar. She told me that she could think of no place better suited than Mar Musa for such an offering. This water was mixed, tear after tear, with the wine of the Eucharistic offering so God may accept the Muslim pilgrimage and the plea for forgiveness that it signifies.

There was also the intercession of this grandma, our neighbour in the village, a burdened woman, because her granddaughter was seriously handicapped. Her son and I had spent months and months trying to drill a well for our monastery. Everything that could go wrong did. She had just returned from the pilgrimage, and I paid her a visit to congratulate her. She said to me: "I prayed a lot for you and your well as I drank the water of Zamzam, and also during my procession around the Holy House of God…" A few days later, the well was functioning and the water still flows to this day.

We Are All God's Children!

A Muslim Sheikh once told us: "The problem is not that you make Jesus the son of God, it's that you don't understand how much we all are God's children!"

This statement can be understood in two ways. The first is that according to Muslim thought, all creatures are "God's family" in the sense that God is like a father who takes care of all creatures with love and benevolence, humans particularly. The human being is God's lieutenant in Creation, like a first-born son whose father entrusts him with his property.

There's a deeper way still to understand why, from a Muslim point of view, it can be said that all humans are God's children. God creates all things through the simple commandment of His Will. In the Qur'an 3:59, it is said: "The similitude of Jesus before God is as that of Adam; He created him from dust, then said to him: 'Be'. And he was." Several times in the Qur'an, God commands the angels: "Prostrate yourselves before Adam!" It is true that to a Christian ear, this divine order immediately brings to mind the angels celebrating the Incarnate Son above the grotto in Bethlehem;

the new, the true, the definitive Adam, "…the firstborn of all creation; for in him were created all things in heaven and on earth: everything visible and everything invisible, Thrones, Dominations, Sovereignties, Powers – all things were created through him and for him."[22]

The Muslim spiritual ear hears other echoes. Indeed, human rationality is the most perfect thing in the world and partakes in the divine Thought that creates and orders the universe. The same applies to other human attributes, which in a totally incomparable way, are also divine attributes. Without saying that Man was created in God's image, in the Qur'an God says: "We have honoured the sons of Adam…and conferred on them special favours, above a great part of our creation."[23] "…Him who created thee, fashioned thee in due proportion, and gave thee a just bias."[24] And yet, Muslim tradition arrives at the interpretation of Muhammad as the model of human perfection. In some branches of Muslim tradition, his light is considered the first creature, and every other creature a reflection of his light… Here we find a type of Arianism with Muhammad rather than Christ as its subject. Besides, Muslim theology often presents Arianism as the true Christianity.

So Adam, father to everyone, is like Christ, Spirit and Word of God. Well, Muhammad is no less than that. All human beings, while aware that they cannot compare themselves to these perfect prophetic models, have to know that their vocation is to imitate them, to get close to God through them, in order to partake in their relationship with God.

The disciples of Jesus have another point of view but are nevertheless not at all displeased to know that Muslims believe in the divine paternity and in our vocation to be His children, even if in a different way.

In obedience to the faith, the Church is fiercely attached to the fact that from the Immaculate Conception to the Ascension, Jesus of Nazareth is an incomparable miracle. Not only because he is admirable, but also because he is the unique, unconditional and radical divine act of Self-Revelation (which logically follows the eternal begetting as divine Self-Consciousness

22   Colossians 1:15–16.
23   Qur'an 17:70.
24   Qur'an 82:7.

and Self-Realisation), uncreated and eternal, original and definitive. As a
result of Christ's divine filiation, Adam and all his children are created in
God's image, in anticipation of their baptism and their life as disciples of
Jesus of Nazareth. Outside the visible Church, the divine act, the death and
Resurrection of Christ, by which every human being is reconciled to God
and welcomed as His child, fulfils the condition for the sanctification of
every soul, always and everywhere. Thus, the universal, spiritual and mystical Church is the family of all the children of God. Because of this, the
person, as an individual who forms relationships, is shown as the height
of the created world, in itself a microcosm of infinite value.

Let us look at it from another point of view, in relation to the consciousness of Christ. We know him to be human-divine, one human-divine
person (meaning a fully human being that coincides entirely with the divine
position). The relational initiative is the divine initiative of the Eternal
Word, the Son, and yet we cannot imagine it to occur elsewhere, neither
in Heaven nor before the world was created, than in the human decision
made by Jesus son of Mary. Jesus in his humanity is aware and intends to
carry out his divinely ordained acts through his human action.

Let us repeat. The night before the Passion, Christ decides to give
himself without limit and to expose himself to torture for love. In terms
of its meaning, this is the contextual action of a man, the Christ-God, who
"makes", provokes and constitutes the event of the divine position regarding
the meaning of the world. It is an "eternal" pronouncement, the impact
of which is everywhere and always. Since then, the universe is entirely this
act of divine self-giving that makes us the children of God the Father, the
paternal-maternal-genitor; and His Spirit of Mercy is the life of the world.

I think of the Christ in Leonardo da Vinci's Last Supper where Jesus
creates the world with his right hand and offers it to God with his left, for
the One to be all in all.

Some might ask: if the point is to be the beloved children of God, why
complicate things so much? Yes, but according to the faith of Christians,
the issue is to see in History the self-giving act of a man who is perfectly
united, to the point where we cannot say what comes before what, to the
divine act of creating, saving and accomplishing the world. It is the gift
of Christian faith that makes the disciple of Jesus aware of the truth, the

coherence and the necessity of these affirmations. We desire to liberate Christian dogma of ideological pretence and of its theological superiority complex. The point is to demonstrate the scope of its truth through the practice of a humble and benevolent hospitality, in love with all the divine beauty that is reflected in the mirror of otherness.

Is There Still Value in Evangelisation?

We will be asked: what remains of preaching the Gospel? What use is there in evangelising in the present time? In my opinion, the basis of such a question can only be the radical separation between the time of the Church and the End Time, and this does not correspond to the logic of Christian faith. The witness of the Church, the love of God and of one's neighbour, espouses the witness of the Spirit in the hearts of people of all traditions; it is a witness that always brings them closer to fully receive grace in the Lord Jesus. Why worry, since the best way to evangelise is to imitate Jesus the way the Little Brother, Father Charles de Foucauld, so humbly and profoundly showed us. Why not offer our witness, in season and out of season, by trusting the Spirit of God that leads everything to its end, which is Christ? Friar Minor Francis of Assisi said it so well in his *Regula Non Bullata*, the first rule he wrote and which wasn't approved in his lifetime:

> Therefore, any brother who…desires to go among the Saracens… As for the brothers who go, they can live spiritually among them in two ways. One way is not to engage in arguments or disputes, but to be subject to every human creature for God's sake and to acknowledge that they are Christians. Another way is to proclaim the word of God when they see that it pleases the Lord, …because whoever has not been born again of water and the Holy Spirit cannot enter into the kingdom of God…[25]

25 François d'Assise, "Écrits [Writings]," in *Sources Chrétiennes.*, no. 285 (1997), 151. English translation from: <https://www.franciscantradition.org/index.php?option=com_content&view=article&id=89&catid=36>.

Do we know the Hour of the Spirit better than God? Let us begin today, in the grace of this *kairos*, of this time full of meaning and urgency, to contemplate the works of the Father in favour of mankind, this marvellous plan so admirably apt to recapitulate all things in Christ.

I certainly desire to go to Mecca as a pilgrim! Maybe not right now, because Muslims would not accept it. And from there, with the Muslims, I want to return to Jerusalem, the first and final direction of prayer in Islam, to contemplate the very humble glory of the Body of Christ, the inclusive Body of Christ, He in whom the entirety of divine works and human efforts find their gracious completion, for all time and in every place.

I want to obstinately repeat that it is given to me to see from this moment (I am not alone but I want to assume responsibility for this witness) how Islam, through the grace of God and according to its own providential destiny, is also engaged in pursuing an inclusive plan of final recapitulation tied to the anticipation of the rightly guided Muhammadan Mahdi.

Muhammad as Model

I have the right and the duty to offer witness, in obedience to charity, to the capacity of the mystical Christ to recapitulate all things by his divine and human offering in the embrace of the Father, so God is all in all. But what does the Kingdom of God gain by my denying the Muslim faith? That faith sees in Muhammad the perfect man, the obedient one, the model made by God and through whom every soul is called and drawn to being perfected in God by faith. Let us Christians try to understand how loving Muslim obedience is! It would be good for us to know that for a great number of Muslims, the Prophet's intercession in favour of the fulfilment of faith in every human soul, according to the model of his prophetic conscience, due to the "Muhammadan Light" and his quality as the perfect man, is effective because it is willed by God. It is a universal intercession comparable to the incomparable intercession of the Incarnate Word. For myself, I ask for infallible fidelity to my *Rabboni* of Nazareth. But it is he who teaches me hospitality and forbids me from excommunicating others. I want to remind my Christian brother, who would be scandalised by my words, of the power and significance of the spiritual reality of the communion of saints. Every faithful soul has by the grace of Christ a sanctifying effect on all souls until the end of the world. The souls of the Just (be they pre-, extra- or post-Christian) are not excluded from the communion of saints! In a way, it is the "sense of the faithful", the devotion of believers, which knows and measures the impact of a soul in favour of others.[26] Well, the impact of the soul of Muhammad is immense for Muslims.

Reading the Scriptures, Rewriting the Future

The work of discernment regarding the Muhammadan prophecy entails for Christians a re-reading of the Biblical revelation. All scriptural re-readings lead to re-writings resulting from the meditation of believers, and they bring an infinite number of new facets to the texts. This doesn't mean reinventing Abraham, Isaac and Jacob. It is precisely the infinite and living possibility of reinterpretation, tied fundamentally to the faith and intercession of the souls of our spiritual ancestors, which makes God, as He says, the God of Abraham, Isaac and Jacob, the God of the living and not of the dead. We worship this God if we are alive, if we welcome His effervescent life! "Now about the dead rising again, have you never read in the Book of Moses, in the passage about the Bush, how God spoke to him and said: I am the God of Abraham, the God of Isaac and the God of Jacob? He is God, not of the dead, but of the living."[27]

26 TN. For further information on the concept of "sense of the faithful" Cf. <https://www.vatican.va/roman_curia/congregations/cfaith/cti_documents/rc_cti_2014 0610_sensus-fidei_en.html>.
27 Mark 12:26–27.

Issa and Jesus

I propose here an example of how to go beyond the exclusivist reading of the sacred texts to attempt a politically engaged reading that tends towards a future harmony. The example is the name of Jesus in the Qur'an. Concerning the question of the Qur'anic name for Jesus, Issa, I would like to first refer to the heavily documented book by Father François Jourdan who dedicates a long chapter to it.[28] His point of view very much differs from mine… And this is why the Church is magnificent!

Some authors rely on the different etymology of the name of Jesus in the Arabic Bible, Yasū', from that of his Qur'anic name, Issa ('Īsa), to deduce that these are two different persons. We must remember that the Qur'an is written in the Arabic language of a part of Arabia, and so in principle there is no problem if the Qur'anic name of Jesus is Issa and not Yasū' as it is in the Arabic (re)transcription of the Syriac and Hebrew form. And also, in the East, Arab Christians give their sons the Qur'anic name Issa. They have no qualms about this! Where does the Qur'anic form of the name come from? It probably relies on the contemptuous form used by the Jews of the Hijaz who wanted to take away from Jesus of Nazareth, the illegitimate son of Mary, the name of Moses' successor Joshua, "God saves", precisely because they do not recognise his role as saviour.

Let it be noted that in French and in European languages in general, the phonetic relationship between Joshua and Jesus is lost. The same is true for the Jacob of the Old Testament and the James of the New Testament, whereas the Arab Christians retain this continuity from the Old to the New Testaments. In any case, the link is not obvious between the Semitic pronunciation of the name of Jesus by his mother and the various European corruptions of the name itself… This starts already in the Greek New Testament.

There might be in the Qur'anic Arabic form "Issa" something that relies on the name Esau who, according to the Bible, lost his position as first-born over a plate of lentils, and who is described as crying out his infinite

28   Jourdan, *Dieu*, 141–51.

distress at being dispossessed of the paternal benediction stolen by Jacob's ruse. It is astonishing to re-read this text because it is a text on exclusion, as is the case with Ishmael.[29] Esau is one of the excluded, one of the losers in the ancient stories of the Patriarchs. He is the father of the people that are the cousins and enemies of Israel, Edom.[30] He is also the father of Amalek. His descendants will become the symbol of absolute evil to be eradicated by genocide.[31] But like Ishmael, he is excluded while also being blessed.[32]

In the awful context of the Near East today, a paradoxical, even inverse reading, and not just an irenically symbolic one, should be proposed. The rise of violence and injustice justified by the texts of the Biblical Covenant has reached such a paroxysm that reading the Bible has become revolting to Christian Arabs. A Palestinian theology of liberation has developed, seeking God in moral justice rather than in the ancestral elections that create chosen peoples.

All the same it is true that the Holy Spirit, experienced from generation to generation, inhabits this Bible, and that a feverish meditation on the texts can quell the thirst of souls seeking the establishment of justice, *al-Haqq*. I have at times called upon Christian scriptural consciousness to read the texts on the banishment of Hagar and the exclusion of Ishmael, the father of Arabs and Muslims, as an illustration of what was later realised through the mystery of Christ and the Church, and which continues to be realised today. Let us open our spiritual eyes! How is it possible to not see in the accounts of Genesis a prophecy of the Passion of Christ and of the sufferings of His Body, the Church?[33] "When the skin of water was finished she abandoned the child under a bush. Then she went and sat down at a distance, about a bowshot away, saying to herself, 'I cannot see the child die'. So, she sat at a distance; and the child wailed and wept. But God heard the boy wailing..."[34] The cry of the child abandoned by his father, linked here with the wood of the bush and with a rejected servant

---

29   Genesis 27.
30   Genesis 36:8.
31   Exodus 17:14; Numbers 24:18–20; Deuteronomy 25:19.
32   Genesis 16:10–12; 27:40.
33   Genesis 21:8–20.
34   Genesis 21:15–17.

mother who weeps desperately... Who has the heart to not recognise the Christ of the excluded, the Christ of those without a homeland, of the "displaced people", crucified before his mother who cannot help him? Do we need to be reminded that for the Muslim Meccan pilgrimage, this image-reality is the origin of one of the most dramatic moments, when Hagar (in Arabic the name *hajar* is linked to the concept of expatriation), distraught, searches for water for the child? Why would the Church be prefigured solely by Sarah, the free woman who has the power of life and death over her servant? Why not listen to Abraham's prayer for his child Ishmael, his first-born?

Further on in the accounts of the Patriarchs, this "great cry of bitterness" uttered by Esau after his brother robs him of the paternal blessing, and this impassioned request: "Father, bless me too!", do they not transport the Christian soul to Golgotha, to hear the cry of the cursed crucified one who echoes it? "Have you not kept a blessing for me?" Esau implored, "Was that your only blessing, father? Father, give me a blessing too." Isaac remained silent, and Esau burst into tears.[35]

Hermeneutics of the Bible by the Bible

In his Epistle to the Galatians, Saint Paul masters a paradoxical reading of the Biblical text. In chapter 4:21-31, he inverts traditional expectations by reinterpreting the text on Hagar and Ishmael. He ends up saying that the real Sarah is the Church of the excluded peoples, that she who thought she was free ultimately reveals herself a slave.

It is always with suffering that the Biblical hermeneutics of our opposed, adversarial histories are conducted in our conflictual present. Why do we persist in seeking a word from God for our times in a macho, ethnocentric and exclusivist Bible? Many ask the same question regarding the Qur'an. Our youths often ask the same question about all our religious

35   Genesis 27:34–38.

traditions… But the cry of divine disarray courses through the Scriptures and through History, it is conjugated and finds a voice in the scorched throats of the outcasts and the tormented. A hopefulness is born from a reading that is always prepared to allow itself to be destabilised by another point of view, the other's point of view.

I love the Church that is always shaken by the deeply moving mystery that keeps surpassing her. Here I think of the Church as she is portrayed in *The Shepherd of Hermas*, as God's very intention when He created the world: "It is for Her that the world was formed."[36] She would ultimately be the gathering of the blessed outcasts.

To conclude the question of the Muslim name for Jesus, I want to say that I like the name Issa in its Qur'anic Arabic. The Qur'anic Jesus is the Messiah of the outcasts! It reminds me of the name Esau, the ancestor of those excluded from the Holy Land. For me, beyond etymology, it is the name of the Saviour. Since our Desert Fathers taught us the prayer of the heart, night and day I repeat it: "*al-Massih* (Christ) *Issa, ibna Maryam* (son of Mary), forgive me the sinner and have mercy on us."

The Aleppo Bus

One day in Aleppo I took a crowded public bus to the countryside. I found a place near the engine, next to the driver, legs and knees crossed like two combs with people beside me on the bench seat. I had already had many theological discussions with more or less friendly Muslims who interrogated me ceaselessly: why do you Christians say this or that? And here, yet again, in front of everyone and loudly, a bearded man started cross-examining me somewhat aggressively, demanding to know how a reasonable person can believe in the Son of God. I answered him: "Wait, for once, you will be the Christian and I will be the Muslim"; and I apostrophised him on all the theological oppositions. I began with the trinitarian

36 Hermas, *Le Pasteur* [*The Shepherd of Hermas*], Sources Chrétiennes (Paris: Le Cerf, 1997).

non-sense, continued with the scandal of the Incarnation, moved on to the absurdity of the Christian cult of Mary, and harshly attacked the priests and bishops who illegitimately hold divine powers, and I described with many arguments how you, Christians and Jews, have corrupted the Scriptures. I expressed being scandalised by the Christian assertion of the Crucifixion of this pure prophet, Jesus of Nazareth. Next, I tackled the dishonest Christian refusal to recognise the Muhammadan prophecy and the obviously divine origin of the Qur'an. I poured oil over the fire with an apologetical attitude that left no space for contradiction and that asked questions only rhetorically, to impose answers. The bus remained in an astonished silence as it swallowed the road. My voice was far louder than the engine itself, which roared underneath me, and my eyes were alight with monotheistic jealousy. At one point an old gentleman said to me: "Stop, we beg your pardon, I understand that this is not the right way to discuss religion, it is not the 'best way' that the Prophet recommended to us." I in turn apologised for having lost my temper so violently, and I promised him that I would never again indulge in polemics. Since then I have systematically avoided the cockfighting of theological discussions. My way of entering into dialogue is first and foremost through a sincere curiosity. I am really interested in understanding something of the particularity of the person facing me, or rather sharing a bench with me. They are dear to me from the start, and I am certain that through their words and experience I will come in contact with something, a new trait, another facet of the Only One who interests me, because He is truly interested in this person that I am meeting. He takes care of me through them and takes care of them through me. A sacred circle comes about and takes shape at this moment; a fruitful circulation beyond the simplicity of our conversation, whether it be directly religious or social, about agriculture, family or technology…the Divine breath is there.

To Conclude

We can make two observations. The first is that we have been caught in a current that started with considerations on Muhammad's prophecy, and has led us to pose the question of hermeneutics, the interpretation of "re-vealed" scripture, in a rather radical way.[37] We have assumed the need for a Christian reflection with its own autonomy in the framework of the collective self-perception of the Church. All the same, we have tried to hold on to the standard of our discourse, which aims for service, *diakonia,* and to the standard of Muslim-Christian harmony in accordance with God's will.

The second consideration, which is connected to the story of the Aleppo bus, is that it is urgent to develop an asceticism of theological thought, so it may renounce the genre of the polemic and of apologetic comparison in favour of a performative theology. Theology is responsible not only for describing phenomena and relating them to one another. In the context of Muslim-Christian dialogue in particular, and naturally also of Christian-Jewish dialogue, this would lead to a series of paralysing dead ends. Theology can from now on aspire only to bear witness, in dialogue, to the personal and communal charismatic events that lead our communities away from identitarian tensions and towards an engagement in the objectivity of the event of mutual spiritual understanding, graced by an evolving harmony.

37   "We" here corresponds to a universal community of persons called to a life of dia-logue. No one has delegated me to represent them, but the exigency that I express immediately necessarily involves the community.

Revelation in Islam

Often in Christian milieux, Christian anthropology and theology are radically opposed to the Muslim vision in terms of the discourse on mankind and the relationship God has established with it. The revelation of Jesus Christ is also considered as definitive and in a way closed; there is hence no room for a tardy Muslim revelation. Recent official Church documents such as *Dominus Iesus* remind us that we should not confuse supernatural theological faith, a grace received through Christ with Christ as the object of our faith, with the natural faith that would be the hallmark of the other religions. In this framework, how can a Christian speak of revelation in Islam? How does the relationship with the Muslim religion, not just with Muslims, flourish in the monastic life of Deir Mar Musa?

The Language of Revelation

In Arabic, "to believe", *āmana*, comes from "faith", *īmān*. In Islam, faith is a divine gift that leads one to gradually perfect one's adherence, until it is complete, to Muhammad's Qur'anic revelation. A revelation is tied to a linguistic context. The eventual recognition of the Muslim revelation cannot happen without an internalisation of the Arabic language. I would even say that it is not exclusively an intellectual process, but also a celebratory one.

Our liturgical language at the Monastery of Mar Musa is Arabic, the language of the Qur'an. It is the Arabic made sacred through the revelation of Islam and used as a sacred and liturgical language by the entire Muslim

Community everywhere in the world, including well beyond the cultural and geographic Arab world. One can speak of a "Muslim catholicism", a religiously and eschatologically projected universality founded on an experience of revelation in History. When Latin was claimed to represent the linguistic medium of Western Catholic homogeneity, there was also an analogy to be made with the Arabic of Islam… The universal Church is conscious of wanting to celebrate God in all languages. Muslims of all languages feel called to celebrate God in Qur'anic Arabic.

Our life choice is unequivocal in its intention to tie our liturgical action and intercession in Arabic to the reality of the Muslim religion, in order to conjugate it to the Christ-Church in light of the Kingdom. The logic is that of inculturation: "Missionaries…must learn the language of the place in which they work, become familiar with the most important expressions of the local culture, and discover its values through direct experience."[1] In a sense, the Arabic language is analogous in terms of value and universal significance to the Hebrew language for the Jewish (and today even Israeli) context. For both communities, it is the language of Heaven, of the God-man conversation, the language that brings these communities together. Both communities are tied to a Holy Land: Jerusalem for the Hebrew language, Mecca (with a view to Jerusalem) for the Arabic language. Each language corresponds to a nation that claims a territory. The two sons of Abraham the wandering Aramean, Isaac and Ishmael, the Hebrew and the Arab, meet again for the burial of the Patriarch, and it is through filial piety that they can get along at last. It happened at the Cave of Machpelah in Hebron-Al-Khalil, the mosque-synagogue where their children are killing each other today.[2]

1   John Paul II, *Redemptoris Missio*, N53.
2   Genesis 25:9.

The Theological Value of the Qur'anic Revelation and the Universality of Revelation

Concerning the eventual Christian theological value of Islam's revelation, I adhere to what is stated in *Dominus Iesus* n.8: "Therefore, the sacred books of other religions, which in actual fact direct and nourish the existence of their followers, receive from the mystery of Christ the elements of goodness and grace which they contain."[3]

It must be said that this text is often misunderstood, either by maintaining that whatever goodness there is in Islam is simply copied from Christianity, or by imagining that only what resembles Christian doctrine can be received as good. In fact, it calls for a different, deeper interpretation.

From the Christian point of view, and I emphasise Christian, Jesus Christ is from the beginning and forever the fundamental, final act of divine Self-Revelation. He is the reason behind all saintliness and the intimate content of all kindness. Hence every human perfection in the full extent of its incredible diversity has its origin and end in the Christ-man-God.

From the Muslim point of view, and in an obviously different sense from the Christian point of view, Muhammad is the summit and the recapitulation of the virtue of faith, which is the primordial and final essence of humanity. As such he is the one for whom every person, everywhere and at all times, produces their mysterious act of faith in life and in its Author.

In Jewish theological anthropology, there is the figure of Abraham by whose faith all nations and individuals are blessed in anticipation of the fulfilment of this blessing in the Messiah, for the sake of all mankind in all ages.

I will not attempt to describe this same universality in a Buddhist or other context. The symbolic colonisation of the world of others is not the point here, but rather the understanding of universality from one's own experience of the Absolute in the context of one's own tradition. We hope

---

3   Congregation for the Doctrine for the Faith, *Declaration Dominus Iesus on the Unicity and Salvific University of Jesus Christ and the Church* (Vatican City: Libreria Editrice Vaticana, 2000).

that we are not mistaken, and that our visions are already one in the heart of God our Father.

A Step Forward

In the same vein comes the felicitous and innovative paragraph on Islam in the "Message to the People of God" of the Synod of Catholic Bishops in October 2008 on the Word of God (the text is particularly felicitous compared to the very weak accents of the preparatory texts). In entry 14, right after underlining the priority of the Church's relationship with the Jewish people, the Synod continues:

> "Blessed be my people Egypt, Assyria my creation, and Israel my heritage."[4] The Lord, then, spreads the protective mantle of his blessing all over the peoples of the earth: "he wants everyone to be saved and reach full knowledge of the truth."[5] We, also as Christians are invited, along the roads of the world, without falling into a syncretism that confuses and humiliates our own spiritual identity, to enter into dialogue with respect towards men and women of the other religions, who faithfully hear and practice the directives of their sacred books, starting with Islam, which welcomes many Biblical figures, symbols and themes in its tradition, and which offers the witness of sincere faith in the One, compassionate and merciful God, the Creator of all beings and Judge of humanity.

It was the first time that the Biblical kinship of Islam was recognised this explicitly, as well as the sincerity of the faith of Muslims; it was also the first time the Qur'anic title of the One God, "Compassionate and Merciful", was received at the level of Catholic collegial authority. The monks of Mar Musa had already done this in the eleventh century, using this same Qur'anic title in their Arabic inscriptions in the church. The entire message of the synod deserves an enthusiastic welcome because of its astonishing novelty, which might indicate a coming spring.

4   Isaiah 19:25.
5   1 Timothy 2:4.

Legitimacy of the Expression "Muslim Revelation"

Let us return to the question of Muslim revelation. I consider the expression to be legitimate first of all on the phenomenological level (the Muslim phenomenon belongs to the category of "revelations"). It is also legitimate as a description of the Muslim conviction and awareness of having received a revelation (recognition based on respect for the symbolic system of others). From the theological point of view, I also think it is legitimate within the limits set by the Church's understanding, keeping intact what is absolute, definitive and normative about Christian revelation, for Christian awareness obviously.

In my opinion, it is theologically legitimate to speak of revelation in Islam by way of analogy, however incomplete and contradictory. The Catechism of the Church mentions the following:

> Those who have not yet received the Gospel are related to the People of God (*Lumen Gentium* 16). …When she delves into her own mystery, the Church, the People of God in the New Covenant, discovers her link with the Jewish People, "the first to hear the Word of God". The Jewish faith, unlike other non-Christian religions, is already a response to God's revelation in the Old Covenant. …And when one considers the future, God's People of the Old Covenant and the new People of God tend towards similar goals: expectation of the coming (or the return) of the Messiah. … The plan of salvation also includes those who acknowledge the Creator, in the first place amongst whom are the Muslims; these profess to hold the faith of Abraham. (*Lumen Gentium* 16)[6]

In terms of the future, we can also remember that Muslims, who are Abrahamic, await the return of Issa-Jesus, son of Mary, the Messiah. Is the Catechism's sentence "The Jewish faith, unlike other non-Christian religions, is already a response to God's revelation in the Old Covenant" to be understood in a strictly exclusive sense? This is not how I see it. Would the theological value of Jewish faith today, relative to this ancient revelation, remain independent from Jesus Christ in his first and second coming? It is not our intention here to wound our elder Jewish brothers when we

6 *Catechism of the Catholic Church,* 839–41.

affirm that the final truth of their Biblical faith ultimately depends, from the Christian point of view, on the mystery of Jesus, son of the Virgin of Nazareth. I find it is legitimate to see by analogy, from a Christian point of view, that the Muslim experience of revelation, insofar as it journeys towards and prepares the full knowledge of Jesus Christ, Master of the Day of Judgement, can be considered, let us repeat by analogy, a revelation.

Belief and Faith

During a colloquium held at the Gregorian University of Rome on the occasion of the 40th anniversary of the Second Vatican Council's Declaration *Nostra Aetate*, which had so radically and positively changed the attitude of the Catholic Church towards Judaism, Islam and other religions, the Islamic scholar and Jesuit theologian Christian van Nipsen stood up and said with much simplicity that in his opinion, the distinction made in the Congregation for the Doctrine of the Faith's declaration *Dominus Iesus* between Christian theologal faith and the beliefs of other religions, was neither in the same vein nor the same logic as the conciliar declaration *Nostra Aetate*. I believe that it is part of the Catholic faith to recognise the virtue of the theological faith of the saints and prophets of the First Testament. Abraham is truly the herald of faith. He belongs to the lineage of men and women of faith magnificently described in the Letter to the Hebrews: "These are all heroes of faith, but they did not receive what was promised, since God had made provision for us to have something better, and they were not to reach perfection except with us."[7]

While these discussions were taking place, I was paying a visit to Cardinal and Patriarch Moussa Daoud in his Syrian village. The Cardinal was a man of the Church to whom our Monastic Community of Mar Musa owed a lot. I asked him what he thought of the faith of Muslims. He told me that he spoke from experience, because in his village Christians and

7   *Letter to the Hebrews* 11:39–40.

Muslims lived side by side; he added that it is often the Muslims who give us the most striking witness of a faith authentically lived.

> Faith, therefore, as "a gift of God" and as "a supernatural virtue infused by Him", involves a dual adherence: to God who reveals and to the truth which He reveals, out of the trust which one has in Him who speaks. Thus, "we must believe in no one but God: the Father, the Son and the Holy Spirit". For this reason, the distinction between theological faith and belief in other religions, must be firmly held. If faith is the acceptance in the grace of revealed truth, which "makes it possible to penetrate the mystery in a way that allows us to understand it coherently", than belief, in the other religions, is that sum of experience and thought that constitutes the human treasury of wisdom and religious aspiration, which man in his search for truth has conceived and acted upon in his relationship to God and the Absolute.[8]

It is not easy to really clarify what it is that "should be firmly held". The question remains open: where does belief end and faith begin? I made the effort to understand the intention and preoccupation of this authoritative text, and it is useful to see things from another point of view. The Church is fiercely attached to the absolute transcendence of the individual act of faith of every person everywhere, always mysteriously tied to Christ and his Church in anticipation of the salvation of all and the final transformation of this world. The Church teaches that only in the historic salvific event of Jesus of Nazareth can the gracious divine act entirely correspond to the grace of individual faith. There is a complete correspondence between the grace given to every person so they may say "yes" to God and the "yes" that God says to every person in Jesus of Nazareth, source of all grace. Indeed, for every Christian, there is a certain level of belief, be it natural or philosophical, which prepares, announces and accompanies the life of faith. And as this is true of the connection between belief and faith among Christians, for it is difficult to grasp the notion of a bare faith that is separate from belief among individual Christians or in the communities of the faithful, it is also true to different degrees and in various ways for the believers of other religions. Nevertheless, the Church is keen on keeping a distinction between a full Christian revelation specific to the Church in

8   *Dominus Iesus*, 7.

its plenitude, and the seeds of the Word, characteristic of the elements of truth in other religions.

In fact, for non-Christians, the mystery of individual faith is always experienced in a cultural, cultic, textual, doctrinal, sacred and finally religious context, which the Church seems to be teaching us to consider as belonging to the domain of belief, for it is united by "ways known to God" to the mystery of the divine action of evangelical preparation. And yet the Church does not teach that the domain of belief is separated from, is in contradiction with or in opposition to the action of God. For if belief is the natural adherence through the natural light of intelligence to what is naturally comprehensible of the world from its origins to its end, one must deduce that this natural knowledge also implies the recognition of the One God, Creator of all things. And yet the Muslim thinks that this belongs to the domain of faith, because it cannot happen without an actual and factual freely given divine light in the individual human soul. In reaction against atheism and agnosticism, the Church insists that the natural knowledge of God's existence is possible without the intervention of the grace of revelation, and therefore is, in a sense, a matter of duty. Muslim philosophers would be divided on this... as would be the Christians! Everyone would however agree that a true knowledge of the true God can only happen through the free and gracious gift of knowledge through which He, the One, manifests Himself to the soul, which is the sphere of revelation.

Again, I want it to be noted that the non-Christian religious structure can be, and in fact is the seminal place for the expression of the faith of persons initiated to the divine mysteries via a particular religious tradition. On this basis, we are not forbidden to listen attentively and to try to deeply understand the Muslim religious spiritual experience, which is centred on the mystery of the Muslim act of faith, considered a grace.

It is not surprising that Eastern Arab Christianity has never, to my knowledge, felt the need to choose a different Arabic term for "faith" than the Qur'anic one; unlike other concepts for which the same words are not so comfortably used.

I think that we can sincerely welcome the teaching of *Dominus Iesus* without necessarily introducing in the relationship with Islam, on the part of Christians, a rejection of the language of faith used by Muslims.

Preceding the Council, Louis Massignon tried to demonstrate through an in-depth study the originality of the Qur'anic source of the Muslim mystical experience, as well as the mysterious transcendence of Muslim faith, which certainly in his opinion anticipates a full and final manifestation of Christ the Redeemer. We are not surprised to find in the Constitution on the Church of the Second Vatican Council, *Lumen Gentium* n.16: "But the plan of salvation also includes those who acknowledge the Creator. In the first place amongst these there are the Muslims, who, professing to hold the faith of Abraham, along with us adore the one and merciful God, who on the last day will judge mankind."

I believe that ultimately it would be useful, in Muslim-Christian relations, as well as on the level of catechism, to learn how to use the distinction between the domain of belief and that of faith, as well as to teach how to discern what is proper to Christian faith and what is particular to the concept of faith in the Muslim experience.[9] It is not so much a question of teaching that we have faith while others have belief, as it is for all of us to try, by benefiting from the pedagogy of belief, to attain faith and the works of faith, the love of God and of our neighbour, through the grace that calls upon us all.

Dialogue, a Gift of the Spirit

I have received some criticism about the fact that in my writings I tend to mix Christian concepts with Muslim concepts and worse, Biblical citations with Qur'anic citations. In dialogue, if we wish to avoid a "dialogue of the deaf", it is necessary to build a common language made of arguments drawn from both religious textual and literary traditions, with both parties learning the other's religious language. This is also true for the process of inculturation of the faith, where the different sources of value and meaning of the culture that is the target of inculturation become, in the mode of dialogue and analogy, the main field of this "new

9   While benefiting from the teachings of *Fides et Ratio*, 30–1.

incarnation". If this process is not led by the Holy Spirit, it is useless. Without a charismatic, "pentecostal" character, inculturation, dialogue and evangelisation become sterile. However, the relationship with Islam is all embroidered with Qur'anic citations. If the fear of syncretism forces us to create independent and parallel conceptual and linguistic worlds, if we want to radically separate the Bible and the Qur'an, this simply means that we are radically separating the Church and the Islamic *Ummah*, by confining ourselves to an ironclad incomprehension.

I am delighted to quote from the speech Pope John Paul II gave on his historic visit to the Umayyad Mosque on 6 May 2001. For us in Mar Musa, this visit was a prophetic blessing for our vocation. He cited the Qur'an alongside the Gospel of Luke by saying:

> As we make our way through existence, we Christians feel the presence of Mary, mother of Jesus; Islam also renders homage to Mary and honours her, she who is "chosen…above the women of all nations". (Qur'an 3:42) The Virgin of Nazareth, the Lady of Saïdnaya has taught us that God protects the humble and "has routed the proud of heart".[10]

Sent by the Church to dialogue with Islam, I still feel less than up to the task of putting the Biblical and Qur'anic texts in deep spiritual semantic interrelation. And besides, I repeat, this work should be carried out by the Church on a theological level, and by communities that meet in dialogue.

The Witness of Christian de Chergé

In the conclusion of his welcome speech to Pope Benedict XVI in Paris, Mr Nicolas Sarkozy, the president of the French Republic, quoted the spiritual testament of Father Christian de Chergé. He presented him as a true French example of contemporary evangelical authenticity at the heart of the cultural and religious differences of the day. I got the impression that he was expressing the need felt by our generation for strong

10   Luke 1:51.

symbolic points of reference to liberate us from this cursed trajectory of the clash of civilisations, the misdeeds of which fill our news. In my opinion, Father Christian is one of Louis Massignon's most accomplished disciples in this spiritual lineage founded by Charles de Foucauld.

This martyr of Christ's love for Muslims internalised Islam in his life as a monk; he welcomed it in his prayer and studied it in depth, starting with the Arabic language, which he perfected with Father Borrmans at the Institute of the White Fathers. We can qualify his spirituality as being Islamic-Christian, and since he wrote in French on the basis of a meditation in Arabic, he also has something fruitful to propose to the French Muslim community:

> *Lectio Divina*: It is a primary and essential reference to "a God who talks to us". Here there is, on both sides, a *REVELATION* that always has something to uncover of itself, that must be allowed to speak, to repeat, to annotate, to interpret, to calligraphy… The spirituality of the Night of Destiny (around the 27th of Ramadan), when a verse can descend upon the believer as a word meant for them, is that of every true monastic *lectio*. It enters the ear: "Listen!", "Read!" ["Listen" is the beginning of Saint Benedict's Rule and "Read" is the beginning of the Qur'anic revelation.][11] We are together engaged in a reading of the "meaning". In the way we read and recite Scripture, there is a path for sharing. A horizon is offered: "come to common terms as between us and you (Qur'an 3:64)."[12]

And again in a speech he gave at the Journées Romaines in September 1989:

> Are we not here together to exercise this prophetic function? Is it not a "project" that we would like to implement together? We are a "people of prophets", and I would testify here, with you, that in Islam as in Christianity, no matter what they say, prophetism is neither dead nor closed (p.2)… The Judgement of this world has already commenced, and reaches us where we are revealed incapable of being faithful to ourselves: "depart from me into the eternal fire…for I was hungry…" (Mtt 25: 41). We can also read: "What led you into Hell Fire…?" (Qur'an 74: 40–46). For thirty years have I carried the existence of Islam within me like a nagging question. My curiosity is immense about the place it holds in God's mysterious plan. Death alone, I think, will give me the answer I await. I am sure to decode it, dazzled, in the pascal light of He

11   Fr. Paolo's clarification.
12   Christian de Chergé, "Dialogue intermonastique et Islam, 1995," in *L'invincible espérance* ed. Bruno Chenu (Paris: Bayard, Centurion, 1997), 208.

who presents himself to me as the only possible Muslim, for he is nothing but "yes" to the will of the Father. But I am convinced that by letting this question haunt me, I learn to better discover the solidarities and even the complicities of today, including that of faith; and to not confine the other to the idea I have of them, which perhaps my Church has transmitted to me, not even to what the majority of them might say of themselves in the present…

The Word of God presents itself to all as a viaticum for the crossing of the desert, for Easter, for the Exodus, for the *Hijra*. The Scriptures are the treasure that the Christians love to search, night and day, for the new and the old, "*Ausculta, o fili*…Listen, son!" These are the first words of Saint Benedict's Rule. "*Iqra',* recite!". This other imperative opens the Qur'an. Every Muslim hears it as addressing them in particular. Here and there, the temptation is to stop at the letter, at a fundamentalist and rigid reading. But many undertake the same common exodus: "Listen with your heart!" specifies Saint Benedict. Must we continue to turn a deaf ear to the message of the other, by contesting, as a matter of principle, their original bond with the Absolute Other… It seems to me that the Paschal Christ would have something to tell us of himself through these [Qur'anic] verses and many others, if we would allow Him to meet us there, as if on a new road to Emmaus. And if His Spirit can make the letter that veiled Him radiate with light and joy, is it not because He who fulfils all Scriptures could also give this one its full sense, without alteration to His Countenance? There is no way to convince oneself of such a thing, unless we approach the Qur'anic text with a humble and disarmed heart, ready to attentively listen to every Word that would come from the Most-High. Because at the end of the day, would we have the audacity and simplicity to take the same ladder together if we refuse from the start to believe that the same Spirit of God is inviting us to do so?[13]

For a disciple of Jesus like Christian de Chergé, sent to the Muslim world by Christ's charity, putting the holy books of other religions on the same level as the Scripture of the Church is not even considered a possibility. The approach in question entails searching the Qur'an, the texts on the life of the Prophet and all the Muslim literature for traces and evidence of the work of the Spirit of God. For it is the Spirit who drives us towards a radical standpoint in dialogue, with a view to the recapitulation of all things in Christ.

13   Christian de Chergé, "Échelle Mystique du Dialogue," *Islamochristiana* (Roma: Pontificio), *Istituto di Studi Arabi e d'Islamistica*, 23 (1997), 10–11.

Eucharistic Savour

A Muslim scholar tried to describe the intimate relationship between the Muslim believer and the Qur'an to a group of Christians.[14] He said that reading the Qur'an with faith is akin to receiving Communion with faith during Mass. The Word of God nourishes the soul of the believer, moving through the body's senses, which are illuminated by the faith of the intellect. I found the analogy remarkable. Moreover, as I think of Christian de Chergé's experience of the monastic *lectio divina* applied to the Qur'an, I can testify to the eucharistic savour that I taste during the recitation and meditation of the Qur'an. For my Christian reader, it would perhaps be easier to think first about the eucharistic savour of the evangelical, Biblical proclamation and meditation. We speak in fact of the table of God's Word to indicate the first part of Mass, by analogy with the actual table of the Eucharist itself, which is the heart of the celebration. Our jealousy over the Body and Blood of Christ is holy, and our theological distinctions appropriate; but through this bread and wine, this body and blood, this objectivation and expansion of His presence, the desire of our Lord is to embrace, penetrate and sanctify all human reality! Does not the bread of friendship, between friends, have a eucharistic flavour?

The Game of Mirrors

I have to acknowledge that in the Church the tendency persists to think of Islam in the framework of a rigid conception of revelation. Considering the Church today, even with the caveat of historical evolution, as the accomplished and definitive form of the religion of Jesus of Nazareth, easily entails the conception of Islam as a late-comer, a false religion. We would recognise its right to exist in the name of human rights and the

---

14   M. Mahmoud Ayoub, "La Parola di Dio nel Corano," *Corano e Bibbia* (Brescia, Morcelliana, 2000): 35.

respect due to everyone. Fundamentally, human history, its perspectives, present and past, are being judged based on a still very literal, fixed, somewhat mechanical, magical and naive conception of revelation featuring a hidden God who plays peek-a-boo. What emerges is the caricature of a God who amuses himself by tricking us with false religions, while leaving the only true religion to languish under the weight of a historical series of scathing, bloody contradictions... I find this path to be a dead-end. It is by way of perplexity that I advance, that of the struggle with the angel to wrest a benediction, of a yet unaccomplished divine adventure; for even the fulfilment of history in Jesus of Nazareth suffers from such an opening on the future, exacting and risky.

Perplexity

We were walking arm in arm in the old city of Aleppo, Dr. Hamed Abou Zayd and I. He had retained the appearance and air of a professor of the Islamic University of al-Azhar, from where he was expelled due to his courageous studies on the Qur'anic text, which forced him to take refuge in Holland. I admit that without going so far as demanding his expulsion, if I were a Muslim, I would have had trouble accepting his views. I find them accurate from the point of view of contemporary hermeneutics, but not sufficiently concerned with carrying the weight and richness of Islamic Tradition; but in this, I am perhaps too much of a Catholic. The events in our Arab and Islamic region were quite gruelling and conflictual. Those who spoke in the name of religions often scandalised us...

We were discussing perplexity, *al-hîra*, as a kind of mystical stage, a moment of unveiling that exposes other veils. He declared to me: "Sometimes, I think that God in Himself is perplexity!" And a burst of laughter unlocked our reflection.

The Adventure of Our Souls

The mystery of Christ is so much a part of the history of our souls that it drives us, more than it slows us down, towards an openness to the journeys of the men and women of our time and of every time. In a sense, we become lovers who seek the traces of our beloved everywhere. Having lost any capacity for objectivity, we look for their features in every face. There is a cultural expatriation, a spiritual ecstasy, a cultural decentring that takes place. I must admit that I am not preoccupied with the fate of Western or any other civilisation. Only my thirst for the infinite drives me, and it seems to me that I can quell it by training my gaze to see this holy water flowing in all flesh. Even the most unsettling contradictions then become the sites of a luminous manifestation, sometimes by way of irony prompting a smile that sees beyond the surface. At other times, this happens by way of the sparks that spring from conceptual contradiction itself, by way of dialectical synthesis, tears or rage in the face of political paralysis and the impasse of thought. Finally, it happens by way of the peace that fills a heart offering up the act of faith on a night blessed by the feeling of being completely surpassed by the absolute. Spiritual people understand each other when they express themselves this way, and feel close to one another. Informed Catholics know that there is an orthodox and dogmatically correct idea here, since the dogma of the Church speaks to us of the courage of God and his friends.

The Qur'an of History and the Qur'an of Faith

Many Christians, or Western ex-Christians, express great difficulty conceptualising the Muslim dogma of the celestial Qur'an, the "Preserved Tablet", this uncreated "Recitation". This is not the place to treat this question exhaustively. The doctrine of the created or uncreated Qur'an was the object of a vast debate within the Muslim Community during the Middle Ages, and one can say that the *Ummah* as a whole has opted to confess the uncreated eternal nature of the Qur'an. There is an ironic dimension to the fact that many Christians think that the Mu'tazilites (the Muslim school of thought that defended the idea of a created Qur'an) are in the right, while symmetrically, Muslim thought tends to hold that the "Arians" (the Christians who defended the thesis of a created Christ, Son of God) are the true monotheistic Christians...

I remember once meeting a Tunisian professor of Qur'anic exegesis in Rome who was influenced by the Western historical-critical method, doubted the uncreated eternal nature of the Qur'an and was inclined to adopt the doubts of the Mu'tazilites. I answered him: "No, in the name of Christian orthodoxy, I confess the Qur'an as uncreated because the truth is indivisible and divine self-communication is inseparable from the uncreated mystery of the One." He gave me a surprised look...

It is not astonishing that it would be difficult for Christians to understand the Muslim position regarding the Qur'an as a book descended from Heaven, an eternal Scripture preserved on a Heavenly Tablet. Moreover, it is not an immediate matter for us to believe in the uncreated eternal nature of the divine Word, never separate from Jesus of Nazareth, the Christ, and to confess the Incarnate Word, fully God and fully human, like you and I, with a spiritual soul, in the East a "spirit", a rational soul, and animate flesh.

Dogmatic Rationalism

It will always be difficult for us to understand our Muslim brothers if we do not free ourselves of a rationalist conceptualism, which in the West is systematically applied to all things divine, resulting in a systematic desacralisation of the world that not only results in empty churches, but also empties souls of meaning. I don't think the theologies of the retreat of God, of His absence etc., are truly fruitful, not even for the sake of founding a more radical human autonomy and for liberating the world from miracles in order to radically submit it to science. Among the religious intellectuals in charge of unifying science and dogma, this is accompanied with a rationalist dogmatism which has its counterpart in Islam as well; it produces a paradoxical incommunicability: Godly matters are henceforth fixed in scholastic systems, and the systems are mutually exclusive.

Inspiration and Revelation

It is certainly possible to conceive that there is a difference between the concept of the inspiration of the Bible and that of the revelation of the Qur'an. But it is true that the concept of revelation is not absent in the Bible itself. Just think of the prophetic oracles, for example. From a literary point of view, it is truly a revealed text tied to a vision. The law given to Moses on Mount Sinaï, beyond any historical-critical consideration, indeed belongs to the genre of revelation from on High, in a single piece, and is even written on tablets by the hand of God. Joseph's dreams in the Gospel of Saint Matthew belong to the revelatory domain, and there are words in the Gospel that come from Heaven; not forgetting the Son who descended from Heaven, and who is the central focus of the Scriptures. The Scriptures are inspired, but they are a vehicle for revelation the way the voice carries speech.

In parallel, the Qur'an is certainly seen by the Muslims in a very different way than the Bible is seen by the Christians. But these ways are not necessarily opposed or irreconcilable. In a sense, the Qur'an descended in its entirety during the Night of Destiny [*laylat al-qadr*]. Moreover, Muslims believe that the same applies to the Torah and the Gospel, which descended on Moses and Jesus on that same night. A Muslim friend told me that this night is like Christmas Eve. At the same time, Muslims acknowledge that the Qur'an descended in verses and groups of verses on specific occasions, related to daily events. This implies that these events were already inscribed in the Preserved Tablet in Heaven. One might get lost in these ideas if one is unable to feel the power of the pre-eternal, uncreated divine command: "*Kun*", "Be!", through which the ineffable God expresses Himself as Creator, and that of "*Iqra'!*", "Recite!", in which God manifests Himself as eternally revelatory. Only through developing an existential and mystical hyperconsciousness of the actuality and immediacy of the presence of the divine creative act, eternally efficacious in relation to that moment where "I write" and "you read", I in the library and you in the subway, that we may touch the mystery of revelation, which is at once entirely historical and perfectly transcendent, entirely human and divinely other.

Predestination and the Freedom of Man

The intellectual dogmatism of medieval Islam and Christianity got entangled in discussions on predestination. If God's eternal Will exerts such a powerful pressure on my existential moment, what becomes of my freedom and of the efficiency of my own will? Muslims will infer a radical atomism whereby the atoms of creation combine, divide and assemble exclusively by divine decree... My Muslim professor in Damascus recognised the difficulty of simultaneously confessing divine omnipotence and human responsibility, of harmonising divine will with human will. Monotheism implies emphasising the absolute priority of the divine decree. But religious practice, moral experience and anthropology demand the recognition of human autonomy... My friend the sheikh used to say that it is like having two threads: "You pull one, and the other follows; you pull the second, and the first follows... There must be a knot but it is hidden." For a Christian, this knot is the Cross, but I didn't say this to him.

I know a woman in Damascus who has visions. The holy oil of hospitality flows in her home and from her hands. She is a very simple Christian; she lets herself be guided by Providence. Many Iranian women visit the Virgin in her home... She once told a group of youths: "When I was a little girl, I studied catechism and I was taught that Christians believe in the freedom of man and Muslims believe in destiny. Now that I love God, I can see more clearly the ineffable union between His absolute decree and my humble freedom."

Divine Writing, Human Writing

Muhammad experienced divine intervention in a verbal form, from Above. He also experienced it through God's providential assistance at the heart of a human group, basically at the heart of history. This idea that things are written in the heavens is as old as writing itself. When ancient man discovered writing, he was moved by the magic and creativity of the gesture that wounds the clay tablet for meaning to emerge from it; it bursts! It is normal in that case to immediately think that the Creator has decreed all His plans by a gesture of Heavenly writing. The human writer feels invested with a divine power; the writing down below corresponds to a writing in the Heavens. The Biblical account that stages God kneading man from clay in a "Mesopotamian" context seems to already indicate this vocation for writing: man is the divine tablet where God inscribes the cuneiform traces of His likeness. Moreover, the Qur'anic event represents from the point of view of Arab civilisation the transition from mnemonic oral culture to the civilisation of the written text.

In the Gospel, Jesus tells his Apostles to rejoice because "… your names are written in Heaven" (Luke 10:20). On which medium would these inscriptions in Heaven be written? "Those who prove victorious will be dressed, like these, in white robes; I shall not blot their names out of the book of life, but acknowledge their names in the presence of my Father and his angels" (Revelation 3:5). So where is the problem with a celestial Qur'an? The theme of the heavenly Book of Life is one of the most shared themes in human spiritual culture. The history of the Muslim hermeneutics of the Qur'an has not been closed, and Christians need to dialogue on this subject respectfully, because Qur'anic hermeneutics has the same importance in Islam as Christology does in the Church.

Is it true that Muslims believe that one cannot interpret the Qur'an? No, not at all. The fourteen and a half centuries of Muslim history are also the history of Qur'anic interpretation, with fine tools and the courage of comprehension through different approaches, which accounts for the pluralism within the Muslim Community.

The Text Lives Only by Tradition

Ultimately, it is not the letter of the text that makes the law. The agreement of different hermeneutical opinions in the fold of the exegetical tradition is what makes the unity of the Community. They say that Muslims are rigid about the content of their text, but Christians should be asked to cast a critical eye upon themselves! Why does the Church believe that bananas and beer can't be used for the Eucharist? Why does the Church believe it is her faithful duty to deny women priesthood? Why does the Church believe that she has no right to allow Holy Communion to divorced individuals? Why does the Church believe that the Pope cannot be elected by universal suffrage of the baptised? All these questions could be considered reasonable and pertinent by people without and even within the Church! Yet the hermeneutical logic, which in the Church guides the discernment of the history of her understanding of her own mystery, lives on a coherence that is intimate and internal to the Church, and cannot be judged from the outside with the tools of another hermeneutical framework. On the contrary, through a respectful dialogue, amiable curiosity and a witness that is fraternal, frank and non-ideological, the conservative and traditionalist anguish fades, and the Spirit of novelty finds its ways to renew the religious face of the world.

CHAPTER 8

Death and Resurrection

The theme of this chapter is one that has been dear to Paolo Dall'Oglio for a long time, since he dedicated his thesis to the perception of the future according to the Muslim faith.[1] Here, Christian hope, represented by the Resurrection of Christ victorious over death, is in dialogue with Muslim hope rooted in the miracle of the Qur'anic text, this witness by God the Compassionate of Himself. It is interesting to see how an entirely historical perspective of political responsibility emerges from this eschatological dialogue.

In the Gregorian University of Rome in 1990, I defended my thesis on "Hope in Islam". It was an exercise in Qur'anic hermeneutics in dialogue with different currents of interpretation. The text I studied was that of *surah* 18, "the Cave", which was very dear to Massignon, and which contains the Qur'anic version of the Christian story of the Seven Sleepers of Ephesus. In this regard, I cannot but refer to the exhaustive work of François Jourdan.[2]

Hope in Islam

In the Qur'an, the question of the resurrection of the dead is conceived as a second creation. God who created the world the first time and gave us life, can give us life anew, either in the form of eternal life and joy or of misfortune and eternal punishment. In this, Islam is entirely "catholic".

---

1   Paolo Dall'Oglio, *Speranza nell'Islām: interpretazione della prospettiva escatologica di Corano XVIII* (Genoa: Marietti, 1991).
2   Jourdan, *Dieu*; François Jourdan, *La Tradition des Sept Dormants* (Paris: Maisonneuve et Larose, 1983).

The general principle in Islam is that every soul will taste death and every human person will be resurrected. To the point where, following the assertion according to which Jesus did not truly die on the Cross but was taken to Heaven by God, Muslims also believe that he will return to earth to die as a martyr and inaugurate the final Resurrection. This is clearly astonishing! How can death on the Cross be unworthy of the sainthood of the Prophet son of Mary, while death during combat against the final Antichrist is glorious? It is an eschatology that is polemical for Christians, given that Jesus must return to open the way for the Muhammadan Mahdi. Among Muslims, some do however believe that Jesus and the Mahdi are ultimately the same person, based on the *hadith*, the prophetic tradition, which says: "There is no Mahdi but Jesus, son of Mary", a sentence I first heard from the lips of the Grand Mufti of Damascus.

For Muslims, there is no contradiction between the negation of the Cross and Christ's martyrdom during the final *jihad*. Death on the Cross represents a shameful defeat and God would not allow this for his beloved Prophet, the son of Mary. But nothing is more glorious than to die in the eschatological and victorious battle against the Antichrist of the End of Times. The Muslim position on this is divided and plural; I believe that it refers to a meaning that goes beyond the Qur'anic letter as well as eschatological projection. Our Islamic-Christian reading would like to journey there.

Veil

Saint Paul speaks of a veil in relation to the incapacity of the majority of Jews to recognise the mystery of the crucified Christ. He thinks of the veil that covered the face of Moses in Sinaï to protect the Hebrews from its radiance as he descended God's Mountain. Saint Paul understands that this veil is before the eyes of the Jews and prevents them from recognising the glorious radiance of God's crucified humility:

Yes, even today, whenever Moses is read, the veil is over their minds. It will not be removed until they turn to the Lord. Now this Lord is the Spirit, and where the Spirit of the Lord is, there is freedom. And we, with our unveiled faces reflecting like mirrors the brightness of the Lord, all grow brighter and brighter as we are turned into the image that we reflect...[3]

From our point of view, this veil is also the one that is stretched between the eyes of the Muslims and the Cross of Jesus. And there is another veil still. The infidelity of Christians towards divine humility and the betrayal of the tortured Christ veils the mystery of Golgotha. The Cross becomes the symbol of a tormenting empire, and the nations are attracted or subjugated through a logic of power, and join the Church with equivocal intention. Jews and Muslims thus find themselves veiled before the Cross. These two communities are then separated from the mystery of Christ. They are separated from it because of the extent of Christian pride. Often, the baptised know nothing of the mystery of their salvation but the Name. Only the outcasts and the humiliated know its taste.

However, I do not doubt the history of Christian sainthood, my position is not a naïve one that puts all the good on the side of Islam and all the bad on the side of the Church. Before and during the Great Jubilee, John Paul II undertook a work of purification of memory in the name of the Church, by asking numerous peoples for forgiveness. This did not please everyone. Some Christians were expecting him to ask forgiveness from the Muslims during his visit to Damascus... I suggest that we accept having different points of view within the Church, that a fruitful complementarity results from this, beyond our contradictions and well beyond our expectations. Moreover, Pope Benedict XVI has created in today's Catholic Church an unprecedented atmosphere of wide and free theological debate.

A final remark concerning the veil: in Europe, the issue of the veil that covers the hair of Muslim women comes up frequently. In a few Muslim trends, women also hide their faces behind a veil. According to the Qur'anic Muslim tradition, Mary stands in the eastern apse of the temple, behind a veil, in spiritual preparation for the Angelic Announcement.[4] In our

3   2 Corinthians 3:15–18.
4   Qur'an 3:37; 19:16–17

Eastern icons, she totally resembles a young Muslim woman. The Muslim Community is in waiting, veiled in modesty before what has not yet been uncovered. At Deir Mar Musa, following the Semitic tradition of our churches, men and women stand before the altar, towards the East, with their heads covered. Our work is to wait in hope for the manifestation of this final Woman-community, "with the twelve stars on her head for a crown".[5] "…as beautiful as a bride all dressed for her husband… He will make his home among them… He will wipe away all tears from their eyes."[6] It is of her that the Qur'an speaks: "…that brings to God a sound heart; To the righteous, the Garden will be brought near."[7] Massignon taught me that the Arabic verb [*uzlifa*] used in this verse, translated here as "will be brought near", is specific to the act of presenting the bride at her wedding.

A Shiite Christmas

A few years ago, my friend Nabil Halbawi, rector of a prominent Shiite Mosque in Damascus, invited me to celebrate Christmas, the birth of Jesus of Nazareth, with "seminarians" at the faculty of theology "Imam Khomeini". That was perhaps the nicest Christmas of my life! During the drive, as I searched my heart for the main thread of a speech that I had not really prepared, my friend told me that Muslims liked Joan of Arc. We did not really explore the matter, but I remembered that Louis Massignon had written that Joan of Arc, the one who heard voices, was loved by Muslims because she embodied the dramatic defence of her sincerity to the point of martyrdom. It is known that Shiites are very touched by the idea of martyrdom, and I said to myself that this might be the right way to begin my talk. I remember asking if Jesus Christ deserved to be considered a martyr. I saw a cloud of anguish in the eyes of my audience. I explained that I obviously knew that for Islam, he did not die on the Cross. But

5   Revelation 12:1.
6   Revelation 21:2–4.
7   Qur'an 26:89–90.

did he not have the intention to radically offer up his life in obedience to God? For Islam, the essence of an action resides in intention. Issa's earthly life having ended with the intention to give his life and his readiness for martyrdom, how can we deny him the title? Especially when we know that in the Muslim account of the End of Times, in Muslim eschatology (that Muslims call the Knowledge of the Hour of Judgement), Jesus the Messiah effectively dies a martyr's death just before Resurrection Day. Everyone found this reasoning to be correct, and we started talking about Mary again, about Nazareth and Bethlehem, because there is not one Shiite home where you wouldn't find a depiction of the birth of Jesus with Mary and Joseph on a wall tapestry or a very colourful print. At the end of the conference, the future imams gifted me a copy of the Qur'an and a bas-relief in copper of the face of the suffering Christ, which they had prepared for me and which admirably corresponded with the subject of our conversation.

Muslim Faith in the Resurrection

Muslims cannot build, as Christians do, their faith in resurrection on the Risen One, Jesus of Nazareth, his empty tomb, and his appearances in the flesh to his Apostles. Neither can they build their faith in the resurrection on the celebration of the mystery of his death and Resurrection; a mystery that is ongoing, enduring and potent in the offering of the bread and wine that become the Body and Blood of his Passion, but also the living body of his Resurrection. They cannot say like the Christians do: we will be resurrected because we have been joined to Christ through baptism; by the Eucharist we have been united to him, to the point where we died in him and now it is He who lives in us, our existence is already in the purview of his Resurrection, and hence of our final resurrection and eternal life with Him and because of Him.

For Muslims, the miraculous witness of the Qur'an is sufficient for believing in the resurrection. It is the sincerity of the heart before the divine sincerity of the text, manifested in its inimitability, its beauty, its ineffable efficacy... The sincerity of the text is one with the Prophet's sincerity. The strength of the text, its might is the same one that created the world and will recreate it on the Last Day. This is sufficient for believing in the resurrection and in eternal life as it is described in Qur'anic verses. This celestial testimony is powerful enough for the most generous youths to engage in holy war, carrying in their souls the full knowledge that death in combat is but the beginning of the most blissful life. Indeed it is the testimony of the Qur'an which kept patience in the hearts of those imprisoned without judgement, of those tortured anonymous ones, the ones buried alive...[8]

Political paralysis, disarray on the symbolical level, the absence of a future and humiliation in the face of the brazen materialism of globalisation provoke a fundamentalist swerve in the relationship to the Qur'anic text, leading to a reading of history without nuance, depth or plurality of layers; Paradise then becomes a mental refuge, a kind of virtual world that has more density than time... That is when one can wear an explosive belt... It is not even always hate that drives one to do it, but rather the unbearable perspective of the present, coupled with an indubitable promise!

Thank goodness, there are other readings in Islam, whether Sunni or Shiite. The symbolic readings peculiar to a certain Sufism and a certain mystical Shiism go in the opposite direction. There is a risk there of a certain political lack of responsibility based on the eruption of the "Other World" in daily life, which then becomes a life of private piety often adapted to social conservatism and to a certain aristocratic traditionalism. The tension is turned towards the perfecting of the soul, sometimes associated with a disdain for social issues.

Today, Qur'anic interpretations find themselves caught between political fundamentalism and ineffective symbolism. And yet Muslim society is experiencing a painful disarray, with a need for reform, participation and the emergence of a civil society that is consciously Muslim and carries a Qur'anic moral and spiritual pathos. We need religious pluralism in Muslim society, and hence a tolerance consciously taken on, because a univocal

---

8   Tahar Ben Jelloun, *Cette aveuglante absence de lumière* [*This Blinding Absence of Light*] (Paris: Le Seuil, 2001). The resistance against despair of these men condemned by the sadism of authorities to the "punishment of the tomb", where they are sustained and saved by repeating Qur'anic verses learned by heart is magnificent.

solution would be deceitful. The same goes for the Church: without pluralism, what we have is ideology. Democratic harmony is the work of the Holy Spirit, and the window of hope is not closed.

Intermediary Eschatology, the Passage

It is interesting however to note that in the Muslim description of the passage from this life to eternal life, there is a certain complexity that very much resembles what in the Church is called intermediary eschatology: the separation of the soul from the body, individual judgement, purgatory, hell or heaven for the separated soul, the final Resurrection and the Final Judgement. In Islam, they speak of the "torment of the grave", a kind of purgatory or anticipated hell. For Muslims as for Christians, the relationship between the souls of the living and those of the dead is very strong. For example, pilgrimage is frequently undertaken on behalf of the soul of a deceased person.

A more current Christian theology, which turns more radically to Biblical sources, highlights the fundamental aspect of the resurrection of the dead, rather than the resurrection of bodies. The mystery of the death of a person already anticipates resurrection. Today, we rarely speak about the different places the soul goes to after death, and we pay more attention to the requirements and conditions of purification of a person, in view of their resurrection and blissful life with God. Today, resurrection is a given of faith. The parallel with Islam is not difficult to make. The Muslim martyr is in a sense immediately resurrected: "And say not of those who are slain in the way of God: 'They are dead.' Nay, they are living."[9] To be a martyr is to already be present at the Final Judgement. When one radically gives one's life, one is already in eternal life with all of one's soul, one's history and one's flesh.

In the Muslim tradition based on the Qur'an, Jesus and Mary are not the only ones to be alive in Paradise. When Muhammad ascended to

---

9   Qur'an 2:154.

Heaven from Jerusalem during his *mi'rāj,* he met the prophets who had preceded him there...

The Living

There are at least three types of persons who are considered to not have died in the Muslim tradition, two of whom are Biblical. The first is Enoch, Idriss in Islam.[10] The second is Elijah, often identified in Islam as *al-Khodr,* the Verdant One, *al-'abd as-sālih,* the Good Servant, who appears in *surah* 18 as Moses' spiritual teacher.[11] In other Islamic regions he is also associated with Saint George "the Peasant", a Christian martyr, and is in turn proclaimed by popular piety as living and not dead, exactly like Elijah. The third type is of Christian origin: the Seven Sleepers of Ephesus, the People of the Cave. Their story is also in *surah* 18, named after the cave. They gave a radical yet non-violent witness to their faith by fleeing the city of Ephesus during persecution in order to keep their faith. Walled-in alive in the cave where they took refuge, they fell asleep, trusting in God despite their dramatic situation. Awakened three hundred and nine years later, they appeared alive to the people of the city before returning to their miraculous sleep. These living figures will all be alongside Jesus on the front of the final battle against the Antichrist, for they all must die in order to be resurrected. The faith of Muslims in the resurrection is illustrated in the Qur'an by the story of the Seven Sleepers, their resurrection is as if demonstrated by their miraculous awakening. They were Christians, Muslims know this. From the point of view of Muslims, they were true Christians, authentic monotheists and thus Muslims before their time, before the term.

10   Genesis 5, Qur'an 19:57.
11   2 Kings 2.

In the Cave

A few days ago I was in the cave of the Seven Sleepers not far from the Monastery of Mar Musa. It is a totally Muslim-Christian place of prayer. In a vast grotto, most certainly a cistern in the past, frescoes tell their story in images and texts on the walls. I was there with American Franciscan friends arriving from Turkey where they had visited the Church of the Seven Sleepers. They were on their way to Damietta in Egypt to visit the place where Saint Francis had his famous irenic, courteous and friendly encounter with the Muslim sultan al-Malik al-Kamil. This encounter took place during the crusade conducted by Saint Louis, during which time he was in fact made prisoner. After months of drought, a blessed rain was falling from the sky as we spoke of these matters. We were interrupted by the voices of two Syrians who came from the neighbouring town of Nebek. There was an old man with the title of *hajj*, one who undertook the pilgrimage to Mecca. It was his first time visiting the cave. And he was well-informed! He knew that there was one in Turkey, one in Damascus, one in Jordan and another in Cairo. (There certainly is another in Tunisia and others elsewhere as well, not counting the one in Vieux Marché in Bretagne…) He summarised for us the story of the Sleepers, specifying that they were Christians. This old Syrian explained to us that this *surah* is read every Friday in mosques, and that its reading allows for the forgiveness of sins from one Friday to another. An astonishing relationship between forgiveness and an account of resurrection… Then we asked him to tell us about his pilgrimage and his experience, that I transcribe here freely:

> The pilgrimage connects the hope of resurrection with the immense gathering of the believers around the house of God founded by Adam, built by Abraham and restored by Muhammad. It is a kind of general rehearsal of the Final Resurrection where there are no more rich nor poor, powerful nor weak, not even a distinction between men and women. They all depart in the white garments of *hajj*, prefiguring their sepulchral burial shroud, assembled to bear witness of their faith, and one would think it was the great pre-eternal assembly of the Primordial Covenant between God and

mankind. The space of the pilgrimage is one of forgiveness and sacrifice, a place of initiation and celebration.[12]

The rain was still falling when we left the cave, with no one around, gathered in this moment to receive this moving and magical testimony. The small coincidences of daily life become touches of presence and meaning for those who believe in the Providential God who likes to be here to take care of us. He spoils us with these signs of His exquisite courtesy.

I remember hearing a lovely story about the prophet Muhammad: he seemed preoccupied, as if sensing something grave, and was asked about his state of mind. He answered his Companions in more or less these terms: "How can I not tremble when I see Israfil, the Angel of Judgement, holding his trumpet to his mouth and pressing it to his lips, puffing up his cheeks ready to blow…" In fact, the death of the Prophet is considered by Muslims as the first in the series of catastrophes that precede Judgement Day.

Imminence and Duration

Current Islamic and Christian interpretations are reassuring, meant to appease souls by estimating that Judgement is not happening just yet, that it is still possible to concern ourselves with our children's inheritance, to buy land and build houses. In contrast, radical believers have the dramatic perception that Judgement is imminent, highly imminent, already here in a moral sense. This entails that we can no longer postpone to a distant future the commitment for justice that leads to peace.

Moreover, from the point of view of a reasonable forecast of humanity's future, it is difficult to think of the end of the world as a matter of a few

12   These are the themes dear to the reflection of Louis Massignon who considers pilgrimage the summit of Muslim spiritual initiation: "Here is Muslim baptism." Massignon, *Les Trois Prières*, 106. Massignon encourages us to see in the gathering of pilgrimage the "covenant", the "coming together" which is a synthesis of gathering and alliance.

generations or even a few millennia. According to this reasonable prediction and barring nuclear conflict or a global environmental catastrophe, the probability of the end of humanity and even more so of all creation is no longer part of the foreseeable future. In contrast, the followers of fundamentalist sects are fixated on the end!

We are left with the existential experience of imminence. Individual mortality and the cataclysms of history call upon us today to take charge of our moral responsibilities in the perspective of a meta-historical end beyond the temporal surface of the created world: the Final Judgement, the resurrection of the flesh and life with God in His Kingdom. The Prophet told his people that if the Day of Judgement comes while they have in their hands a young sapling, they should still plant it. This paradoxical attitude indicates that the value of a righteous deed can ultimately dispense with its historical visibility; for beyond the crust of history as a chronicle of power, true history happens elsewhere. Christians say that true history unfolds in the communion of saints, and Muslims believe that history is accomplished in the unity and faithfulness of the invisible *Ummah* of believers.

Prophecy, Person, Futures

At the turn of the millennium, my thoughts rather tended towards a rejection of this objectification of time by Christians; it seemed too absolute to me, and completely oblivious of temporal conceptions and of the division of time in other religions. At the time I was visiting my sister who is married to a Jewish man, both of them ex-communists. Their home is located in the countryside north of Rome, in a very small valley crossed by a stream. The valley had been long used as a cemetery by Etruscan farmers. It seemed like a place inhabited by atemporal depths. I lay down on a huge rock shaded by leaves. Awakened from my sleep by I know not what, I wrote in one go the gist of the following text:

> It is opportune to take up the theme of prophecy in the Mediterranean context, but also from a global point of view, and not only according to the Muslim-Christian

relationship. Prophecy and the act of faith constitute two aspects of one reality, which is about the possibility and capacity to welcome the presence and initiative of the personal God deep within the heart, at the summit of the soul in communion with the Spirit. This presence of the Divine Host within the person is rational and creative: Adam is a microcosm, created in the Qur'anic view in the image of the universe by divine decree: "Be!", and "he was" in history until its consummation.[13] The angels, the spiritual powers, are invited to prostrate themselves before Adam who is formed from earth and breath, because he is a prophet.[14] He pronounces the names and the meanings revealed to him by God. He knows what the angels do not.[15] Earth receives form like letters receive meaning. The person is inscribed like a clay tablet styled in cuneiform. Adam is taken from earth, Eve is taken from Adam. It is a perfect correspondence. The breath enters Mary and the Word is formed into man inside her. The idea of our Adamic origins is now being lost in the rear view of infinite evolutionary processes; whereas our vision of the future, which it is possible and dutiful to imagine as a prolongation of the human beyond the limits of the planet (towards a potentially infinite dispersion in space and time), becomes a "nebulisation" of the present moment. Only the arc of personal life, stretched between a creative start and an ineluctable end, constitutes the remaining key analogy to interpret existence. This is why Jesus son of Mary, the Person, in the dramatic claim to in himself destroy and reconstruct the Temple, image of the Cosmos and site of Glory, proposes himself as pinnacle and source of meaning, life and light for his disciples when they recognise in Him, in the arc of his own life, the designs of a benevolence that embraces everything. For this, after he and Mary tasted abandonment, he declared that all is fulfilled. But the disciple who recognised the mystical birth of the Church when the blood and water flowed from the right side of this Temple, declared that only now does everything begin. The Qur'an underlines the analogy, the very identity of Adam with Christ. The fidelity of the Church to Jesus of Nazareth is inscribed, as a surpassing of the Law, in the re-creation of the person, the other of the relationship: man and woman, God and I, the summit of the Sinaï (Mosaic prophecy) and the grotto of Hira (the Muhammadan prophecy). On the other hand Elijah, or rather the spirit of Elijah, of Enoch and of John the Baptist return repeatedly to be carried to Heaven on a chariot of divine fire. Moses, with whom God speaks face-to-face, always announces the coming of the Anointed one; and Muhammad, upon whom the Word descends in the form of the oracle, announces His final return.

Each prophecy plays out in a specific and necessarily equivocal linguistic arena. This neither justifies the fundamentalist absolutising of the

13   Quran 3:59.
14   Qur'an 2:34; 7:11; 38:71–73 & 15:28–29; 38:71–71.
15   Qur'an 3:59; Romans 5:14; 1 Corinthians 15:20–22, 45–49.

prophetic expression, nor does it permit the exercise of ingenious doubt concerning the truth and sincerity of the prophetic expression itself. Only through spiritual intelligence, practised in future dialogue and communion, can we encounter the truth of a monotheistic prophecy so radical, so polemical, and apparently anti-Christian as that of Muhammad. This can be achieved by following, in spirit, the course of the devotional tradition to the Prophet of Islam, to which belong the sincere souls, the souls of invocation, the sacrificed souls of Muslim saints, men and women. A disciple of Jesus spoke of Moses' veil, opportunely descended to prevent the understanding of the pivotal mystery of Golgotha, so it does not remain captive to particularism.[16] This same veil is laid in the Qur'an, in order to forbid, to prevent and to chastise the use of this holy mystery for means that have to do with power and appropriation in the "Christian" world. There are different post-Christianities: historically post-Christian prophecies like Islam, or the ulterior and constant pursuits of pre-Christian religious traditions, like Judaism, or also extra-Christian ones, like Hinduism and Buddhism, and finally the modern and postmodern rejection of the claim of the witnesses of the empty tomb. And all this turns in a centrifugal or centripetal way around this axis, casting a vast shroud on Christ. So what will they do, the disciples of Christ, of these post-Christianities? They could reject them as works of Satan, or tolerate them in anticipation of the final manifestation of the Light, or finally they could love, in a dynamic of functions relative to one another, in order to build shared hopes in common futures.

The year 2000, a period during which the Churches endeavoured to demonstrate the historical centrality of the Christ-event, seemed on the contrary to indicate, between the lines, the historic failure of Christianity. This failure of Christian universalism does not however consecrate the success of another form of globalism, which is in appearance more powerful and efficient. This failure of the Christian system does nevertheless appear to correspond to a process that fosters the rebuilding of the discipleship of Jesus as an interpersonal relationship. From this rebuilding stems the

---

16   2 Corinthians 3:7–18.

attachment to the mystical, meta-historical value of the human person in a divine being-child.

Future, hence eschatology; we will rewrite them together, us men and women of this plural time, which is at once dispersed, global, homogenising and tendentiously imperial. The so very peripheral Nazarene man and his disciples wanted to be witnesses to the definitive dynamic of giving, of the offering and of communion; the symbolic, effective site of the passage to the infinite, the eternal. Other traditions, by other paths, are witnesses to these same exigencies, and to others which are their own. And so we will rewrite eschatology, we will make it, we will realise it together if we are capable of penitence, of forgiveness, of communion, of tolerant dialogue and loving relationships, accessing with devotion the truth of the other as a condition for witnessing to the truth which is within us. This is why it is good to be able to dialectically practise a sense of belonging that is plural and dynamic in order to foster intersecting future hermeneutics. This will only be possible through the attentive reception and development of the prophetic gift at the centre of every person's personality, in silence, in listening, in the oracle. An infinite Pentecost of the Spirit in the present: in an effort to the death, in divinisation through relationship, all relationships, from the most mystical to the most material. Spirit beyond the letter; Word in the moist soil of this day, in the common body of the Word, the world.

Humbly, firmly, we will oppose closed affiliations. Nevertheless, we will remain faithful to the truth of traditions in their originality, their complementary and corrective interconnections, sometimes punitive, ultimately salvific.

In various places and in different ways, bridging identities, more or less solid, are being constituted. Even more, a cybernetic fabric covers the world with a new and common linguistic cloth, a virtual image of a more real and effective communion of saints. It is the hour of a new prophecy; not so much of a new prophet as of all of us prophets. And so, as we look back and ahead, we are gripped by infinite emotion, compunction and consolation.

The Failure of Christianity

As I tried to explain my text following a request for clarification from the Church Authority, I specified that by the words "it seems on the contrary to indicate, between the lines, the historic failure of Christianity", I meant to suggest that this failure seems sometimes to be demonstrated by the divisions, the shortfalls, the treasons, the infidelities, the half-heartedness, the thirst for power, etc. ...But in fact the term "seems" indicates the duty to go beyond the appearance of "this failure of the Christian system", which "appear(s) to correspond to a process that fosters the rebuilding of the discipleship of Jesus as an interpersonal relationship". It is upon the discipleship to Jesus that is founded, despite the contradictions in Christian history, the eternal youth of the Church. I said: "But the disciple who recognises the mystical birth of the Church when the blood and water flowed from the right side of this Temple, declared that only now does everything begin." Here, Christianity is understood as a reality which is internal to cultural and social history, as it may be seen from the outside, beset by incoherence and human limitations.

My text wants to take on the difficulties of those who find themselves outside the visible Church, and the doubts of those who are inside but are troubled, in order to find anew the source-experience of being a disciple of Jesus Christ, on the basis of which the Church is gathered by the Spirit at all times, even in the year 2000, the Jubilee Year.

If we meditate on the tragedies of the twentieth century, on the division between the Churches and within the Church, on the massive impermeability of these huge human groups from the great religions to the Christian faith and on the incapacity to communicate in depth with them, on the anguishing phenomenon of secularisation and the astonishing spread of a vain and immanentist hedonism, etc., we could reach the conclusion that the year 2000 was not only an occasion for a joyful and legitimate celebration of God's faithfulness and of the obedience of Jesus' disciples who form the Ecclesial assembly in its most sound theological and evangelical dimension; it was also an occasion for a great conversion.

Relaunching evangelisation is a priority, because it confronts a grave deficiency which needs to be addressed. It is this deficiency that I have paradoxically called the failure of Christian universalism, because the latter has not yet succeeded in bringing together the plurality of humanity in faithfulness to the Christ of the Beatitudes, and must today rethink universality through a rediscovery of the Gospel, in profound dialogue with all human religious realities and a new hearkening to the Spirit of prophecy.

Nevertheless, I do not want to make a gnostic separation between Christianity and the transcendent mystery of the Church. This failure of Christianity is ours, but at the same time, it is we who are called to form the Body of Christ in our time. We have often reduced the mystery of the Christ-Church to an ideology and a power structure. But Christ is faithful, and calls us to a renewed faithfulness. The model inspired by a universalised uniformity, built on the global spread of a mainly Western historical form of a monocultural Christianity that attempts to substitute itself to other religions and cultures; this is what I consider in my text as having failed. But I do not at all consider a failure the human-divine project constituted by Jesus and his Church, a project we still carry in vases of clay.

Conclusion

Islamophilia in All Cases

A Catholic man has just died. His life was exemplary, he attended Mass every Sunday and could even celebrate it in Latin. He went to confession every year, and now he arrives light-hearted at the gates of Paradise, confident in his rights. Saint Peter receives him and consults his registers, then the computer. The Catholic man is indeed registered, everything seems to be fine. But Saint Peter frowns, he seems to be searching for something. The Catholic man waits patiently, he knows how computers are… After a while, Saint Peter says:

- It's annoying, something is missing…
- This is a surprise, answers the Catholic, everything was in order when I left!
- Yes, but I am looking, and I cannot find your Muslim friend.
- My…what?
- Your Muslim friend, there is no indication of him.
- Come on, why would I have a Muslim friend?

Saint Peter answers: "To enter Paradise, you need to have a Muslim friend…" Seeing the scandalised expression on the man's face, he adds gently: "It will surely work out, why don't you wait a little while on the bench next to the entrance door."

Beside himself, the rejected candidate sits on the bench, fuming. Someone else is waiting also. Without looking at him, he exclaims: "Administration, it is not any better here! Now they have something missing from my file!" The other answers in anger: "It's the same with me, they didn't let me in! Computers complicate everything, things were simpler before!"

"It's scandalous, we must complain!" He looks at his neighbour. He's a dark-skinned, turbaned and bearded man who goes on to explain: "Everything was perfect for me, I recited my prayers five times a day, I was in the front row in the mosque every Friday to hear the sermon, I even went to Mecca, I don't understand what could be missing!" He also had presented himself in vain at the counter.

But then here they are, discussing the dysfunction of the modern world! They talk and talk, each one tells the other his life story, speaks of his entitlement and good deeds... After a while, lowering their voices, they confide their small lapses, their small infidelities...

It looks like this just might work out after all...[1]

As I revised the text, I searched, I asked for a title for the writing effort we had undertaken. It was dawn on Friday morning, I was still half-asleep in a state of passive prayer, when the title "Islamophilia" sprang up; the same way that the word "Islam" had appeared on the far horizon when I was a novice, meditating and asking Heaven how I could commit my life to the service of the Kingdom.

Clearly, the term Islamophilia is the opposite of Islamophobia, as there is a fear of Islam and Muslims that becomes a phobia, a blinding obsession.

Certainly, the word Islamophilia can sound to some like a psychological and social pathology. And we are aware that this entire book can be interpreted as the expression of a typically Western guilty naïvety, as the exercise of a masochistic capitulation provoked by a poorly assumed culpability. It's not even a case of cultural relativism anymore, for here the weapons of Christian civilisation have been consigned to its age-old enemy.

In the first verses of the Gospel of Saint Luke as well as at the start of the Acts of the Apostles, the author addresses one Theophilus, "he who loves God". In this book, we have addressed the love of Islam in the name of the love of God. A few months ago, 138 Muslim representatives sent the Pope and other Christian leaders a letter inviting them to come "to a common word" on the love of God and the love of one's neighbour ["A Common Word between Us and You", 13 October 2007]. Its central idea

1　Story told by Paolo Dall'Oglio in Le Vieux Marché on his return from the pilgrimage to the Seven Sleepers, transcribed by Christine de Pas.

was that there are essential elements for reciprocal understanding and hence collaboration between Muslims and Christians, without excluding the Jews. It was intended as an irenic response, the "best response" to Pope [Benedict XVI]'s address at Regensburg, which one could say removed diplomatic good manners from interreligious dialogue in order to inaugurate a dynamic of frankness between brothers and a dialogue of common responsibility towards today's world.

To love is to think differently. Saint Paul teaches us:

> Love is always patient and kind; it is never jealous; love is never boastful or conceited; it is never rude or selfish; it does not take offence, and is not resentful. Love takes no pleasure in other people's sins but delights in the truth; it is always ready to excuse, to trust, to hope, and to endure whatever comes. Love does not come to an end.[2]

Here is a hermeneutical programme for the interpretation of the event of Islam, and a political programme worth sharing.

It is perhaps more realistic to think in terms of a clash of civilisations, but that is not a Christian approach. In fact, the Church teaches Christians that there is a logic in this world that leads to everyone's perdition. It is the logic of individual interest, to which the Gospel opposes with a logic of hope. We hope that God does not despair of us or of Muslims. The logic of the Kingdom of God is the logic of charity in everything and despite everything. We hope that everything moving within this logic is stronger than death, and already partakes in the eternal Kingdom. On the contrary, what does not live with this logic is already dead and disappears!

Nevertheless, I am sensitive to the anguish of those who are concerned with the future of Western civilisation, and who feel threatened… And yet, I surprise myself wondering if it is truly worth it to save the West. Some worry that the Basilica of Saint Peter would be turned into a mosque and that the bell towers of Notre Dame would become minarets. In my view, the West's only richness is that which can be offered fraternally, as a valuable experience humbly proposed to the evolving human universality. The first step is to rediscover our roots in the East. I am thinking here of the Christian East.

---

2   1 Corinthians 13: 4–8.

Allow me to express my filial gratitude to the Church of the East. She never renounced her constitutional pluralist structure. Ultimately, she did not give in to the imperial logic of undifferentiated uniformity. I thank my Eastern Christian friends, including when they manifest resistance to my statements. This is how cultural, psychological and spiritual emigration are accomplished. I thank them for their hospitable welcome, their patience and their trust. First of all, I think of the Eastern sisters and brothers of our Monastic Community, then also of the Christians of the town of Nebek nearby. I also think of the bishops of our Syriac Catholic Eparchy: Hanna Dahi, Moussa Daoud, now also George Kassab, as well as of the community of priests. I would like to also mention three Easterners here: the late Melkite bishop of Aleppo, Neophytos Edelby, the lamented Damascene philosopher Antoun Maqdissi and my venerable Jesuit colleague Father Antoun Massamiri. All three knew and loved Louis Massignon, all three offered hospitality to my burning soul.

During a wedding dinner, I asked my great friend the *Mufti* of Nebek, Sheikh Yasser Hafez, to give me some ideas for a conference I was to participate in at the European Parliament during the "Arab Week" in Brussels. He proposed that I tell them on his behalf to what extent the Europeans have disappointed his hope in democracy. I will join my thoughts to his and those of other friends to declare here: the democratic Europeans seem to us incapable of controlling their economic appetites, paralysed by mafia-like tendencies and political corruption. They say that they love the Arabs and Muslims but they easily side with their enemies! They do not know how to make the necessary distinction between people, society and the power systems that people have to endure! I wondered then what could be the alternative to democracy. I side with those who think that there is no such alternative and on the contrary, I demand it for everyone, albeit in plural forms adapted to cultures and situations.

It is true in my view that a democracy devoid of values becomes corrupted to the point of tyranny. I am surprised to see societies with a slow democratic evolution, like Syria, for example, express nevertheless profound and shared values. In the absence of a civil culture of human rights, religious culture and spiritual experience rooted in solidary social groups are capable of transmitting these values. Schools, municipal offices, workplaces, markets, classes in mosques and churches, the tents and living rooms of tribal chiefs... They represent spaces of transmission, certainly imperfect, still spaces of implementation of authentic values... It is thanks to this that society does not go under. People believe that it is better to create consensus around a de-facto power than lose the peace and unity of the country by a majorities game, led, when all is said and done, by foreign actors. Far be it for me to imagine that this is a sufficient justification for the current stagnation in many countries of the Muslim world.

My aim is to point out, based on my experience, that religions, and particularly the Muslim religion, are depositories of values and of the pedagogical paths of initiation necessary to re-enchant democratic societies with humaneness, faithfulness, gratuitousness, beauty, a sense of sacrifice, tenderness and mystery.

We are moving towards a global society which we hope is democratic and capable of expressing in the best way the wealth of our spiritual traditions. Trust is what inspires the gift of what is best. I am addressing Christians as well as Muslims and others. Everyone will meet the other they dared hope for. Trust your Muslim neighbour, they will be for you a source of life. Imagine a positive development for your Christian neighbour... You would have gained a generous friend. Try to carve out a constructive role for yourself towards your work colleagues who are from a different religion... They will play a positive role in your life. Take the initiative during Eid to visit the stranger living across from you... You will gain an affectionate friend. Rather than ceaselessly wonder which conservative attitude, which religious war, which spiteful reciprocity and which feeling of being a persecuted victim will keep us faithful to the gods of our ancestors, let us ask ourselves to which generous and genial evolution is the One God of our future communion inviting us.

Nobody can imagine that a Muslim world which is theologically despised, humiliated by the nuclear might of its enemies, exploited in its resources, instrumentalised by perverse strategic designs, impoverished of its best youths, delivered to tribal and archaic conservative structures as well as to the most dangerous revolutionary drifts, judged *en bloc* as the root of all terrorism, could offer globalised society the best of itself. We will get the Islam that we knew to hope for!

Ultimately, I recognise the duty of the Community of Jesus' disciples, the Church to which I belong by vocation, to judge my words. I have the deep desire that we may advance together. I ask forgiveness in advance from Muslims, my brothers, for any form of expression that might seem infelicitous or unjust to them. If I have decided to publish my reflections, which remain to be refined, here in this book, it is because I believe in all conscience that it is urgent, in the current time, to share my experience and my vision in this way.

I conclude with the Muslim invocation upon the Prophet which concludes every prayer:

> My God, sanctify Muhammad and the family of Muhammad, as you have sanctified Abraham and the family of Abraham, bless Muhammad and the family of Muhammad, as you have blessed Abraham and the family of Abraham. Praise and glory to You. *As-salamu 'alaykom wa rahmatu-Allah.* May God's salvation and Mercy be with you.

Appendix

Excerpts from the Rule of Mar Musa Monastery Including the Statutes of the Monastic Confederation of al-Khalil Regarding Relations with Islam

It seemed to me useful to include an appendix with some key texts from the Monastic Rule of Deir Mar Musa concerning its relationship with Islam. The translation from Italian to French (the original is in Arabic) is the work of Nathalie Vierrucci, for which she is warmly thanked. My intention is to show that this book cannot be considered an altogether complete expression of the Community's shared vocation. This vocation corresponds to the ecclesiastical consciousness of our time, while this book is a more personal attempt towards further development. At the end of the day, we are convinced that it is better to advance a metre together than a kilometre alone. This text received the *nulla osta* of the Congregation for the Doctrine of the Faith in 2006, and is today the object of a vast discussion within our Eastern diocese.

Excerpt from the Introduction

(1) "The particular vocation of the monastery of Saint Moses the Abyssinian and of the monastic Confederation of al-Khalil (The Friend of God) comprises three priorities:
   – Contemplative life according to the Syriac tradition, with a spiritual engagement in the Middle-Eastern Christian and Arab Islamic context.
   – Engagement in manual work according to the great example of the Nazarene family.
   – Abrahamic hospitality."

(4) The particularity of the charism of the Monastic Community of Saint Moses the Abyssinian is based on a few elements which constitute a strong symbolic unity for us who have been called to this kind of monastic life, for the Churches we live with, the societies where we live and the Universal Church for whom we live. The Monastery of Saint Moses the Abyssinian is an important symbol for the Eastern Churches, who have always found the monasteries of the desert to be sources of evangelical spiritual renewal, following the example of the people of Moses in the Sinaï, the trail of the Desert Fathers of Egypt and Palestine, and on the basis of the teachings of Ephrem and Isaac the Syrians.

Moreover, and in addition to the importance of the desert monastery for the Eastern Church across the centuries, as Islam spread and even at its inception, the symbolism of monastic life, particularly hermetism, was important for and had a direct impact on the formation of Muslim spirituality and of the Sufi tradition. Sufism gained the esteem and even legal recognition of the entire Muslim Community. In addition to this important element, we have been called to follow in the footsteps of the Eastern saints, men and women who knew how to offer a perfect Christian witness based on the Gospel and the teachings of the Fathers, with respect, a spirit of service and the exercise of mercifulness in the Muslim context for fourteen centuries. There are also saints, men and women from every Church who were driven by the Holy Spirit to offer themselves alongside Christ for the sake of Muslims. We are thinking here of Saint Francis of Assisi and Saint Ignatius of Loyola. In the same way, we are aware that our particular vocation is built on this renewal of religious life, especially in a Muslim context, that the Holy Spirit performed in the life of Charles de Foucauld. Our vocation is also rooted in the intellectual and spiritual profundity, the serious dialogue, the science and wisdom of Louis Massignon, which are the basis of the inculturation of his and our Christian faith in the language, the civilisation and the spiritual experience of these countries and their people. This has driven him to found, alongside our Eastern sister Mary Kahil, the brotherhood of the *Badaliyya* for mainly Eastern men and women disciples of Jesus, dedicated to manifesting the love of Christ, Jesus of Nazareth, towards Muslims and Islam.

Likewise, the great change in the Church in terms of its openness to other religions, particularly to Islam as an Abrahamic religion, which happened during the Second Vatican Council, bore fruit, and intensified during the last quarter of the twentieth century with the involvement of the Churches and the believers of other religions. This change has undoubtedly been a strong basis and a dynamic motor for our particular vocation. The latter saw its most exalted sign in Pope John Paul II's visit to the Great Umayyad Mosque in Damascus on 6 May 2001, and received the effectual Apostolic seal in the special benediction he bestowed the next day on the monastic Community of the Monastery of Saint Moses the Abyssinian. (See also the "Explanatory Note" below.)

Canon II: "The monastery is a religious house in which the members tend towards evangelical perfection by the observation of the rules and traditions of monastic life" (Can. 433 – § 1) of the Code of Canons of the Eastern Churches (hereafter CCEO). Additionally, monastic life at the Monastery of Saint Moses the Abyssinian is characterised by three priorities and one horizon.

The first priority is contemplative life according to our Syriac tradition with a spiritual engagement in the framework of our Christian Middle-Eastern and Arab Islamic context. It is a personal and communal contemplative life, marked by the simplicity that we find among the old Desert Fathers and closer to us, in Charles de Foucauld. The Virgin of Nazareth, Mary Mother of the Word, remains our foremost teacher in contemplative spiritual life.

The second priority is the engagement in manual work following the example of the Nazarene family, which constitutes an accomplished anthropological project that successfully unifies the human person in body and mind, and is responsible for the tending of the material world and society towards the horizons of the Kingdom.

The third priority is Abrahamic hospitality, which monks have practised throughout the ages: a hospitality made of service, mercy and forgiveness; a hospitality of wisdom and spiritual guidance; a hospitality of the common table and of silence, of welcoming the other in their hour of wealth and in their hour of need, with their particular charism and spiritual thirst.

The horizon is our particular dedication to Jesus the Redeemer's love for Muslims as persons, and for the Muslim world as *Ummah*. We offer our life so the evangelical leaven is efficiently present in Muslim society according to the spirit of discernment, hope and charity, which is capable of transforming yesterday and today's suffering into a basis for mutual understanding and love, in mutual esteem and respect. This love of Christ for Muslim men and women is an authentic aspect of His love for all humanity, and it demands to be fulfilled according to Saint Paul's Hymn of Love (1 Corinthians 13), and to the teachings of Chapter 6 of the Gospel according to Saint Luke. Moreover, the practice of charity excludes neither the recognition of the rights of human individuals and groups, nor the defence of minorities. On the contrary, it gives rights their ultimate goal and the efficient evangelical method to safeguard them.

Excerpt from Canon IV

On the basis of this catholic affiliation, the Community will be able to sincerely fulfil its ecumenical dimension, with equilibrium and harmony, by prophesying days of unity to come, not only for the visible Church but also for all the children of Abraham and for the human family, by the grace of our Lord Jesus Christ.

Excerpt from Canon XIII

In this Eastern monastic life, all members of the Monastic Community, superiors and all others will have to faithfully and perfectly observe their vows to God of chastity, poverty and obedience, as well as their vows of contemplative life, manual work and hospitality, projecting the special offering of themselves towards expressing the love of the Lord Jesus for Muslims and for the Muslim world. They must not forget that this love is particular, given their vocation which emerges from the heart of Christ who loves in a particular manner the people of all religions, cultures and social communities. When preferential love is expressed in the Gospel, it is towards the poor, the humble and the marginal; in this as well we are entirely engaged. Each member of this Community will always heed this Rule as well as the first legislative and spiritual texts expressing the special character of this vocation and this charism as the source of their spirituality (Can. 426 of CCEO).

The particular identity of the al-Khalil Community in relation to the Muslim world obeys the vision of the Church's Second Vatican Council and the teachings of the Magisterium that followed. Theological research in this domain, so delicate and decisive in our time, is certainly one of the characteristic duties of the Community. This theological engagement is at all times tied to the spirit of contemplation and to the practice of spiritual dialogue, the dialogue of shared social engagement and the dialogue of life, which characterises our experience.[1]

However, it should always be very clear, especially for the Superiors of the Monasteries and the President of the Confederation, that the theological opinions of the members will constitute the common teachings of this Community only when their conformity to the teachings of the Magisterium of the Church has been verified. It remains that the Superiors and the members have the duty to practise charitable and attentive respect for the diversity of opinions, for evangelical correction and discernment in a spirit of mutual openness and shared hope. Always preserving charity, we should fraternally correct, sometimes also firmly, the members who by their particular outlook on the interreligious question, adopt attitudes that

---

1   TN. "The concept of dialogue of life was endorsed by Pope John Paul II in his 1990 encyclical letter *Redemptoris missio*. There he described the dialogue of life as one in which 'believers of various religions bear witness to one another in daily life concerning human and spiritual values and help one another to live them in order to build a more just and fraternal society...all the faithful and every Christian community is called to practice dialogue, although not in the same way nor to the same degree.'" Synod of Bishops Special Assembly for Asia, "Jesus Christ the Saviour and His Mission of Love and Service in Asia: That They May Have Life and Have it Abundantly" (JN 10:10). (1998): 49, citing John Paul II, Encyclical Letter *Redemptoris missio*, 57; AAS 83 (1991) 305.

contradict the teachings of the Church; this as much for their spiritual good as for the protection of the transparency of the evangelical witness of the Monastic Community.

Excerpt from Canon XIV

The clerical members of the Monastery should have acquired an authentic Eastern liturgic sensibility, theoretical as much as practical, under the direction of experts recognised as such. They must also develop a profound ecumenical sensibility rooted in Patristic theology, in the knowledge of the different stages of the ecumenical movement and in Catholic doctrine. Similarly, they must have acquired an adequate knowledge of the Muslim world, the context where they exercise their ecclesial ministry. The formation of future clerical members must also take into great consideration spiritual theology and missiology in order to exercise ordained ministry in the particular framework of the Monastic Community of al-Khalil.

The clerical members of the Monastery will not neglect ongoing education or the importance of acquiring the sciences that are strictly related to the particular charism of this Community and to the practice of priesthood, both within the Community and towards hosts and visitors (Can. 372 of the CCEO).

Excerpt from Canon XXIV

One of the duties of the independent Monastery Superior is to take care of the Fraternities of al-Khalil, made up of friends of the Monastery who join together to share, according to their own charism and situation, the spirituality of our Monastic Community. He gives his consent to the election of the coordinator of this Fraternity. Likewise, it is he who must, if necessary and with the consent of his council, dissolve a Fraternity.

The independent Monastery Superior must spiritually guide the persons who have realised that God is calling them to participate, according to their own charism and situation, in the spirituality of the al-Khalil Community. He can delegate this function to a member of the Monastic Community and to a dependent Monastery Superior, both filial and subsidiary.

Canon XXXIV: It is very important that assemblies are held at least once a year, where all the members of the Monastic Community are gathered, or at least a certain number of monks and nuns named by the Superior, alongside persons who share with the Monastic Community some of its spiritual objectives and who, in one way or another, are connected to the life of the Monastery. The Monastery Superior will invite them with the agreement of his council. These assemblies will make it possible to study the reality and context of the Monastery, to listen to different opinions and to make propositions on ways to improve and reform the situation.

Excerpt from Canon XXXV

Whoever joins one of the Monasteries of the al-Khalil Confederation must first be driven by the Holy Spirit. They must know that they are a sinner forgiven because of the blood of Christ, and a poor soul that the Spirit has brought to the mountains of solitude to hear His call in secret, to meditate on God's Word and to obtain freedom through the evangelical law and the logic of gratuitousness. They ask to be sanctified in humility, they desire to put all their natural and spiritual charisms at the service of the Kingdom, they aspire to total dedication to God through loving Him and loving each human being, and, in a special manner, they desire to associate themselves with the intercession of Mary, Mother of the Redeemer, and that of Abraham, father of believers, for Islam and Muslims, for whose sake Christ sacrificed himself also, for their redemption and atonement. It is Christ who, by the power of his Resurrection, renders those who desire to adhere to monastic life capable of standing as candidates for this life, trusting only in God.

Excerpt from Canon LI

At the appropriate time, the one getting ready for monastic vows says: "I, so and so, forgiven sinner, dedicate myself perpetually to the Father, the Son and the Holy Spirit, the One and True God, through monastic vows in the Monastery (they name the Monastery and if there is more than one independent Monastery, they will add: "and in the al-Khalil Monastic Confederation"), in evangelical chastity, poverty and obedience, in a life of prayer, of manual work and of welcoming guests, and I commit myself, with this Community and according to the charism and the mission of the Church, to the service of the Muslim world until the Kingdom of Heaven comes" (Can. 462 of the CCEO).

Excerpt from Canon LXIV

They [the members] all demonstrate great devotion for the Cross of the Saviour mounted in the church of the Monastery. They commend the practice of wearing the cross around the neck or of the tattooed cross, according to the more balanced customs of the local Christians. If discrete charity and missionary discernment, not human fear, lukewarm faith, a secular attitude or the fear of martyrdom advise, especially in a Muslim milieu, to not wear the cross over the habit, and to replace it or not by another Christian sign, they should remember that they are called to an ever more perfect union with Christ, the humble and suffering servant for the redemption of all. Every decision in this regard will be taken by the ordinary synaxis.

Canon LXXXVI: "The monks and nuns of the al-Khalil Confederation are willing candidates, by the very fact of their monastic vows, driven by love for martyrdom in all its forms: the martyrdom of weariness, the martyrdom of illness, the martyrdom of failure, the martyrdom of their close ones and their family, as well as the martyrdom of blood and the martyrdom of obedience and patience. They must renew the perfect offering every day by thanking God for the grace of partaking in the suffering of Christ on the horizon of the light of eternal life."

Excerpt from Canon LXXXVII

The members of the Monastic Community who pass away in the monastery in the hope of eternal life must be buried in the monastery's cemetery in the way suited to our particular vocation and according to what we know of the wishes of the deceased.

Explanatory Note on the Particular Vocation of the Monastic Community in the Muslim World

We are going to reflect here on the texts of the Magisterium, which in the Spirit we consider as the constitutional texts of our particular vocation in the Muslim world. Evidently, we do not intend by the selection of these texts to circumvent their integrity and that of the Catholic doctrine that they carry.

Above all, we draw inspiration from the Declaration *Nostra Aetate* on the relationship of the Church with non-Christian religions. "The Catholic Church rejects nothing that is true and holy in these religions … The Church, therefore, exhorts her sons, that through dialogue and collaboration with the followers of other religions, carried out with prudence and love and in witness to the Christian faith and life, they recognise, preserve and promote the good things, spiritual and moral, as well as the socio-cultural values found among these men (2)." Concerning Muslims specifically, after recalling their adoration of the One God, the submission of Abraham, their reverence for Jesus, their honouring of Mary, their expectation of Judgement Day and their esteem for culture and moral life, the text concludes: "Since in the course of centuries not a few quarrels and hostilities have arisen between Christians and Muslims, this sacred synod urges all to forget the past and to work sincerely for mutual understanding and to preserve as well as to promote together for the benefit of all mankind social justice and moral welfare, as well as peace and freedom (3)." "We cannot truly call on God, the Father of all, if we refuse to treat in a brotherly way any man, created as he is in the image of God (5)."

Perhaps an even more important text is the one concerning Muslims in *Lumen Gentium*, in the framework of the mystical ecclesiology taught by the Council. The Monastic Community of al-Khalil really wishes to situate itself within the perspective of "Christ the Light of nations" and also "eagerly desires…to bring the light of Christ to all men, a light brightly visible on the countenance of the Church (1)". The Spirit introduces us into the intention of the eternal Father who created the world "by a free and hidden plan of His own wisdom and goodness" and calls us to the Holy

Church, which at the end of time "will gloriously achieve completion, when, as is read in the Fathers, all the just, from Adam and 'from Abel, the just one, to the last of the elect', will be gathered together with the Father in the universal Church (2)". The Father wanted to draw all things to Him in Christ, the image of the invisible God. Christ inaugurates the Kingdom of God on earth, and the Church, or rather the Kingdom of Christ already mysteriously present, grows visibly in the world by the grace of God. By virtue of the blood and water that flowed from the side of Jesus who, once lifted up, draws us all to him, and by virtue of the ecclesial celebration of the Eucharist where the work of our redemption is renewed, "all men are called to this union with Christ, who is the light of the world, from whom we go forth, through whom we live, and toward whom our whole life strains (3)". "Just as Christ carried out the work of redemption in poverty and persecution, so the Church is called to follow the same route that it might communicate the fruits of salvation to men (8)." "By the power of the risen Lord it [the Church] is given strength that it might, in patience and in love, overcome its sorrows and its challenges, both within itself and from without, and that it might reveal to the world, faithfully though darkly, the mystery of its Lord until, in the end, it will be manifested in full light (8)." "At all times and in every race, God has given welcome to whosoever fears Him and does what is right… So it is that messianic people, although it does not actually include all men, and at times may look like a small flock, is nonetheless a lasting and sure seed of unity, hope and salvation for the whole human race (9)." "All men are called to be part of this catholic unity of the people of God which in promoting universal peace presages it. And there belong to or are related to it in various ways, the Catholic faithful, all who believe in Christ, and indeed the whole of mankind, for all men are called by the grace of God to salvation (13)." "Finally, those who have not yet received the Gospel are related in various ways to the people of God. In the first place we must recall the people to whom the testament and the promises were given and from whom Christ was born according to the flesh (Romans 9:4-5). On account of their fathers this people remains most dear to God, for God does not repent of the gifts He makes nor of the calls He issues (Romans 11: 28-29). But the plan of salvation also includes those who acknowledge the Creator. In the first place amongst these there are the Muslims, who, professing to hold the faith of Abraham, along with us adore the one and merciful God, who on the last day will judge mankind (16)." The missionary Church has but one goal: "Whatever good is in the minds and hearts of men, whatever good lies latent in the religious practices and cultures of diverse peoples, is not only saved from destruction but is also cleansed, raised up and perfected unto the glory of God, the confusion of the devil and the happiness of man. The obligation of spreading the faith is imposed on every disciple of Christ, according to his state…In this way the Church both prays and labours in order that the entire world may become the People of God, the Body of the Lord and the Temple of the Holy Spirit, and that in Christ, the Head of all, all honour and glory may be rendered to the Creator and Father of the Universe (17)."

In the conclusion to the Constitution *Gaudium et Spes* the Council Fathers express themselves as follows: "We think cordially too of all who acknowledge God, and who preserve in their traditions precious elements of religion and humanity. We want frank conversation to compel us all to receive the impulses of the Spirit faithfully and to act on them energetically. …Since God the Father is the origin and purpose of all men, we are all called to be brothers. Therefore, if we have been summoned to the same destiny, human and divine, we can and we should work together without violence and deceit in order to build up the world in genuine peace (92)."

In *Evangelii Nuntiandi*, Pope Paul VI tells us regarding the Proclamation: "This first proclamation is also addressed to the immense sections of mankind who practice non-Christian religions. The Church respects and esteems these non-Christian religions because they are the living expression of the soul of vast groups of people. They carry within them the echo of thousands of years of searching for God, a quest which is incomplete but often made with great sincerity and righteousness of heart. They possess an impressive patrimony of deeply religious texts. They have taught generations of people how to pray. They are all impregnated with innumerable 'seeds of the Word' and can constitute a true 'preparation for the Gospel' (53)."

For the Monastic Community of al-Khalil, it is spiritually clear that its particular charism for Muslim-Christian dialogue and for the inculturation of the faith in the Muslim world cannot, ultimately, be separated from the evangelising mission of the Church, and that it participates dynamically in it. "Therefore though God in ways known to Himself can lead those inculpably ignorant of the Gospel to find that faith without which it is impossible to please Him (Heb. 11:6), yet a necessity lies upon the Church (1 Cor. 9:16), and at the same time a sacred duty, to preach the Gospel. And hence missionary activity today as always retains its power and necessity (*Ad Gentes* 7)." Underlining the importance of "in ways known to Himself", the Declaration *Dominus Iesus* of the Congregation for the Doctrine of the Faith encourages theological engagement: "Theologians are seeking to understand this question more fully. Their work is to be encouraged, since it is certainly useful for understanding better God's salvific plan and the ways in which it is accomplished (21)." We would like to engage in exploring these divine ways, not only intellectually, but also in a vital, contemplative, relational and evangelical way, with prudence and humility, faithful obedience and true ecclesiastical spirit. Indeed it is by these same mysterious ways that the Church will be able to experience the ultimate harmony between evangelisation and dialogue. This engagement, which we consider as profoundly Catholic and to be lived in a spirit of communion, must be realised in a concrete and continuous relationship with the local Church, the Patriarchal See and the Holy See.

The Magisterium of the Church has on various occasions emphasised the charism of religious life, particularly of contemplative life and especially of Eastern monasticism when it comes to evangelisation, interreligious dialogue and inculturation. "Indeed it can be said that monasticism in antiquity, and at various times in subsequent ages too, has been the privileged means for the evangelisation of peoples" (*Orientale Lumen* 14).

In the Apostolic Post-Synodal Exhortation *Vita Consecrata*, Pope John Paul II says: "The Church entrusts to communities of consecrated life the particular task of spreading the spirituality of communion, [they] are signs that dialogue is always possible and that communion can bring differences into harmony (51)." And we see in no. 76: "The specific contribution of consecrated persons, both men and women, to evangelisation is first of all the witness of a life given totally to God and to their brothers and sisters, in imitation of the Saviour who, out of love for humanity, made himself a servant." The missionary drive *ad gentes* "is felt above all by the members of Institutes, whether of the contemplative or of the active life. Consecrated persons, in fact, have the task of making-present, even among non-Christians, Christ who is chaste, poor, obedient, prayerful and missionary (77)." "It should be emphasised that in countries where non-Christian religions are firmly established, the presence of the consecrated life is of great importance, whether through its educational, charitable and cultural activities, or through the witness of the contemplative life (78)." "In the context of missionary activity the process of inculturation and interreligious dialogue have a role to play…in many ancient cultures religious expression is so deeply ingrained that religion often represents the transcendent dimension of the culture itself. In this case true inculturation necessarily entails a serious and open interreligious dialogue, which 'is not in opposition to the mission *ad gentes*' and 'does not dispense from evangelisation' (79)." No. 102 in its entirety deals with the role of consecrated life in relation to interreligious dialogue: "…the freedom of spirit proper to the consecrated life will favour that 'dialogue of life' which embodies a basic model of mission and of the proclamation of Christ's Gospel."

Again, in the Post-Synodal Exhortation *Ecclesia in Asia*, the Successor of Peter validates us by saying: "I repeat how important it is to revitalise prayer and contemplation in the process of dialogue. Men and women in the consecrated life can contribute very significantly to interreligious dialogue by witnessing to the vitality of the great Christian traditions of asceticism and mysticism (31)."

In the Post-Synodal Exhortation "A New Hope for Lebanon" the Pope returns to the Apostolic Letter *Orientale Lumen* and says: "Monasteries can become 'the prophetic place where creation becomes praise of God and the precept of concretely lived charity becomes the ideal of human coexistence; it is where the human being seeks God without limitation or impediment, becoming a reference point for all people, bearing them in his heart and helping them to seek God.' …Monks will be, as they were before, spiritual guides and teachers, and their monasteries the spaces of ecumenical and interreligious meetings (57)."[2] And then, the chapter on

2   TN. Cf. For a link to the full text in French, an official English language translation is not available: <https://www.vatican.va/content/john-paul-ii/fr/apost_exhortations/documents/hf_jp-ii_exh_19970510_lebanon.html>.

interreligious dialogue, in particular with Islam, is for us fundamental: "I invite them to consider their insertion in Arab culture, to which they have contributed so much, as a privileged space to conduct, in concert with the other Christians of the Arab world, an authentic and profound dialogue with Muslim believers (93)."

The scope of dialogue in the Community of al-Khalil will be open to universality, and above all to brotherhood between all the children of Abraham, with a view to overcoming and rejecting the logic of violence. Pope John Paul II is also, in so many of his addresses, a master in this. During the Holy Mass celebrated on the occasion of the 35th World Day of Peace, he tells us that his call is first and foremost addressed to those who believe in God, in particular "the three Abrahamic religions", Judaism, Christianity and Islam; he reminds us that from this earth rises the sound of the blood that cries out to God, the blood of brethren shed by their brethren; that they all descend from the same "Patriarch Abraham", and are the children of the same Heavenly Father, like all men.

We should listen to the Spirit of God with devout and constant attention. The Pope explicitly recognises the active presence of the Holy Spirit in the life of the members of other religious traditions; this is the case in *Redemptor hominis,* where he asserts "the firm belief of the followers of the non-Christian religions, a belief that is also an effect of the Spirit of truth operating outside the visible confines of the Mystical Body (6)". In his encyclical *Dominum et vivificantem,* John Paul II goes further and affirms the universal activity of the Holy Spirit in the world before the Economy of the Gospel, to whom this action was ordained, and he speaks of this same universal activity of the Spirit present today "also outside the visible Body of the Church (53)".

The Declaration *Dominus Iesus* by the Congregation for the Doctrine of the Faith is an important document of the Magisterium, decisive in regards to our Community's ecumenical dimension as well as its commitment to interreligious dialogue. Since its publication, this Declaration has been the subject of a fruitful series of reflections within the Community and a good opportunity for listening with filial devotion and exercising our judgement in theological obedience. Today, the study of this Declaration is part of the formation of the members of the Community and must be considered as an encouragement to unite fidelity and courage in our engagement: fidelity to the objectivity of what is prescribed by the Catholic Christian faith, and courage to open ourselves to the action of Christ and the Holy Spirit, also beyond the visible limits of the Church, still within the ecclesial perspective of the Kingdom of God.

Our loyal efforts towards inculturation will be exempt from any indifferentism and nihilistic relativism, as well as from any equivocal and superficial syncretism. Our love for Muslims is guided by the discernment of this "ray of that truth which enlightens all men (*Nostra Aetate* 2)" towards the fullness of the truth. Our presence in the Muslim world where the love of Christ sends us does not indicate a dual belonging in terms of faith. On the contrary, it is our unconditional belonging to the mystery of Christ and of the Church, His bride, that determines the depth of our commitment to dialogue.

It seems to us that Pope John Paul II, with his prophetic initiative of the Interreligious Prayer Meeting for Peace in Assisi has somehow designated Saint Francis as the patron of dialogue, in particular with Islam. The Saint, in the *Regula non bullata* (The Earlier Rule), indicates to the Brothers two ways to live spiritually among Muslims: "One way is not to engage in arguments or disputes, but to be subject to every human creature for God's sake and to acknowledge that they are Christians. Another way is to proclaim the word of God…" Our hope, and already our experience in the daily practice of respectful and valorising hospitality, is that openness to one's neighbour, which finds in inculturation its dimension of faith and in dialogue its natural domain of expression, and evangelisation, when more in tune with the moderation and humility of the Divine Master, converge in perspective, in a unique communion.

Through their faith in the prophecy of Muhammad the Arab, Muslims consider themselves the descendants of Ishmael and heirs to the blessings bestowed on him through the intercession of the Holy Patriarch Abraham. Early on, Saint John of Damascus said: "They are also called Saracens, which means divested by Sarah. (Saint John of Damascus, *Écrits sur l'Islam*, Paris, Le Cerf, 1992, p. 211)." Cardinal Carlo Maria Martini, in his capacity as bishop of the Universal Church, tells us:

The account we heard is taken from the oldest book of Scripture, the book of Genesis (Ch.21). It tells us of a son of Abraham who was not the ancestor of the Hebrew people as Isaac will be, but upon whom God's blessings were also bestowed. "But the slave-girl's son I will also make into a nation, for he is your child too" (Genesis 21:13). And at the end of the story, it is said: "God was with the boy" (21:20). The real vicissitudes of Ishmael and his offspring remain obscure in the history of the second and first millennium B.C.E., but it is clear that the Biblical reference concerns a few Bedouin tribes that were settled around the Arabian Peninsula. From such tribes, many centuries later, Muhammad the Prophet of Islam would be born. Today, at a time when the Arab world has assumed extraordinary importance on the international scene, and partly in our country also, we cannot forget this ancient blessing that shows God's fatherly Providence towards all His children. (*Noi e l'Islam*, Milano, 1990, pp. 11–12)

In the same perspective of reconciliation, Cardinal Kasper recalls: "Moreover, neither Hagar nor Ishmael were ever repudiated by God, who made him a great nation" ("Antisemitismo una piaga da guarire", *L'Osservatore Romano*, 7 September 2003).

Our monastic life in the Muslim world must be lived within a prophetic and eschatological dimension, projected towards the realisation of the promise made to Abraham and which the Virgin Mary sings as being already fulfilled in the Magnificat. The Book of Genesis gives a glimpse of this eschatological reconciliation with the presence of both Isaac and Ishmael at the Patriarch's tomb (Genesis 25:9). It is in the perspective of this finality of people and the cosmos that we understand the confident wish of Pope Gregory VII as he formulated it to Sultan al-Nasir in 1076 CE (*Epistola XXI:*452): "And we pray, with our heart and our word, that after the long period of this life, God lead you in the embrace of blessing of the most holy patriarch Abraham" (Fr. Thomas Michel & Mgr. Michel Fitzgerald, Conseil Pontifical pour le Dialogue Interreligieux, *Reconnaître les liens spirituels qui nous unissen*t, Cité du Vatican, 1994, p. 4).[3]

Great attention is paid by the Monastic Community of al-Khalil to the other documents issued by the Catholic Hierarchy, especially to the

---

3 TN, English translation from the Latin by Ozden Mercan, "Constructing a Self-Image in the Image of the Other: Political and Religious Interpretations of Pope Pius II's Letter to Mehmed II (1461)" (Masters, Central European University, Budapest, 2008), 23.

Pastoral Letters of the Catholic Patriarchs of the Orient as well as to the documents written together with the pastors of other Christian Churches in the Muslim world. These texts, such as the letter by the Catholic Patriarchs entitled *Christian Presence in the Orient* (1992), and the letter *Together before God for the Welfare of the Individual and of Society* (1994), are often the thesis of monastic catechisms, and nourish our prayer and praxis.

In conclusion, it is right that we address ourselves to Mary, to whom we entrust our vocation, with the words of Pope John Paul II in the Damascus Mosque:

> As we make our way through life towards our heavenly destiny, Christians feel the company of Mary, the Mother of Jesus; and Islam too pays tribute to Mary and hails her as "chosen above the women of the world" (Qur'an 3:42). The Virgin of Nazareth, the Lady of *Saydnâya,* has taught us that God protects the humble and "scatters the proud in the imagination of their hearts" (Lk 1:51). May the hearts of Christians and Muslims turn to one another with feelings of brotherhood and friendship, so that the Almighty may bless us with the peace which Heaven alone can give. To the One and Merciful God, praise and glory for all eternity. Amen. (Easter Celebrations, 2006)

Bibliography

Ayoub, M. Mahmoud. "La Parola di Dio nel Corano," *Corano e Bibbia*, Brescia: Morcelliana (2000).

Chouraqui, André. *Moïse*. Paris: Éditions du Rocher, 1995. Flammarion, 1997.

Congregation for the Doctrine for the Faith. *Declaration Dominus Iesus on the Unicity and Salvific University of Jesus Christ and the Church*. Vatican City: Libreria Editrice Vaticana, 2000.

D'Assise, François. *Écrits* [Writings]. Sources Chrétiennes, no. 285, 1997.

Dall'Oglio, Paolo. *Speranza nell'Islām: Interpretazione della Prospettiva Escatologica di Corano XVIII*. Genoa: Marietti, 1991.

Damascène, Jean. *Écrits sur L'islam*. Sources Chrétiennes, no. 383, Paris: Éditions Le Cerf, 1992.

D'Assise, François. "Écrits [Writings]," *Sources Chrétiennes*, 151 (1997).

De Chergé, Christian. "Échelle mystique du dialogue," *Islamochristiana* 23, Roma: Pontificio Istituto di Studi Arabi e d'Islamistica (1997).

——. "Dialogue Intermonastique et Islam," 1995, in *Christian de Chergé: L'invincible Espérance*. Paris: Bayard Éditions-Centurion, 1997.

De Cyr, Théodoret. *Histoire des Moines en Syrie* [History of the Monks of Syria]. Sources Chrétiennes. Vol. 257, Paris: Le Cerf, 1979.

De Pury, Albert & Macchi, Jean-Daniel, *Juifs, Chrétiens, Musulmans, Que Pensent Les Uns Des Autres?*. Paris: Labor & Fides, 2004.

De Montjou, Guyonne. *Mar Musa, Un Monastère, Un Homme, Un Désert*. Paris: Albin Michel, 2006.

Hermas, *Le Pasteur [the Shepherd]*. Sources Chrétiennes. Paris: Le Cerf, 1997.

Huntington, Samuel. *Le Choc des Civilisations [Clash of Civilizations]*. Paris: Odile Jacob, 2007.

Hussein, Mahmoud. *Al-Sîra*. Vol. II, Paris: Grasset, 2007.

Jelloun, Tahar Ben. *Cette Aveuglante Absence de Lumière* [This Blinding Absence of Light]. Paris: Le Seuil, 2001.

Jourdan, François. *La Tradition des Sept Dormants*. Paris: Maisonneuve et Larose, 1983.

——. *Dieu des Chrétiens, Dieu des Musulmans*. Paris: Éditions de l'Œuvre, 2007.

Le Coran. Translated by Jacques Berque. Paris: Albin Michel, 2000.

Maalouf, Amin. *Les Croisades Vues par les Arabes [the Crusades through Arab Eyes]*. Paris: J'ai Lu, 1999.

——. *Les Identités Meurtrières [in the Name of Identity]*. Livre De Poche. Paris: Grasset & Fasquelle, 1998.

——. *In the Name of Identity, Violence and the Need to Belong*. Translated by Barbara Bray. New York: Penguin Books, 2003.

Marchesi, Fr Giovanni S. J. *La Civiltà Cattolica* 3636 (15 December 2001).

Martini, Cardinal Carlo Maria. *Noi e l'Islam*. Milan: Centro Ambrosiano, 1990.

Massignon, Louis. *Les Trois Prières d'Abraham*. Patrimoines Islam. Edited by Daniel Massignon. 1997 edn, 9 vols. Paris: Le Cerf, 1997.

——. *Opera Minora: Nazareth et Nous, Nazaréens, Nasara*, Collection Recherches et Documents. Edited by Youakim Moubarac. Vol. III, Beirut: Dar al Maaref, 1963.

Mercan, Ozden. "Constructing a Self-Image in the Image of the Other: Political and Religious Interpretations of Pope Pius II's Letter to Mehmed II (1461)." Masters Thesis, Central European University, Budapest, 2008.

Pittau, Giuseppe. "Culture in Dialogo. L'attualità di Matteo Ricci," in *Vita e Pensiero*, January/February (2000).

Ploux, Jean-Marie. *John-Paul II, Textes Essentiels*. Paris: Éditions de l'Atelier, 2005.

Six, Jean-François. *Charles de Foucauld Autrement*. Paris: DDB, 2008.

Tot Sevenaer, Christian Van Nispen. *Chrétiens et Musulmans: Frères Devant Dieu?* Paris: Éditions de l'Atelier, 2009.

Pontifical Council for Interreligious Dialogue. "Reconnaître Les Liens Spirituels qui Nous Unissent, 16 Ans De Dialogue Islamo-Chrétien [Recognize the Spiritual Bonds that Unite Us, 16 Years of Christian-Muslim Dialogue]," Vatican City (1994).

"Réflexions du Cardinal Walter Kasper." *Service d'Information*, Conseil Pontifical pour la Promotion de l'Unité des Chrétiens [Pontifical Council for Promoting Christian Unity], n.113, 2003/II-III.

Synod of Bishops Special Assembly for Asia. "Jesus Christ the Saviour and His Mission of Love and Service in Asia: 'That They May Have Life and Have It Abundantly'. (Jn 10:10)." (1998). Accessed 14 March 2022. <https://www.vati can.va/roman_curia/synod/documents/rc_synod_doc_20021998_asia-instrl abor_en.html>.

STUDIES IN THEOLOGY
SOCIETY AND CULTURE

Religious and theological reflection has often been confined to the realm of the private, the personal or the Church. In Europe this restriction of religion and theology can be traced back to the Enlightenment and has had long-lasting and pernicious consequences for the understanding of religious faith and society. On the one hand, there has been a rise in religious fundamentalisms around the globe, while, on the other hand, so-called advanced societies are constructed mainly along economic, pragmatic and rationalistic lines. Added to this is the reality that religious faith is increasingly lived out in pluralistic and multi-faith contexts with all the challenges and opportunities this offers to denominational religion.

This series explores what it means to be 'religious' in such contexts. It invites scholarly contributions to themes including patterns of secularisation, postmodern challenges to religion, and the relation of faith and culture. From a theological perspective it seeks constructive re-interpretations of traditional Christian topics – including God, creation, salvation, Christology, ecclesiology, etc. – in a way that makes them more credible for today. It also welcomes studies on religion and science, and on theology and the arts.

The series publishes monographs, comparative studies, interdisciplinary projects, conference proceedings and edited books. It attracts well-researched, especially interdisciplinary, studies which open new approaches to religion or focus on interesting case studies. The language of the series is English. Book proposals should be emailed to any, or all, of the following:

SERIES EDITORS:

- Dr Judith Gruber, Research Professor, Leuven University (judith.gruber@kuleuven.be)
- Dr Norbert Hintersteiner, University of Münster (norbert.hintersteiner@uni-muenster.de)
- Dr Declan Marmion, St Patrick's College, Maynooth (Declan.Marmion@spcm.ie)
- Dr Gesa Thiessen, Trinity College, The University of Dublin (gesa.thiessen@tcd.ie)

Vol. 11   Leah E. Robinson:
           Embodied Peacebuilding: Reconciliation as Practical Theology.
           293 pages. 2015. ISBN 978-3-0343-1858-7.

Vol. 12   Dermot A. Lane (ed.):
           Vatican II in Ireland, Fifty Years On: Essays in Honour of Pádraic Conway.
           421 pages. 2015. ISBN 978-3-0343-1874-7.

Vol. 13   Wilfred Asampambila Agana:
           "Succeed Here and in Eternity": The Prosperity Gospel in Ghana.
           379 pages. 2016. ISBN 978-3-0343-1932-4.

Vol. 14   Richard Lawrence Kimball:
           The People of the Book (ahl al-kitāb): A Comparative Theological Exploration.
           342 pages. 2019. ISBN 978-1-78874-268-9.

Vol. 15   Marthinus J. Havenga:
           Performing Christ: South African Protest Theatre and the Theological Dramatic
           Theory of Hans Urs von Balthasar.
           246 pages. 2021. ISBN 978-1-80079-028-5.

Vol. 16   Leopold Leeb:
           One Dragon, Two Doves: A Comparative History of the Catholic Church in
           China and in Vietnam.
           356 pages. 2022. ISBN 978-1-80079-796-3.

Vol. 17   Richard Kimball, Marie Salaün and Masha Refka:
           In Love with Islam, Believing in Jesus.
           230 pages. 2023. ISBN 978-1-78997-996-1.

Printed by
CPI books GmbH, Leck